D0908222

Money and Calculation

Bocconi on Management Series

Series Editor: **Robert Grant**, Eni Professor of Strategic Management, Department of Management, Università Commerciale Luigi Bocconi, Italy.

The *Bocconi on Management* series addresses a broad range of contemporary and cutting-edge issues relating to the management of organizations and the environment in which they operate. Consistent with Bocconi University's ongoing mission to link good science with practical usefulness, the series is characterized by its integration of relevance, accessibility and rigor. It showcases the work of scholars from all over the world, who have produced contributions to the advancement of knowledge building on theoretical, disciplinary, cultural or methodological traditions with the potential to improve management practice.

The series is edited by the Center for Research in Organization and Management (CROMA) at Bocconi University and is published through an agreement between Palgrave Macmillan and Bocconi University Press, an imprint of Egea.

For information about submissions of book proposals or the series in general, please contact Maurizio Zollo at maurizio.zollo@unibocconi.it or Robert Grant at grant@unibocconi.it.

Titles include:

Massimo Amato, Luigi Doria and Luca Fantacci (*editors*)
MONEY AND CALCULATION
Economic and Sociological Perspectives

Vittorio Coda
ENTREPRENEURIAL VALUES AND STRATEGIC MANAGEMENT
Essays in Management Theory

Bocconi on Management Series
Series Standing Order ISBN 978-0-230-27766-3

You can receive future titles in this series as they are published by placing a standing order. Please contact your bookseller or, in case of difficulty, write to us at the address below with your name and address, the title of the series and the ISBN quoted above.

Customer Services Department, Macmillan Distribution Ltd, Houndmills, Basingstoke, Hampshire RG21 6XS, England.

Money and Calculation

Economic and Sociological Perspectives

Edited by

Massimo Amato
Bocconi University, Italy

and

Luigi Doria
Bocconi University, Italy

and

Luca Fantacci
Bocconi University, Italy

First published 2010 by
PALGRAVE MACMILLAN

Palgrave Macmillan in the UK is an imprint of Macmillan Publishers Limited, registered in England, company number 785998, of Houndmills, Basingstoke, Hampshire RG21 6XS.

Palgrave Macmillan in the US is a division of St Martin's Press LLC, 175 Fifth Avenue, New York, NY 10010.

Palgrave Macmillan is the global academic imprint of the above companies and has companies and representatives throughout the world.

Palgrave® and Macmillan® are registered trademarks in the United States, the United Kingdom, Europe and other countries.

ISBN: 978-0-230-27777-9 hardback

This book is printed on paper suitable for recycling and made from fully managed and sustained forest sources. Logging, pulping and manufacturing processes are expected to conform to the environmental regulations of the country of origin.

A catalogue record for this book is available from the British Library.

Library of Congress Cataloging-in-Publication Data

    Money and calculation : economic and sociological perspectives / edited by Massimo Amato, Luigi Doria, Luca Fantacci.
       p. cm.—(Bocconi on management series)
    Includes bibliographical references.
    ISBN 978-0-230-27777-9
       1. Money. 2. Finance. 3. Management. 4. Economics. I. Amato, Massimo. II. Doria, Luigi, 1969– III. Fantacci, Luca, 1971–
HG221.M81556 2010
332.4—dc22   2010027486

10 9 8 7 6 5 4 3 2 1
19 18 17 16 15 14 13 12 11 10

Printed and bound in Great Britain by
CPI Antony Rowe, Chippenham and Eastbourne

Contents

Contributors

Massimo Amato is tenured researcher at Bocconi University, Milan, and Fellow of the Institute of Advances Studies, Nantes. His fields of interest range from economic history and the history of economic thought to phenomenology. He is the author of *Il bivio della moneta* (*The Money Junction*, Egea, 1999), *Le radici di una fede. Per una storia del rapporto fra moneta e credito in Occidente* (*The Roots of a Faith. Outline of a History of the Helationship between Money and Credit in the West*, Bruno Mondadori, 2008) and *L'enigma della moneta e l'inizio dell'economia* (*The Enigma of Money and the Inception of the Economy*, to be published in 2010). He is co-author with L. Fantacci of *The End of Finance. Where the Crisis Comes from and How we can Conceive a Way Out*, Polity, to be published in 2011.

Yuri Biondi is Research Fellow for the French Institute of Research (www.cnrs.fr) at the Ecole Polytechnique of Paris (www.polytechnique.fr) and affiliated Professor of Corporate Governance and Social Responsibility at CNAM (www.cnam.fr). He is promoter and main editor of *The Firm as an Entity: Implications for Economics, Accounting, and Law* (Routledge, 2007) and co-editor, with Tomo Suzuki, of *The Socio-Economics of Accounting* (*Socio-Economic Review* special issue, October 2007). His current research interests are the interdisciplinary connections of firms, money and accounting, at the theoretical and applied levels.

Dick Bryan is Professor of Political Economy at the University of Sydney. He has for a number of years researched Marxian value theory and international capital movement. For the past decade his specific focus has been financial markets, and especially financial derivatives. With Michael Rafferty, he is the author of *Capitalism with Derivatives: A Political Economy of Financial Derivatives, Capital and Class* (Palgrave 2006).

Jean Cartelier is Emeritus Professor at Paris X-Nanterre University. His main fields of research are general economic theory, the theory of money and the history of economic thought. He has published many articles and books in defence of the 'monetary approach'.

Luigi Doria carries out research at Bocconi University, Milan. He has been Fellow of the Nantes Institute for Advanced Studies. He has done research at the University IUAV of Venice. He has co-edited (together with Valeria Fedeli and Carla Tedesco) *Rethinking European Spatial Policy as a Hologram: Actions, Institutions, Discourses*, Ashgate, 2006. His most recent research interest is economic sociology, focusing on the relation between quality and calculation.

Luca Fantacci is Assistant Professor of Economic History at Bocconi University. He is the author of *La moneta. Storia di un'istituzione mancata* (*Money. History of a Failed Institution*, Marsilio, 2005), and co-author with Massimo Amato of *the End of Finance. Where the Crisis Comes From and How we can Conceive a Way Out*, Polity, forthcoming 2011), in addition to several articles on monetary and financial history and, more recently, on the thought and activities of J. M. Keynes.

Herbert Kalthoff is Professor of Sociology at the University of Mainz, Department of Sociology, in Germany. His research interests are the sociology of knowledge and practices in the field of finance, banking and teaching, focusing on qualitative methods. He is co-editor of *Facts and Figures* (Metropolis, 2000) and *Theoretische Empirie* (Suhrkamp, 2008), and author of 'Practices of Calculation' (*Theory, Culture and Society* 22, 2005) and 'The Launch of Banking Instruments and the Figuration of Markets' (*Journal for the Theory of Social Behaviour* 36, 2006).

Bill Maurer is Professor of Anthropology and Director of the Institute for Money, Technology and Financial Inclusion at the University of California, Irvine. He is the editor of several collections, as well as the author of *Recharting the Caribbean: Land, Law and Citizenship in the British Virgin Islands* (University of Michigan Press, 1997), *Pious Property: Islamic Mortgages in the United States* (Russell Sage Foundation, 2006) and *Mutual Life, Limited: Islamic Banking, Alternative Currencies, Lateral Reason* (Princeton University Press, 2005), which was awarded the Victor Turner Prize in 2005.

Alex Preda is Reader in Sociology at the University of Edinburgh, UK. He is the author of *Framing Finance. The Boundaries of Markets and Modern Capitalism* (University of Chicago Press, 2009) and *Information, Knowledge, and Economic Life. An Introduction to the Sociology of Markets* (Oxford University Press, 2009), in addition to several articles. His current research focuses on anonymous transactions in online financial markets and on the activities of non-professional traders.

Michael Rafferty is Senior Researcher at the Workplace Research Centre, University of Sydney. His research is at the interface of international

capital and labour markets, and most recently he has been research-
ing the operation and performance of pension funds. He also works
extensively on financial innovation. With Dick Bryan, he is the author
of *Capitalism with Derivatives: A Political Economy of Financial Derivatives,
Capital and Class* (Palgrave, 2006).

Uwe Vormbusch is Senior Research Fellow at the Department of
Sociology, Mainz University. He received his PhD from Frankfurt
University in 2002 and finished his Habilitation at Jena University in
2008. He teaches economic sociology, the sociology of accounting and
the sociology of technology. His most recent book is about govern-
ing by numbers in contemporary capitalism: *Herrschaft der Zahlen.
Zur Kalkulation des Sozialen in der kapitalistischen Moderne* (Campus, 2010).
He has also written 'Talking Numbers – Governing Immaterial Labour'
(*Economic Sociology Newsletter* 10, 2008) and 'Accounting. Die Macht der
Zahlen im gegenwärtigen Kapitalismus' (*Berliner Journal für Soziologie* 14,
2004).

1
Introduction

Massimo Amato, Luigi Doria and Luca Fantacci

Emotions, identity, values, happiness – all different aspects of life are pervaded by a growing complex of calculative practices. Calculation, ubiquitous and multifarious, is driven not merely by an extension of the scope of exchange, but by a deeper urge towards generalized equalization and totalization. Money is the measure of exchange. As a unit of account and a means of payment, it serves the purpose of exchange. Yet, money increasingly has become itself an object of exchange and calculation on financial markets that tend less to the production and exchange of actual goods, and more to the elimination of all uncertainty by means of universal exchangeability. How is it that, in this overwhelming plethora of money and calculation, the economy seems to have lost its measure? The essays collected here investigate, from various viewpoints, how calculation and money, in their nature, relations and transformations, bear upon the meaning of measure in economic life.

The volume does not merely intend to present an array of various scholarly positions concerning money and calculation. Nor does it intend to be a systematic treatise on the notions of money and calculation, on their historical forms or their current embodiments.

The guiding idea of the book is that questions on the nature of money and the nature of economic calculation are bound by a constitutive co-belonging. The central assumption is, in other words, that the understanding of key dimensions of economic life continuously involves interpretations of the relationship between money and calculation.

Despite its importance, this relationship tends to remain unexplored or implicit. The interrogation of how money calculates and is calculated tends in fact to remain on a different plane than the interrogation of *what calculation is*, of what characterizes *economic calculation* as such, and of how calculation *shapes* economic and financial life.

With a view to overcoming this impasse and bringing to light non-obvious relations, the book intends to facilitate a dialogue between reflections on money and reflections on calculation in the light of certain issues that, in their uncomfortable radicalness, remain yet to be addressed in an open debate.

What does it mean to say that money calculates? How does the answer to that question depend on the way in which the nature of money is conceived, for example, in the framework of a commodity – or a credit-theory of money? And conversely, how ought the meaning, the boundaries and the 'finalization' of calculation be seen in relation to the phenomenon of money? Is the apparently ubiquitous calculation really related to a monetization of social life? And how are both these tendencies related to the fact that money itself is treated as a commodity exchangeable on particular markets?

If calculation (also in the form of models, formulas and accounting procedures) *makes* financial markets, how does this 'performativity', in turn, depend upon and reinforce a particular understanding of the relationship between money and credit? What does it mean when, with the establishment of modern financial markets, money itself is made the object of calculation or when, with more recent financial innovation, derivatives appear as a new form of money, entirely shaped by calculation? In what sense, and from what perspective on money and calculation, does the *calculation of money* become a problem? Ultimately, if money and calculation have to do with *measure*, how are they both related to the meaning of measure in economic life?

It is through these questions that the book aims to facilitate an encounter between different disciplinary and theoretical positions on the ways in which money and calculation relate to each other.

Sketch of the debates on money and on calculation

Money and calculation have been at the centre of a renewed scientific interest in recent years, which has addressed the variety of forms that both take in contemporary economies. However, money and calculation have been considered mostly separately, and not in terms of their relationship. Or, rather, their relationship has not been treated systematically and explicitly, but has remained in the background of various specific lines of research.

The revival of the reflection on money has drawn together different scientific fields – economics, political economy, history of economic thought, economic history, economic sociology, anthropology, philosophy – and is characterized by the range of its scope and the plurality of its interpretive perspectives.

Within the field of economics, recent years have witnessed a renewed interest in money, for example in the attempt to provide microfoundations for explaining the existence of money within a theoretical framework that traditionally excludes it, namely that of general economic equilibrium. These contributions, however, have continued to see money as a commodity, or in any case a *thing*, designed to facilitate exchanges, without questioning the nature of money (Cartelier 2009). A wider debate, involving mainly political economists, sociologists, anthropologists and historians, has concerned questions of the nature and functions of money,[1] covering broad issues related to the historical and logical conditions of money and its conceptualization (e.g., money as a universal equivalent in commodity exchange versus money as defined by the social relations characteristic of credit).

One of the major themes which continue to animate the debate concerns the relationship between money and social life.[2] A tradition that builds on the classic works of Marx, Weber and Simmel, and continues to this day, understands money as an entity which produces an abstraction and a rationalization of social relations, and entails an unconditional comparability of everything with everything, thus making commensurable what is not commensurable. Despite their diversity, these different approaches share the idea that the abstractive and desacralizing violence of money causes a 'calculative' erosion of the social fabric. Another line of argument asserts that money is a social construct and in many ways is embedded in social relations, variously perceived and experienced. We refer here to studies that focus on the pluralization of monetary forms, on the social and spatial embeddedness of money and on the diversity of its meanings (Zelizer 1994, Guyer 2004 and Gilbert 2005), studies that in some cases demand a re-socialization and re-culturalization of money.

Within this theoretical scenario, the richness and diversity of different positions are deemed by some scholars to depend upon the inevitable indeterminacy of money. According to these positions, the intersection of 'traditional' problems with new issues creates a multidimensional situation, which makes it allegedly problematic if not impossible to provide a coherent answer to the ontological question about money. According to other lines of thought, what is at stake is not only an investigation of contemporary monetary forms, but the question of what money is. For those who address this issue, the tradition of money-thinking, from Aristotle to Keynes, is not a corpus of stratified and fixed knowledge, but rather a series of questions waiting to be answered (Ingham 2005 and Amato 2006). In this perspective, all the titles under which money is commonly understood – money as a measure, as a social institution, as a means of exchange, as a commodity, as a symbol, as a form of language – need to be reconsidered.

Reflections on calculation,[3] in turn, are characterized by two main trends. On one hand, calculation tends to enlarge its frontiers, covering 'objects' which have historically been beyond its scope. On the other hand, calculation is being radically redefined. Calculation is no longer seen as exclusively related to the sphere of numerical/quantitative operations, which are associated with the concept of 'abstract calculation'. A wide range of practices – such as formatting, figuring, displaying, classifying, timing, legally framing – are interpreted as having calculative performativity.[4]

In general terms, we could say that a double indistinctness seems to emerge: both the difference between what is and what is not a calculative tool, and the difference between what can and what cannot be calculated tend to vanish, and hence need to be reassessed.

The diversification of calculative practices is often associated with a proliferation of *calculative agencies*. According to the actor-network theory, these calculative agencies may be seen as resulting from the continuous interaction between human agents (from market professionals to consumers, from public institutions to non-governmental organizations), non-human elements (technical devices, algorithms, software, formulas, models, metrological standards, and so on) and the networks that emerge from their relations.

In general terms, a field of socio-economic thought is devoted to the diverse 'dimensions' of calculation: the role of calculative tools, the profile of calculative practices, the relationships between calculation and social interactions and the ideas and programmes which underlie calculative operations.

Within certain sociological debates, the discourse on the nature and structure of calculation goes hand in hand with a reinterpretation of the relationship between calculation and the institutions of economic life, and particularly the market. This is the case with the vast area of research in which market behaviour becomes largely understood in terms of social processes of calculation. Recent analyses concerning the calculative character of markets – and particularly the way in which processes of calculation construct material and immaterial objects as tradable goods – constitute one of the most lively areas of current economic sociology.[5]

This topic is related to the macro-issue of the performativity of calculation, that is, the question of how calculative tools, practices and agencies shape economic structures and behaviours. A first approach to calculative performativity insists on the impact of the 'calculative abstractions' of modern finance. In particular, ever more sophisticated mathematical models for the quantification of risk are interpreted as instruments that, by means of an 'infinite extendibility' of calculation, shape money and credit markets. This dominance of certain abstract fictions within economics and finance leads to an ever more decisive deconstruction and marketization of social relations.

A second approach highlights the distributed nature of computational processes, the multiplicity of calculative agencies and hence the possibility that the *politicization* of calculation calls into question its potential hegemony (Callon and Muniesa 2005). In a context in which calculation is allegedly ever more socially constructed and distributed, markets appear as differentiated devices, which (as well as the calculative tools themselves) are constantly reshaped by actors and social sciences (Callon 1998).

How money and calculation call into question management in times of crisis

The structure of the present volume derives from the peculiar character of the issues it addresses. More precisely, it derives from the radical way in which those issues question consolidated theoretical approaches in different disciplines. In particular, the issues relating to calculation and money confront managerial and economic sciences with questions that, by their very nature, tend to escape any reassuring theoretical framing, even with the concurrence of various approaches. In fact, despite the extraordinary proliferation of analyses, theories and debates around those issues, the questions that they raise remain, in a certain sense, intact – simply because they are unfathomable questions.

It is for this very reason that these questions run the risk of being merely repressed. On one hand, it is difficult to deny their relevance (on the basis of a purely empirical analysis); yet, on the other hand, it is impossible to address them within the ordinary framework of scientific debate. They run the risk, therefore, of remaining at the margin of scientific enquiry, thus generating a sort of diffused and impalpable disquiet, which one tries to set aside, assuming that sooner or later they will be addressed.

Let us now take a closer look at how this risk applies to calculation and money, particularly in relation to management. Managerial disciplines are intensely engaged in what we may broadly call the 'universe of calculation'. This is an extremely complex and ever-changing universe that includes practices of accounting, control, forecast, quality assurance, business and social auditing, calculation of the performance of human resources, and evaluation of a growing array of intangibles such as customer care, interpersonal relations, stakeholder satisfaction and so on. Managerial sciences are continuously confronted with this universe of practices (which involve measurement, evaluation, control, certification, ranking and auditing) and with a related range of calculative methodologies (see, e.g. the application of portfolio theory to human resource management). It could be argued that the theoretical and methodological debate concerning this universe of calculation represents one of the frontiers of management (of private businesses as well as public entities).

All spheres of management (but also, more and more clearly, of the entire society) are thus pervaded by an urge to measure everything, which involves both the adoption of ever more complicated techniques of calculation and risk management, and the assumption within the scope of calculation of an ever wider array of objects, including emotions, feelings and relationships.

Despite the uneasiness which it generates, this calculative proliferation seems to resist criticism. The condemnation of the 'unintended consequences' and the dysfunctional nature of certain calculative processes and of the disembedding of the new social objects produced by calculation tends to lead to a mere revision of calculation methods (Power 2004).

Against this trend, strong critical positions have emerged, even within managerial sciences. 'In the end, we probably measure more things in more detail than is functionally necessary'. This statement was made by an eminent scholar in managerial studies, who goes on to ask: 'Is it really necessary to measure in order to manage? Is the attempt to measure performance in finely tuned detail simply a symptom of social and economic decline? Do societies and organizations only invest in elaborate and pseudo-precise measurement systems in time of crisis, when social and economic order must be preserved?' (Power 2004, pp. 779–780).

To ask to what extent calculation is functionally necessary leads us not only to question the apparently indefinite enlargement of the scope of calculation, but also to raise the issue of the reference of calculation. In other terms, the question concerning what is measurable and to what extent it is measurable goes hand in hand with the question of the measure of value, particularly in relation to the calculation of organizational and social phenomena. The debate on this point is certainly characterized by a wealth of critical positions. However, as long as the overall value produced by a firm is measured by money, the question of how money, as we know it, constitutes a measure of value deeply affects managerial studies and practices, and particularly accounting theory. If the relationship between money and calculation concerns management, this is particularly true in times of crisis. In fact, the crisis is not merely something that managerial practices have to take into account as an exogenous shock (to be included in budgets, forecasts and calculations) or something that they have to deal with in terms of crisis management. It is, rather, something that demands a deeper interrogation of what kind of measure of value businesses can actually rely on as a reference for their calculative practices.

It has been repeatedly stated, even with alarm, that the financial crisis is not merely an incident of market mismanagement, but an event that questions our way of seeing the economy, money, risk and creditor-debtor relationships. This interrogation pervades the present volume, even if none of the contributors directly address the issue of the crisis.

Can we blame the crisis simply on a series of errors in the processes of calculating financial risk, and on ineffective regulation? Or rather, is it the result of an unsound relationship between the calculation of risk, according to certain financial models, and the regulation of financial markets based on those same models? And in what sense does the crisis urge us to reflect on money as an institution, and on its relationship to credit, to risk, to calculation and, particularly, to accounting? To what extent does the possibility of booms and busts depend on the peculiar way in which debtor-creditor relationships are conceived and treated as calculable and exchangeable entities?

The economic and philosophical investigations concerning money which are included in this volume, are an attempt to reopen key questions on the nature of money and on its role in economic life. In this respect, as the reader will see, the question of calculation is not at all marginal, but rather a fundamental dimension. In particular, the relevance of the relationship between money and calculation is clearly felt, even by laypeople, in the issue of derivatives, which has come to the fore in the debate concerning the crisis. As a technology of assurance for the commodification and management of risk, derivatives are, deliberately, the focus of two contributions to this volume, which address the issue in its economic and anthropological perspective. And in these contributions, once again deliberately, the question of the relationship between calculative technologies, money and the objective measure of value is widely discussed.

We hope that this brief discussion has served to show how the problematic nexus between money and calculation calls into question management, economics and social sciences in a very direct way. To help bring those questions out of the shade, and to use them as the occasion for a renewed relationship with the tradition of social thought, and as the opportunity for a new reflection on the life of business and economic systems, is indeed one the main objectives of this book.

The character of an unusual book: different approaches to a common set of questions

It is precisely in relation to the tone of the questions outlined above that the structure of this volume, and the degree of risk that it involves, ought to be understood.

The volume is indeed built upon a dialogue between different scientific perspectives, ranging from economics to sociology to anthropology. Such diversity is essential for an inquiry into a phenomenon, such as the relationship between money and calculation, which interrogates various social sciences.

The diversity involved is not merely between different disciplines, but between various points of departure. Considered as a whole, the volume is not the outcome of shallow interdisciplinarity, but rather it responds to an essential freedom of movement. In fact, it arises from a set of questions that provoke each of the contributors individually.

It is in this sense that we may claim that the volume does not intend to provide an array of different interpretative positions. Nor does it aim at gaining a common interpretive framework. Rather, the various contributions are given consistency by the fact that they all acknowledge the importance of seeing money and calculation as phenomena that mirror one another. It is the exposure to a common phenomenon, even from different perspectives, that opens the possibility of communication. The reader will find evidence of the latter in the cross-connections between these chapters, even beyond those that have been explicitly pointed out by the authors. This approach has been successfully tested in a workshop in which some of the contributors participated. The workshop was held in May 2008 at Bocconi University. The editors are thankful to the Department of Institutional Analysis and Public Management of Bocconi University for financial and organizational support.

Synopsis of the book's contents

A first issue that the volume addresses concerns the way in which money calculates in a market economy. As the contribution by Jean Cartelier suggests, this issue calls into question both the nature of calculation and the nature and economic role of money. Cartelier discusses recent developments within general economic equilibrium theory aimed at explaining the existence of money, and appreciates the idea that money allows decentralized control over social relations. However, these developments continue to represent money as a peculiar commodity, that is, as 'fiat money', without any reference to sovereignty. According to Cartelier, money should be thought of primarily as a unit of account, that is, as an 'accounting institution', as the mode of expression and calculation with which individuals relate to one another on the market. The existence and definition of money as a unit of account depend on a sovereignty which is intrinsic to a market economy.

In a similar vein, Yuri Biondi argues against the theories which assume that money, in the form of a thing or a sign, is the general means allowing or at least facilitating generalized exchange, that is, the market. He believes, following a neglected tradition of economic thought, that money should be understood not only as a means of exchange but also as a unit of account. Whilst money as a means of exchange relates to transactions and payments in a given space and time, money as a unit of account is essential to economic relations which extend over space and time. Moreover, the understanding of money as a unit of account calls into question accounting as a crucial form of economic calculation. In accounting systems the temporal dimension appears both in the way debt-credit relations are taken into account, and by the application of accruals and other accounting techniques that are conceived to cope with space, time and hazard. The ideas and practices of accounting and the 'accounting' function of money are tightly intertwined: if, on one hand, accounting relies on the conception of money as a unit of account, then on the other hand, it expands that conception well beyond the notion of a mere unit of denomination for the prices of goods and financial assets. In this perspective, the logic of that peculiar form of economic calculation which is embodied in accounting systems, and the nature of money as a unit of account, are addressed in terms of their constitutive co-belonging.

A second line of interrogation in the contributions to the volume concerns money as an object of calculation in the light of the interpretation of money as an institution, and more specifically as an institutional measure of exchange. How can money, understood as an institution, be subject to processes of calculation? In what way does the demand for unconditional calculation affect money as a measure? These issues are addressed by the following two contributions.

Massimo Amato's approach is not strictly economic, but rather aims at a phenomenological clarification of the relationship between money and calculation that is implicit in economics. Money plays its role as a measure only insofar as it is established as an institution. Yet, with the act of institution, language is at stake. It is not by chance that, since the beginning of reflection on money, it has been associated by analogy with language. Today, that analogy is understood in terms of a purely conventional conception of both money and language as means of communication. Is this a reductive, or rather reductionist, understanding of that analogy? And if so, what is lost? Amato argues that what is lost is not only or even primarily the *finality*, but the very *sense* of communication itself, and more precisely the possibility of limiting the use of money and language as means of communication. Since language is originally, in the West, *logos*, and *logos* is also the root of calculation, the reduction of language to a mere means of communication coincides with a representation of calculation as a global logistical process. Within their technological interpretation, both money and calculation become instruments of a totalization, by which what calculates and measures is treated at the same time as an object of calculation and measurement. The ultimate effect is a totalization of exchange, that is, a structural loss of the limit and of the end of exchange itself.

Luca Fantacci questions the rate of interest as the peculiar feature of modern financial systems that sanctions money as an object of calculation and hence denies its nature as a measure for exchange. If it is obvious that the rate of interest is a crucial factor in monetary calculations, Fantacci asks, on the basis of an interpretation of Keynes's work, what kind of calculation is implied in the money rate of interest? The question is traditionally settled simply by accepting the hypothesis that money is a commodity and that the rate of interest is its price. The calculation involved appears therefore merely as a quantitative calculation of costs and benefits. However, the premises and implications of this hypothesis are exactly what this contribution discusses, showing that money as a store of value is complementary to its role as a form of financial calculation that claims to describe all phenomena in terms of quantitative probabilities, leaving no room for what is fundamentally imponderable.

This peculiar form of finance is also discussed by the next contribution to the volume, which considers financial derivatives and their implications for the theory of money. As Bryan and Rafferty argue, if derivatives are to be understood as money, they are essentially a kind of money based on unlimited computation. Derivatives perform, as they say, 'a binding and blending role'. They establish price relations that both bind the future to the present or one place to another, and convert between different forms of asset. Derivatives compare money and assets with respect to their future, and at the same time compare a wide range of physical and financial assets (and different forms of money). Therefore, they represent a form of money which is constructed around the unconditional calculative commensurability of everything with everything (every kind of currency and asset with other kind of currency and asset, over time). This 'new commodity money' implies a more radical confusion between money and commodity than the one implied by the classical concept of commodity money: monetary equivalence itself appears now as a commodity of variable value. This conception of equivalence implies an extreme commodification of risk, which pretends to cover even incalculable risk, that is, uncertainty. The development and growth of derivatives has appeared, in the past few decades, as the way to eliminate risk by means of its generalized calculability and exchangeability. However, in the context of the global financial crisis we see that the conception of equivalence borne by this new commodity money is systemically fragile.

All this follows from the fact that derivatives do not imply ownership or exchange of the underlying commodity (be it currency or goods): their original, however indirect, relationship with ownership and exchange of goods, which legitimized derivatives as opposed to mere bets, has progressively disappeared. The issue of the exchange of commodities as the purpose of calculation (or conversely, the issue of a sort of self-referentiality of calculation no longer linked to ownership and exchange of commodities) is a crucial question for the analysis of the new horizons of calculation.

Within the scenario of 'universal calculability' described above, there is an issue that continues to concern, more or less tacitly, social sciences. It is the issue raised by the question *what calculation is referred to?*. Is the calculation of a growing range of social dimensions directed towards market exchange? Is the exchange of tradable commodities the *end* of calculation? Can we still accept the proposition of von Mises that 'Economic calculation cannot comprehend things which are not sold and bought against money' (Von Mises 1966)? Or is calculation separated from the framework in which it has historically operated as *economic* calculation?

The hypothesis formulated by Luigi Doria is that the calculation of social reality is driven not so much by the production of transactable commodities, as by the valorization of human, technical, cultural, territorial, monetary *resources*. *Resource*, as an enigmatic keyword of the modern socio-economic lexicon, designates a totalizing mobilization that transcends the exchange of commodities, and obliterates the element of clearing and distinction which exchange brings into economic life. The project of calculating money in terms of *financial resources* and calculating the life of *human resources* should be seen as a significant trend in the current socio-economic scenario.

Akin to the problem concerning the 'finalization of calculation' is the issue regarding the relationship between calculation, numbers and the religious dimension. In this respect, Bill Maurer questions the argument according to which calculation, and especially the paraphernalia of quantitative finance, entail a 'quantitative reduction' of social phenomena, a depersonalization and dehumanization of economic life that demand a counteraction in the form of a re-socialization and re-culturalization of money and finance (Maurer 2008). According to Maurer, the task of social sciences is not so much to condemn the numerical, building on an allegedly obvious identification of number with calculation, but to reflect on how the arithmetical procedures and stochastic models that shape trading in derivatives cause calculations to become separated from any transcendental dimension.

A final important area of interrogation concerns the sociological analysis of the morphology and role of calculation with respect to a set of practices and technical tools, particularly in the realm of finance. The analysis of the relationship between calculation, social practices and tools is central to the contribution by Herbert Kalthoff and Uwe Vormbusch. On the basis of an empirical analysis of a specific field of financial activity, portfolio management, the authors argue that the heterogeneity of these procedures leads to a variety of results, expectations and efficiency lines (calculations). In the case of portfolio management no strong codification of calculation exists which could describe the calculation of a value in a standardized way. According to the authors, we are no longer concerned with calculation in the strict sense of the word, but with the simulation of events and their developments. Therefore, it is of no significance whether the actors employ codified models or proceed idiosyncratically. They simulate the characteristics and growth prospects of their portfolios within specific market surroundings, and thereby visualize possible developments that they can react to in consequence. In this context, the infrastructure of the calculation culture is regarded as a toolbox for a plethora of uses, in a scenario in which the generation of knowledge about relationships and connections between data, models, implementation and theory is pivotal.

A sociological interpretation of calculation in financial markets is at the core of the contribution by Alex Preda. Preda's analysis, which focuses on the significant case of lay online trading, questions the possibility of understanding calculation as the application of a set of formulas and general models which would then be situated (and thus modified, adapted and reshaped) in the field of practice by traders. Calculation is not merely a situated action, but a situational action: it is shaped by the interaction order of trading, and the resources in the situation are not simply vehicles for a strategic calculative action which remains independent of these resources.

These sociological analyses provide valuable information on the profile, operation and power of the concrete processes of calculation, even while they offer an important perspective from which to reconsider questions on the nature of calculation, its legitimacy, its limits and its peculiar position within modern economy and finance.

Acknowledgments

A slightly different version of Chapter 8 by Bill Maurer originally appeared in *Economy and Society* 31(1): 15–36, 2002. An extended version of Chapter 10 by Alex Preda has been published in *Accounting, Organizations and Society* 34(5): 675–693, 2009. The editors are very grateful to the journals for kindly granting the permission to republish the articles.

Notes

1. See, for example, the important debate in *Economy and Society* with articles by Geoffrey Ingham, Costas Lapavitsas, Ben Fine, Dick Bryan and Michael Rafferty, in Volume 30, Issue 3, 2001; Volume 34, Issue 3, 2005; Volume 35, Issue 2, 2006.
2. For a presentation of different lines of thought with regard to this issue see Maurer (2006).
3. The 'new' profile and role of calculation have recently been, more or less directly, addressed by a wide and well-argued interdisciplinary reflection, in which a major role has been played by sociological studies, comprising the contributions of Michel Callon and Fabian Muniesa (on markets and calculation), Franck Cochoy (on the notion of *qualculation*), Andrew Barry and Don Slater (on calculation and the *technological turn* in the economy), Herbert Kalthoff (on the practices of economic calculation in the economic and financial sectors), Donald MacKenzie (on the performavity of calculation with particular regard to financial markets), Peter Miller and Nicolas Rose (on programmes and ideas of calculation and their relation with the governing of economic life), Andrea Menniken (on the calculative features of accounting), Michael Power (on auditing as a peculiar calculative universe), Karin Knorr-Cetina and Alex Preda (on calculation in the sociology of financial markets). For an analysis of important themes of the debate on economic calculation, with particular regard to the relationship between the tools and practices of calculation on one side, and the 'ideas' of calculation and the meanings it is endowed with on the other, see Miller (2008).
4. We refer, in particular, to the debate on the notion of *qualculation* proposed by Franck Cochoy. See Callon and Law (2005).
5. On calculation, agency and markets, see Callon and Muniesa (2005).

References

Amato, M. (2006) 'Notes on the (Im)Proper Use of Money. From an Openly Hidden Tradition of Money-Thinking', paper presented at the IEHC Helsinki, 2006. Accessible online at: http://www.helsinki.fi/iehc2006/papers2/Amato.pdf.

Callon, M. (1998) 'Introduction: The Embeddedness of Economic Markets in Economics', in M. Callon (ed.) *The Laws of the Market* (Oxford: Blackwell), 1–57.

Callon, M. and Law, J. (2005) 'On Qualculation, Agency, and Otherness', *Environment and Planning D: Society and Space*, 23 (5), pp. 717–733.

Callon, M. and Muniesa, F. (2005) 'Economic Markets as Calculative Collective Devices', *Organization Studies*, 26 (8), 1229–1250.

Cartelier, J. (2009) 'Fiat Money or Minimal Set of Rules? What Concept of Money for a Market Economy?', mimeo. The text may be requested to jcartel@club-internet.fr.

Gilbert, E. (2005) 'Common Cents: Situating Money in Time and Place', *Economy and Society*, 34 (3), 357–388.

Guyer, J. (2004) *Marginal Gains: Monetary Transactions in Atlantic Africa* (Chicago: University of Chicago Press).

Ingham, G. (ed.) (2005) *Concepts of Money: Interdisciplinary Perspectives from Economics, Sociology and Political Science* (Cheltenham: Edward Elgar).

Maurer, B. (2006) 'The Anthropology of Money', *Annual Review of Anthropology*, 35, 15–36.

Maurer, B. (2008) 'Re-socialising Finance? Or Dressing It in Mufti? Calculating Alternatives for Cultural Economies', *Journal of Cultural Economy*, 1 (1), 65–78.

Miller, P. (2008), 'Calculating Economic Life', *Journal of Cultural Economy*, 1 (1), 51–64.

Power, M. (2004) 'Counting, Control and Calculation: Reflections on Measuring and Management', *Human Relations*, 57 (6), 765–783.

Von Mises, L. (1966) *Human Action: A Treatise on Economics*, 3rd edn (Chicago: H. Regnery Co.).

Zelizer, V. A. (1994) *The Social Meaning of Money* (New York: Basic Books).

2
Money Is the Scribe of a Market Economy

Jean Cartelier

The purpose of this chapter is to give an alternative version and interpretation of Kocherlakota's argument that money is a memory (bookkeeping technology). There seems to be some confusion in the way in which the conception of a memory-money is presented and understood today. What is acceptable is the idea that money allows a decentralized control over the actions of individuals in the market, thus providing an alternative to centralized control which is incompatible with a market economy. Such an idea is old, going back at least to Galiani. What impairs its presentation in Kocherlakota's version is a double confusion between money and capital (due to the assumption of durability of fiat money) on the one hand, and between accounting and centralization on the other. Even a brief explanation of the relationship between money and accounting allows us to dispel these confusions and to propose a different idea of what money really does in a market economy. An essential component of money is the nominal unit of account, an aspect completely disregarded by academic theory. The unit of account is the language of individuals in the market. It is the mode of expression and computation of individuals in their relationships with one another. Its existence and its definition depend upon a sovereignty which is inherent to the market economy, and which is completely obscured by academic theory, where money is conceived as a particular commodity, that is, fiat money.

A 'spontaneous' empirical view of money may lead theoreticians on to the wrong track.[1] The ritual list of monetary objects that opens most textbooks on money makes readers believe that money is basically a thing or a special commodity. Conceiving of money as an abstract system of rules or as an institution is not mentioned at this stage. Later on, when abstract theory enters the scene, readers find it quite natural that 'fiat money' is the central concept in academic theory (Shi 2006). 'Fiat money' is a good, a special one indeed since it is absent from utility and production functions. Its exclusive role, theoreticians say, is to be used as an intermediary of exchange. Abstract theory here appears to rest on a sound and realistic view. But this is not the case. If academic theoreticians conceive money as 'fiat money' and not as an institution, it is not for empirical but for very abstract reasons. There is nothing wrong with that. But a straightforward consequence is that an academic theory of money can only be understood through a careful examination of the theoretical arguments leading to the notion of 'fiat money'. When theoreticians maintain that *money is what money does*, they relate less to real life than to what money does in their abstract models. For instance, money remedies the absence of a double coincidence of wants in Kiyotaki and Wright 1993, private information on the quality of goods in Williamson and Wright 1994, the impossibility for individuals to credibly commit themselves to acting decisively in Kocherlakota 1998a, and so on, depending on the context of the model and its special assumptions. Such an epistemology is legitimate, no doubt. But it shows that a critical assessment of an academic theory of money requires a study of its internal logic which is free from pseudo-empirical evidence.

The most outstanding instance of such pseudo-empirical evidence is the so-called 'durability' of 'fiat money'. In theoretical models, durability of 'fiat money' is the necessary and sufficient condition for money to be a store of value. Why call it 'pseudo-empirical' evidence? Are metal coins, banknotes, cheques, and so on, not durable objects? Of course they are. But it would be erroneous to infer from the durability of monetary objects that money is a store of value. For instance, in a metallic system, money is not gold or silver but coins issued by the mint. Coins are issued according to legal rules. If these rules change, existing coins are no longer a means of payment or intermediary of exchange. They must be melted and coined anew, according to new *legal rules*. Neither from the durability of metal nor that of demonetized coins can we infer that money is a store of value. *Money* (legally acceptable coins) should not be confused with *capital* (gold, silver and other durable commodities). This is even clearer in modern monetary systems where credit money depends entirely on banks' financial viability, which is clearly not a tangible entity. Nevertheless, academic theoreticians have built models in which 'fiat money' is assumed to be durable – not resulting from a careful examination of empirical evidence, but because such an assumption is crucial for their fundamental propositions of the essence of money and the role it performs in an exchange economy. In what follows, emphasis will be placed on the logical structure of the academic theory of money, in order to avoid over-emphasizing monetary objects.

The demonstration of the existence of a general monetary equilibrium, with money being a pure intermediary of exchange, is relatively recent (Iwai 1988, Kiyotaki and Wright 1993). Two major propositions are combined with that demonstration: (i) the *essentiality* of money (a monetary economy is better at maintaining equilibrium in terms of welfare than the same economy without money) (Wallace 2001); (ii) the equivalence of money with a social memory when anonymity prevents individuals from credibly committing themselves (Kocherlakota 1998a and 1998b). Claiming that 'money is memory' – which assumes the durability of 'fiat money' – is very appealing. The proposition is not only brilliant but seems perfectly in line with the idea that money, even conceived of as purely intermediary, is also necessarily a store of value. As a store of value money is an element of capital (which is in fact the unique element of capital highlighted in Kocherlakota's seminal article).

Kocherlakota's basic tenet is now accepted by almost all academic theoreticians: money is seen to play in a decentralized economy the role played by a record of all past monetary transactions in a centralized economy. The idea of money as memory seems to be in accordance both with a long tradition – that of *money pledge* – rehabilitated recently by Ostroy and Starr (1990), and also with the interpretations of some anthropologists (Hart 2009).

The purpose of the present contribution is to present a different interpretation of Kocherlakota's thesis and, incidentally, to suggest an alternative theory of money. Previous misunderstandings have rendered 'money is memory' a misleading concept. What Kocherlakota convincingly shows is that money effects a decentralized control over individuals when they make transactions in the market. In this sense money may be opposed to centralized control or, similarly, to total transparency based on public records of past transactions. Money allows individuals to make exchanges with each other despite a lack of information. That idea is a profound and interesting one. It is also a very old one. It can be traced back at least to Galiani (1977) (see Spahn, 2007), and it has always been present at every stage in the history of economic thought. What causes a problem with Kocherlakota's version is a double confusion: (i) between money and capital (due to the assumed durability of 'fiat money'); and (ii) between accounting and centralization.

Even a rudimentary examination of the relations between money and accounting is sufficient to clarify these confusions and suggest another view of what money really does in a market economy. A basic component of money is the *nominal unit of account*, an element which plays no specific role in academic theory. The nominal unit of account is just the language used by individuals when they are operating in the market.[2] The nominal unit of account, the primary concept in the theory of money according to Keynes, is the means by which individuals determine and express their actions towards others. Its existence and definition has something to do with sovereignty, an underrated notion in academic theory. Conceiving money as *fiat money* allows academic theoreticians to avoid dealing explicitly with the concept of sovereignty.

Money, anonymous scribe rather than memory

The proposition that 'money is memory' derives directly from money being seen as a good, a special good indeed, called 'fiat money'; and indirectly from individuals being seen in an *a priori* given space of goods or commodities. Note that in academic theory, individuals are seen only as an initial endowment (a point of the commodity space), preferences (functions defined by the commodity space) and access to techniques of production and transaction. An alternative view is possible, according to which individuals are *accounts* interlinked by *flow of payments*. Clearly, (i) the latter view has no less empirical legitimacy than the academic alternative; (ii) it raises the problem of money in a very different way. While agreeing with the implicit concept of Kocherlakota's article – money as a decentralized control over individuals – such an approach avoids confusing money with capital, by attributing to the former a property specific of the latter (to be a store of value). It also avoids considering money and accounting as substitutes. Accounting does not necessarily imply a centralized economy. That individuals may be described by their accounts does not mean that any of them has a free access to others accounts.[3] Individual accounts are like many private memories written in a common language, the nominal unit of account. Individual accounts rather than money play the 'technological role of memory'. Money, instead of being a special commodity called 'fiat money', appears rather as a device allowing individuals to inscribe determinate amounts of nominal units in their accounts.

Scribe *versus* memory

An *a priori* given commodity space is the necessary starting point of any value theory. We are so used to that approach that we do not inquire into its relevance or legitimacy. Explicit justifications of that starting point are rare and poor.[4] It is sometimes called into question through the introduction of some uncertainty about goods quality (private information). Williamson and Wright (1994) see in that private information a reason for the acceptance of money as the only perfectly recognized good in that context.

It is not possible here to develop a discussion on the merits and drawbacks of the assumption of a given commodity space. What must be said, however, is that such an assumption should not be interpreted in a naturalistic manner, as it is too often the case. Rather than being part of a naturalistic description of the world in which we live, commodity space is an abstract notion appropriate only to specific theoretical considerations. In the history of economic analysis, the concept of commodity space appears as an alternative to an exclusively monetary description of the economy, which was rejected by Adam Smith as irrelevant. Authors who adopted that monetary view were criticized by Smith, who coined the term 'mercantilists' to denounce them. Commodity space should be interpreted as using the *language* of value theory (and also the language of individuals who are described by value theory).

What is at stake is whether money as a term is an optional part of the language of value theory (does money belong to the commodity space?), or part of the exclusive language of a market economy. Is it possible to describe what happens in a market economy using only money quantities? The answer is: yes.

Instead of describing economic agents as starting from a commodity space (endowments, preferences and techniques), it is quite possible to conceive of them as *accounts in which various quantities of the same nominal unit of account (the dollar) are inscribed*. Dollar, rather than commodities, is a term common to everybody. Each individual has his/her own account where quantities of dollars at a given date represent either assets or liabilities (the time dimension is zero). Individuals meet randomly (or not). The unique visible consequence of a (bilateral or multilateral) meeting may be the transfer of dollars from one account to another. If this happens, amounts of assets and liabilities are instantly modified (flows of payment have a time dimension of –1). Transfers are recorded as transactions at the very time they take place. They measure the *variations* at time *t* (or during an accounting period) of the assets and liabilities. *Amounts* of dollars inscribed in the balance-sheets are part of a history: they are accumulated over time according to legal or conventional rules (often independently of the rules governing transactions).[5] What matters here is not the more or less durability of commodities (given by assumption) but the validity over time of the unit of account, which is the real problem obscured by the misleading expression (when applied to money) 'store of value'.

Regarding transactions, the relevant question is not to know whether they are realized by barter or thanks to a special element of the commodity space ('fiat money'). The crucial point is knowing how transfers of units of account (dollars) are realized. *Who (or which device) is in charge of inscribing into accounts dollar transfers between individuals?*

Two opposite answers may be given to that question. They differ in the same way as the two considered by Kocherlakota when he tries to remedy the no-commitment problem. The first solution is a *direct social control*: a clearing center *à la* Debreu makes sure that all agents respect their budgetary constraints. Anonymity is broken and individuals strictly comply with the rules of the market (equivalence): there is a centralization achieved by a non-individual, an auctioneer-accountant. A second solution is an *indirect social control*: a payment system allows individuals to find some means of payment, transferring dollars from one account to another. Money here is no longer a special commodity but a *set of rules*. For instance, payments which are not durable (credit money) have to be paid back to the bank. Equivalence is imposed on individuals, but only *a posteriori* (accounts should be balanced at the end of the period). Money is the device by which accounts are managed. In this view, money may be said to be *the scribe of a market economy*. Money is seen *not as a concrete object, not as a commodity, but as a set of rules performing the inscription and transfer of nominal units of account in an economy characterized by decentralization and equivalence.*

All monetary organizations in the history of market economies may be conceived of as different realizations of the same set of rules which combine three basic principles: a nominal unit of account; a procedure to obtain the means of payment; and a procedure to settle the balance necessary due to a lack of *a priori* co-ordination among decentralized individuals.[6] When equilibrium situations only are taken into consideration, as with Kocherlakota, the first two rules are sufficient.[7]

Without a clearing central system or a system of payment, it would be impossible to transfer dollars and achieve positive balance-sheets, a situation equivalent to that of autarky in the academic model. With money, dollar transfers may take place and autarky is avoided. Money here is *essential* in the sense described by Wallace.[8] Finally, money is as efficient as centralized clearing if demand for money is not rationed (money is no better than clearing).

In both previous versions of the theory, money only is compatible with decentralization and anonymity. But money is substitutable for memory only in Kocherlakota's view. This is in accordance with the logic of value theory in which money is conceived as a special commodity used as an intermediary of exchange – 'fiat money'– but contrary to parsimony (Occam's razor), since durability has nothing to do with intermediation in exchange. In the monetary approach adopted here, money does not play the role of memory. It ensures, however, decentralized control of budgetary constraints and equivalence.

Money: net wealth or institution?

Following a monetary approach does not mean refusing to take goods into consideration. It means only that a purely monetary description of an economy is possible and sensible. But nothing prevents this description including commodities and various assets, drawing a parallel with value theory. Individual net wealth may be defined by the *scalar product* of the vector of quantities (positive) of assets, that is, durable commodities or financial assets, and the quantities (negative) of liabilities defined by the vector of money prices. But, according to the Mengerian principle, prices are meaningful only for those commodities or assets negotiated in the market at time t.[9] In other terms, at t only purchase flows are correctly evaluated by market prices, but not stocks formed by past transactions. Market prices at t should not be applied to all the commodities and assets inscribed in balance-sheets. The principle *marked to market* is no more justified than that of historical or replacement prices. Amounts of units of account inscribed in balance-sheets (zero time dimension) are partly arbitrary and conventional. It is not the case for flows (time dimension -1). In short, amounts of wealth are arbitrary, but variations of wealth are not. They are determined by transfers of dollars recorded at t (remember that money is the exclusive intermediary of exchange, and that transactions are all sales or purchases and not barter).

The evaluation of wealth depends also on the durability of goods. If all commodities were perishable, individual and social wealth would be zero.

If, by contrast, all commodities lasted forever, the wealth of individual i in a pure-exchange economy would be $\langle p(t), x_i(t) \rangle$. Exchange would modify the physical composition of wealth, but at each point of time the wealth variation would be zero. But, despite that fact, the amount of wealth may vary according to the accepted convention for accounting prices.

Let us assume commodities and assets lasting forever, and non-durable money (IOUs paid back at each transaction round). Transactions are subject to monetary equivalence: purchases $\left(\langle p(t), x_i^+(t) \rangle \right)$ tend to create a negative balance of payment and sales $\left(\langle p(t), x_i^-(t) \rangle \right)$ a positive one. The difference between purchases $(+)$ and sales $(-)$ is the balance of payment. To maintain the parallel with Kocherlakota, it is assumed that equivalence between purchases and sales applies so that:

$$\langle p(t), x_i'(t) \rangle = 0.$$

Individual wealth i evolves according to:

$$\frac{d}{dt} w_i(t) = \langle p'(t), x_i(t) \rangle + \langle p(t), x_i'(t) \rangle = \langle p'(t), x_i(t) \rangle.$$

Here, the principle of historical prices is implicitly adopted and wealth evolves according to variation of prices over time. If the *marked to market* principle has been adopted ($p'(t) = 0$), individual wealth would be constant.

Money, if assumed to be non-durable, is not part of individual or social wealth. Money is present only in transactions, as an exclusive means of transferring units of account. A non-durable form of money perfectly performs the transaction function. Being necessarily present in transactions, money affects wealth variation. It is not the case here because disequilibrium situations are not considered (in order to keep in step with academic theory).

The place of money relative to wealth entirely depends on how we conceive it: as a special commodity, or as an institution.

In models where money is assumed to be durable and to play the role of memory, like other durable or capital goods, money is logically an element of wealth.[10] This is the case in value theory, when the so-called 'problem of integration of money into value theory' is solved. Money, being positively priced at equilibrium, becomes part of capital and appears in the balance-sheet. But if we consider money as a substitute for social clearing (without costs), then money is no longer an element of wealth, but merely an institutional device. The fact that money is essential – because it allows greater social wealth than bartering – does not make it saleable in the market. Law is essential (think of a lawless society!), but law is not part of social wealth either. When money is not seen as a good or a commodity, there is no possibility of relating it to social wealth. Only 'fiat money' has a (relative) price.

To think of money as an institution rather than a commodity has another interesting consequence. It connects money and sovereignty. Money is among the rules of the market game. Where do these rules come from? Money is the set of rules governing the inscription of monetary amounts in individual accounts. Individuals are subject to these rules, as they are subject to laws. Rules and laws evolve. Who has the power to institute and to modify these rules? This question brings us to key problems in the formation of money theory (think of the debates about the legitimacy of monetary reforms), which have been overlooked since the notion of 'fiat money' came into the foreground.

Monetary theory abounds in metaphors (the 'veil', the 'lubricant', and so on) and images (the 'wheel of commerce', and so on). Money in the economy is like blood in the human body, information in communications systems, or words in a language. The view adopted here of the relation of money to wealth is relatively unusual, so it may be useful to recast it with the help of a new metaphor. Money is to wealth what the RAM of a computer is to its ROM, that is, the totality of orders and instructions allowing the operator to write information on hard disks. Money, like the RAM, is active only when the computer is active (when transactions take place) whereas wealth, like the ROM, exists independently. Another metaphor may be suggested: money is to the economy what the operating system is to the computer.[11] Such metaphors are a way to underline the radical difference between money and wealth, and between money and capital. Money is a decentralized means of social control (the position shared by Kocherlakota and academic theory), and as such should not be separated from sovereignty. In this scenario 'fiat money' seems a misleading notion: it prevents us from seeing money as a necessary component of the accounting system through which a market economy attains a representation of itself.

Money and accounting

Kocherlakota takes a wrong track when he assimilates accounting to centralization.[12] It is true that accountants have to follow common rules imposed by the state for fiscal and other reasons. But information relating to accounts is private except when firms try to borrow in the market. And even in that case, only part of the account information is publicly available. In other words, we should not confuse two different oppositions: one is relative to information and its distribution among individuals – centralization *versus* decentralization; the other concerns the description of individuals – commodity space *versus* amounts of the nominal unit of accounts. The former introduces the longstanding, plausible idea that money is a decentralized social control providing an alternative to centralized control; on that idea academic theoreticians and others may, and perhaps should, agree. The latter, by contrast, reveals a strong opposition between value theories (a real approach) and a monetary approach. Accounting may find a place in both, but it is only in the monetary approach that accounting achieves its full identity.

Accounting and theory of a market economy

Empirical arguments are not the only ones which prefer a description of agents as individual accounts rather than as points in the commodity space. The special affinity between accounting and the monetary approach is decisive (see Cartelier 2006). The outstanding point is that accounting and the monetary approach take into consideration *out-of-equilibrium situations*, whereas academic theory deals only with equilibria.

Out-of-equilibrium situations are characterized by non-zero monetary balances between voluntary purchases and sales. Such balances must be settled (by constrained operations) as a consequence of the equivalence principle. Assume, for the sake of simplicity, that the only possible settlement of a balance is to sell (if the balance is negative) or to buy (if the balance is positive) a perpetual financial asset yielding at each point of time one unit of account (Keynes's consols).[13] The positive or negative quantity of consols held by individual i at time t is $\mu_i(t) = \int_0^t \mu_i'(t)dt$, which is also the amount of interest (received or paid) while $P_\mu(t) = \int_0^\infty e^{-rt}dt$ is the price of the consols.

The aggregate quantity of consols and its variation at each t are identically equal to zero: $\sum_i \mu_i(t) = 0$ and $\sum_i \mu_i'(t) = 0$. Applying the terms used in the preceding section and using for the money balance of individual i at time t, the relation is now:

$$-\langle p(t), x_i'(t) \rangle - \mu_i(t) = \sigma_i(t).$$

Involuntary balances have to be compensated by an equivalent sale or purchase of consols $p_\mu(t)\mu_i'(t)$ where $\mu_i(t) = \int_0^t \mu_i'(t)dt$. The total amount of interest paid or received results from the history of balances experienced by individual i.

The evolution of individual wealth is still zero, due to equivalence, but here its composition changes over time in a way that is *non-desired* by individuals. If purchases exceed sales, the involuntary increase in commodities is balanced by an involuntary loss in consols:

$$v_i(t) = \frac{d}{dt} w_i(t) = p_\mu(t)\mu_i'(t) + \langle p(t), x_i'(t) \rangle = 0.$$

At each point of time there is a 'market sanction' expressed by $p_\mu(t)\mu_i'(t)$.

In contrast, in academic theory $\mu_i(t) = 0$ and $p_\mu(t)\mu_i'(t) = 0$, $\forall i,t$. In other words, value theory, despite its high degree of rigor and sophistication, does not account for a system where anonymous forces of competition encourage or repress individual actions in the market when they are not in accordance with those of others. In academic theory there is room neither for 'market sanctions', nor for competition as a co-ordination device. But in a decentralized economy, equilibrium is a very special case and non-equilibrium is the general rule. Double-entry accounting and the monetary approach combine the equivalence principle (the obligation to settle balances) with instant variation of wealth composition. They therefore provide a more appropriate description of a market economy than academic theory does.

Money theory and disequilibrium

In disequilibrium situations, balance settlement is crucial. Consequently, monetary rules are essential for these situations and the dynamics they trigger. Money is present 'in person', to use Marx's expression. Wicksell and the Swedish School, Hawtrey, Schumpeter and Keynes in the *Treatise on Money* have foregrounded the study of monetary dynamics. Global stability and general equilibrium on the one hand, and accounting and monetary organization on the other, are very closely related. But economists have largely neglected this connection due to the dominance of 'fiat money' in the value approach (see Cartelier 2007).

The heart of the matter is how to combine the two fundamental characteristics of a market economy: (i) transactions are multilateral (at a given point of time or accounting period, any individual may transact with any other); (ii) decentralization means a great dispersion of information among individuals. Academic theory does not succeed in combining these two features. Search-theoretic models of money essentially consider bilateral relations.[14] Here, equilibrium is the rule. In a sense, such a restriction is acceptable since it would be difficult to understand why two agents would transact without agreeing on the transaction. In this framework, money is naturally justified to remedy the lack of a double coincidence of wants. In other words, money and equilibrium may be related, given this special environment. But when multilateral transactions are acknowledged, as is the case with the strategic market games approach, it becomes clear that disequilibrium is the rule. Some general principle of price determination has to be imagined in order to explain disequilibrium situations. Shapley-Shubik's rule provides for this necessity. But Shapley-Shubik's rule requires that money is presupposed at the very start. In sum, there is a gap which is difficult to fill between a theory which pretends to explain why money is used at equilibrium in a bilateral setting, and one which admits general disequilibrium in a multilateral monetary setting.

Conceiving money as a decentralized social control hopefully contributes to closing this gap. Barter complies only with partial budgetary constraints. In contrast, monetary exchange takes place necessarily under multilateral budgetary constraints. Each individual is constrained not to spend in units of account more than he gets from *all other individuals*. Such a constraint leaves room for non-zero bilateral balances. Decentralization, at the same time, makes it difficult or impossible for individuals to control their total balance by a lack of information about their partners. In this sense, it may be said that money is co-extensive in a market economy. If this is true then trying to provide microfoundations for money, as academic theoreticians claim to do, is misleading and unsuccessful.

Money, as mentioned above, is a combination of three components: (i) a unit of account providing for a common language; (ii) a procedure to obtain means of payment, allowing individuals to realize their plans in the market independently from each other; and (iii) a constrained procedure of balance settlement imposing equivalence to all individuals. Balance settlement (or report over time) is the tangible form taken by disequilibria. Individuals react to these unexpected situations by triggering in a decentralized way (there is no auctioneer) monetary disequilibrium dynamics. What is at stake here is the viability of the economy and, more precisely in relation to money, the maintenance of the monetary organization and the unit of account.

Economists defending a monetary approach (the Wicksell connection in general, including Keynes in the *Treatise*) have not really succeeded in building a fully-fledged theory of dynamics. As in the case of value theory, no general proposition has been established yet. Some stumbling-blocks are common to both approaches, in particular the complex interdependence between individuals in a dynamic setting. However, prospects seem better for the monetary approach since *market mechanisms* determine disequilibrium prices, which is not the case in the academic theory where prices are only determined by equilibrium conditions. The most adaptable price mechanism is the Shapley-Shubik rule (described in the writings of traditional economists like Cantillon and Smith), which makes sense only in a monetary economy, that is a market economy where money is not optional and does not need any microfoundation (see Benetti and Cartelier 2001).

Money and payment

A negative characteristic of 'fiat money' must be added to those mentioned above (non-consumable, non-input and non-privately producible goods): *'fiat money' is not a nominal unit of account*. As a commodity, although very special, it may be used only as a *numéraire* and not as a nominal unit of account. Being a *numéraire* is possible for any commodity (simple or composite) having a positive price at equilibrium. Being a nominal unit of account is the most specific property of money according to the intellectual tradition which Schumpeter calls the 'monetary approach'. The first sentence of Keynes's *Treatise on Money* expresses this idea: 'Money of account, namely that in which debts and prices and general purchasing power are *expressed*, is the primary concept of a theory of money' (Keynes 1930, p. 3, italics in the original). The opposition to value theory, where no room is left for any nominal unit of account, cannot be more clearly affirmed. Another way of defending this idea, which is very similar to that of Keynes, is Sraffa's proposition that a monetary economy is an economy where there is only one way of expressing prices (Sraffa 1932).

The impossibility for value theoreticians of dealing with a nominal unit of account is at the heart of a confusion about the permanence of money over time. The existence of a monetary equilibrium is not relevant to that issue, but only to the question of 'fiat money'. The assumption of the durability of 'fiat money' is not a solution either. It makes money a store of value depending on its quantity (according to the quantitative theory of money), but that quantity is exogenous and arbitrary. Moreover, as seen above, durability is not a necessary characteristic of an intermediary of exchange. Following Occam's principle, one should refrain from such redundant and unwise assumptions. The permanence of money should not be reduced to the question of the store of value. It is rather a question of the viability of the monetary organization and of the economy. Does the current set of monetary rules ensure that economic activity never experiences an instability such as to make these rules unacceptable? Permanence of the unit of account over time is a very specific problem, distinct from that of conservation of value, which concerns capital goods and assets.[15] It relates to the forms of money, and to the rules by which transactions are realized and inscribed in accounts.

To get rid of the nominal unit of account (and, incidentally, get rid of any reference to sovereignty) may be considered the founding act of value theory. Aiming to base economic theory on real wealth, and not on nominal values that are too linked with politics, value theoreticians (Smith, Ricardo and Walras, to mention only our distinguished predecessors) have assumed a commodity space as their starting point. Such calculations need to homogenize commodities in relation to prices or values. For Ricardo the notion of *production difficulty* does the job; for Walras it is *marginal utility*. In both cases no nominal unit of account, no 'editing of a dictionary' (Keynes's metaphor) are needed. Individuals are supposedly free from any nominal illusion. Claiming that the nominal unit of account should be at the center of the analysis is not only in radically opposition to value theory, it also requires a new economic concept. Nominal illusion no longer makes sense. Nominal amounts matter, and so-called 'real values' are nothing but deflated quantities, which are generally unsuitable for a rigorous analysis.[16] Since accounting is not a measure of something which could exist independently, monetary evaluation of wealth is not external to wealth.[17] Market transactions, that is, transfers of units of account, are the very condition of any measure of wealth.

Money differs radically from commodities; however, it differs also from credit. Credit money, that is private means of payment, cannot achieve a transaction. Credit is not anonymous. These two points are tightly related. The cheque drawn by individual i from bank A and passed to individual j in order to settle a transaction does not terminate that transaction unless a sufficient amount of units of account are inscribed in i's account, and unless bank A is solvent. The transaction is said to be finished, and i and j free from any obligation to each other, only when units of account are definitely transferred to j's account, which requires that banks settle interbank balances. *Payment* is the term for that definitive transfer of a given amount of units of account from an individual to another (through banks, or not). As long as a transfer is conditional on the individual's and the bank's situation (private information), a payment does not take place. *Payment is the very principle of money*: the identity of private individuals does not matter any longer; individuals are totally independent from each other once the payment is realized.[18]

When money is considered from the point of view of payment, money may be contrasted with credit. This opposition is traditional in the banking school tradition (initiated by Smith and developed by Tooke, Marx and later by Hawtrey): money, by contrast with credit, is viewed as the device by which debts are legally settled. Hawtrey rightly maintains that money is the name of the rule allowing stabilization of a credit system which is unstable by nature. The concrete form taken by this device (gold standard, central banking policy, or whatever) is secondary to the abstract definition. Money must be distinguished from monetary objects.[19] In this view, money may be called a rule, a device or an institution, but certainly not a commodity, not even a special commodity. The assimilation of money and capital, which is typical of academic theory, is the antithesis of this concept.

To maintain, as we do in the present text, that money is the scribe of a market economy, is an attempt to get rid of misleading metaphors (veil, wheel of commerce, and so on), which have in common the reduction of money to empirical objects, characterizing money at a theoretical level as a special commodity called 'fiat money'. Money, as the scribe of a market economy, is the common language allowing communication between individual and decentralized accounts. It also provides the rules by which market relations determine the wealth of individuals, and its variation. Whatever else they may be, monetary objects are essentially a concrete realization of an abstract principle.[20] Their basic role is to terminate a transaction by a definitive transfer of units of account, and to relate all individual transactions by subjecting them to the equivalence principle. Beyond their various empirical functions, they act as a decentralized social control. Keeping this point in mind may help us not to give in too easily to money fetishism.

Notes

1. I am grateful to Luigi Doria and Luca Fantacci for their suggestions and comments on a first version of this paper. The usual disclaimer applies.

2. For a very clear account of the differences between money and language, see Ganssmann, forthcoming.
3. Shubik regrets the neglect of accounting by theoreticians, which he considers to be a serious oversight in economic theory (Shubik 2002).
4. To take a recent example, Wallace (2001) writes: 'Tastes and technologies are given building blocks of economic models mainly because the assumed description can, in principle, be provided by other disciplines. Agronomists describe the various ways to grow wheat, chemists describe how molecules are constructed, and so on. But no other disciplines will tell economists how real cash balances contribute to utility or reduce time spent shopping or what constitutes those real balances' (p. 849). Wallace's argument is not acceptable: the way academic theory describes commodities (Euclidian space, continuum, and so on) is not inspired by any other discipline except mathematics. Presupposition of commodities in terms of a Euclidian space is a theoretical proposition and not an empirical observation. In order to justify such a view, only theoretical arguments make sense.
5. It is the case when assets are measured by their historic values. But this is equally true when the principle *marked to market* applies because the commodities or assets concerned have not all been negotiated in the market at *t*. If they had been, prices would have been different.
6. A more explicit but non-technical presentation of money as a system of payment may be found in Cartelier 1996.
7. Due to the failure of the study of general competitive equilibrium global stability in the 1970s, theoreticians have ceased to consider non-equilibrium situations. Even if serious reasons may be invoked to explain that failure, it has dramatic consequences for the relevance of academic theory.
8. But there is here no temptation to use essentiality as a justification for the existence of money. The notion of the logical genesis of money is useless (money must be presupposed in order to reveal the conditions under which it is accepted), and the so-called 'microfoundation' of money is an illusion.
9. Academic theoreticians of money rightly follow Menger and not Walras when they link prices and effective realization of transactions ('It is an error in economics, as prevalent as it is patent, that all commodities, at a definite point of time and in a given market, may be assumed to stand to each other in a definite relation of exchange, in other words, may be mutually exchanged in definite quantities at will' [Menger 1892]).
10. Luca Fantacci rightly observes that in Keynes's view of the rate of interest, money becomes a commodity, 'which leaves open, not only the question concerning the legitimacy of considering and treating money as a commodity, but also the question of what the peculiarities of money with respect to other commodities are' (Fantacci, this volume).
11. See more on all this in Kalthoff (Chapter 9 of this volume).
12. Ernest Solvay, in his time, considered also that money and accounting were two alternative modes of co-ordination in a market economy.
13. In observable economies, processes are more complex: balance settlement is realized by various procedures, moving from bankruptcies, mergers, LBOs and so on, to financial operations.

14. Search-theoretic models are at a loss on this point. Agents cannot transact more than once at each t. Here is a reason to emphasize the so-called store of value function of money.
15. The fact that agents may not accept legal means of payment – as was the case in Germany after World War Two, according to Vincent Bignon (Bignon 2007) – can be interpreted as reluctance toward the unit of account, as much as toward the monetary objects. To remedy that crisis usually implies the need for a new nominal unit of account.
16. 'To say that net output today is greater but the price-level lower, than ten years ago or one year ago, is a proposition of similar character to the statement that Queen Victoria was a better queen but not a happier woman than Queen Elizabeth – a proposition not without meaning and not without interest, but unsuitable as material for the differential calculus' (Keynes 1936, p. 40).
17. On the performative aspect of accounting, and of calculation more generally, see Doria (Chapter 7 of this volume).
18. One may think at first sight that such a proposition is contrary to Ingham's money theory. It is not the case. Ingham assimilates money and credit. But Ingham distinguishes between bilateral trust, which corresponds to credit, and multilateral trust, which corresponds to money (see Ingham 2004).
19. Empirically the distinction between money and credit evolves over time. In the nineteenth century convertible banknotes and checks were credit instruments, according to Tooke. They were not money because they needed to be convertible into money, that is legally acceptable coins. Nowadays, big banks are considered to be 'too big to fail', and deposits are insured. Cheques can be accepted as equivalent to legal money if they are certified. The distinction between money and credit is conceptual, and its application may vary according to time and place.
20. Dick Bryan and Michael Rafferty's contribution to this volume (see Chapter 6) should probably be read in this spirit.

References

Benetti, Carlo and Cartelier, Jean (2001) 'Money and Price Theory', *International Journal of Applied Economics and Econometrics*, 9 (2), 203–223.

Bignon, Vincent (2007) 'La crise monétaire allemande de 1945–1948', in Bruno Théret (ed.) *La monnaie dévoilée par ses crises* (Paris: Editions de l'EHESS), 221–248.

Cartelier, Jean (1996) *La monnaie* (Paris: Flammarion).

Cartelier, Jean (2006) 'Comptabilité et pensée économique, Introduction à une réflexion théorique', *Revue économique*, 57 (5), 1009–1032.

Cartelier, Jean (2007) 'Money and Markets as Twin Concepts?', in A. Giacomin and C. Marcuzzo (eds) *Money and Markets, a Doctrinal Approach* (London: Routledge), 79–95.

Galiani, Ferdinando (1977) *On Money [Della Moneta]*, in Peter R. Toscano (ed.) University Microfilms International (Chicago: University of Chicago [1751]).

Ganssmann, Heiner (forthcoming) *Doing Money, Elementary Monetary Theory from a Sociological Standpoint* mimeo.

Hart, Keith (2009) 'Mediation and Memory in the Theory of Money', Workshop 'On Either Side of the Economic Science of Money', University of Paris-Ouest-Nanterre, September 2009 mimeo.

Ingham, Geoffrey (2004) *The Nature of Money* (Cambridge: Polity Press).

Iwai, Katsuhito (1988) 'The Evolution of Money: A Search-Theoretic Foundation of Monetary Economics', CARESS Working Paper No. 88–03, University of Pennsylvania.

Keynes, John Maynard (1930) *A Treatise on Money*, vols. 5 and 6 of *The Collected Writings of John Maynard Keynes* (London: Macmillan, 1971).

Keynes, John Maynard (1936) *The General Theory of Money, Interest and Employment*, vol. 7 of *The Collected Writings of John Maynard Keynes* (London: Macmillan, 1971).

Kiyotaki, Nobuhiro and Wright, Randall (1993) 'A Search-Theoretic Approach to Monetary Economics', *The American Economic Review*, 83 (1), 63–77.

Kocherlakota, Narayana, R. (1998a) 'Money Is Memory', *Journal of Economic Theory*, 81, 232–251.

Kocherlakota, Narayana, R. (1998b) 'The Technological Role of Fiat Money', *Federal Reserve Bank of Minneapolis Quarterly Review*, 22 (3), Summer, 2–10.

Menger, Carl (1892) 'On the Origin of Money', *Economic Journal*, 2, reprinted in R. M. Starr (ed.) *General Equilibrium Models of Monetary Economies* (Boston: Academic Press, 1989).

Ostroy, J. M. and Starr, R. M. (1990) 'The Transactions Role of Money', in B. M. Friedman and F. Hahn (eds) *Handbook of Monetary Economics*, 1 (Amsterdam: North-Holland), 3–62.

Shi, Shouyong (2006) 'Viewpoint: A Microfoundation of Monetary Economics', *Canadian Journal of Economics*, 39 (3), 643–688.

Shubik, Martin (2002) 'Accounting and Economic Theory', Working Papers AC and ES, Working Paper No. 16, Yale School of Management. Accessible online at: http://www.ssrn.com/abstractid=344421.

Spahn, Heinz-Peter (2007) 'Money as a Social Bookkeeping Device', in A. Giacomin and C. Marcuzzo (eds) *Money and Markets, a Doctrinal Approach* (London: Routledge), 150–165.

Sraffa, Piero (1932) 'Dr Hayek on Money and Capital', *The Economic Journal*, 42 (165), 42–53.

Wallace, Neil (2001) 'Whither Monetary Economics?', *International Economic Review*, 42 (4), 847–869.

Willamson, Steve and Wright, Randall (1994) 'Barter and Monetary Exchange under Private Information', *The American Economic Review*, 84, 104–123.

3

Money without Value, Accounting without Measure: How Economic Theory Can Better Fit the Economic and Monetary System We Live in

Yuri Biondi

Introduction

The financial crisis of 2007 was unanimously declared a liquidity crisis, and governments and central banks worldwide reacted by injecting massive amounts of fresh money to rescue the financial system. Whilst this response succeeded in effectively restoring ordinary inter-bank credit, it did not address the systemic issues raised by the crisis.

Empirical evidence of price levels for durable goods, commodities, real estate or corporate shares, as well as of monetary aggregates, does not point to a lack of liquidity as the proper explanation of the crisis. On the contrary, some key elements suggest an *excess of liquidity* that implied disruptive speculative waves, including overwhelming *inflation* of financial assets and real estate. At the corporate level, such excess liquidity was enhanced by corporate policies fostering leverage: by debt financing for leveraged buy-outs or to pay down shareholders' equity through stock repurchases; by leased and off-balance-sheet financing – but also by issuing shares as means of payment for mergers and acquisitions, in some cases; by borrowing and share-issuance by financial organizations; by securitization (i.e., commoditization) of simple or sophisticated financial contracts that displaced those financial investments in the realm of money, giving them an apparent monetary dimension; and by the market liberalization of derivatives' origination and distribution.

Such a liquidity problem confronts policy-makers and theorists with two distinct issues, already recognized by von Hayek and Keynes[1] respectively: the distinction between money and investment can be weakened and eventually lost by modern financial practices; consequently, secondly, the proper relationship between the monetary and the economic dimension may be muddled by the evaporation of that critical distinction.

Theoretically speaking, then, our problem with liquidity refers to the proper understanding of money and of its role in economy and society. Our problem relates to the confusion between price and value that leads us to misconceive money as a 'measure of value'. This confusion appears to survive from the classical economic English tradition which dominated the nineteenth century and the birth of the political economy. The following analysis will show that this peculiar understanding of money is inappropriate to the current financial and economic conditions, and does not properly capture the functioning of money in either financial or non-financial organizations.

This paper aims therefore at developing a constructive critique of the concept of money as a measure of value. This concept creates a quantitative correspondence of money to everything, and reduces its fundamental roles – as a means of payment and a mode of accounting – to the quantity of money that is supposed to be the *general equivalent* for everything. However, advances in economics and accounting allow us to better understand money without value, and accounting without measure. Money may then be interpreted as a socio-economic medium without intrinsic content, and its accounting function may be effectively inscribed into the set of relationships that constitutes every economic organization which is accounted for on a monetary basis – whether public or private, business or non-business, financial or non-financial. This institutional economic approach to money *and* accounting may enhance our understanding of the socio-economic system as a dynamic system of relationships based upon both monetary and economic dimensions.

The surviving preconception of classical economics

Limiting our attention to modern economic thought, the idea of money as a measure of value belongs to the classical economic English tradition. Those economists were fascinated by the accumulation of capital that was then understood as the ultimate source of wealth. Consequently, they tried to explain the working of the whole economic system from the viewpoint of that accumulation. The place and role of money is problematic in such perspective. On one hand, money appears to exemplify the functioning of capital: money-capital is then invested and produces more money-capital. Saving and usury can be and have been identified as the proper basis of the working of the economy. On the other hand, the 'popular confusion of money and capital' (in Schumpeter's terms) must be avoided: wealth ultimately does not consist of mere money, which is nothing but a medium towards wealth as the ultimate end. Therefore, money should be a 'veil' of the overarching production of wealth through the accumulation of capital (i.e., productive wealth). Money should eventually disappear, leaving wealth and capital standing alone as proper foundations of the *real* economic system. As a consequence, following Schumpeter, the classical English thesis cannot explain the significance of *business income to the firm nor financial interest,* but only the significance of salaries to workers and rents for properties. The proprietor who personifies the business firm is then understood as a modern *King Midas* who owns the productive capital that has to be accumulated, that is maintained and increased. This capital is the ultimate source of such income, which generates wealth. Business profits and financial interests are then reduced to rents or quasi-rents on the underlying properties which provide the kingdom's worth.

From this classical perspective, money is certainly a 'veil', but it is also understood as a *general equivalent,* making each good convertible into every other good. It acts then as a standard of value, since it determines the unique market price that incorporates that value. This idea appears to survive in the neoclassical theory, even though it no longer fits the new conceptual framework. Since Edgeworth's box at least, the bilateral market exchange is not *equivalent,* since both potential participants aim at gaining from their subjective viewpoints. Exchanges no longer have recourse to the notion of money as a permanent standard of value, but only as a general means of exchange. The direct connection between value and price is definitively cut off. Any notion of equivalence becomes even more problematic when multilateral equilibrium is considered, since the co-ordination and regulation of the economic system is then assured by general competition between agents, not by equivalence attained in each isolated exchange.

Schumpeter and Menger's monetary ingenuity

Carl Menger in particular led the critique of the classical English notion of money as a measure of value, which he contrasted with the concept

of money as a measure of price. Accordingly, money cannot be understood as an objective measure of values that intrinsically belong to economic goods – their 'gold soul' conferred by King Midas's touch – but
should be related to subjective and interactive price formation and then
considered only as an expression of determined prices. Menger (1892,
p. 159, our translation) claimed that 'according to mainstream theory,
the chief and primitive function of money consists in *measuring* the
exchange value of goods on the basis of *its own exchange value*. This
implies therefore that the value of cash is a known quantity, whilst the
value of other things should be determined by measuring it through
that value ...' (italics in original). This extremely important statement
identifies two mistakes that have to be rectified before we can develop a
positive conception of money as a means to measure value:

(a) The idea that one given exchange value is a definitive *quantum*
    intrinsic to each separate good;
(b) The idea that such a quantum is supposed to be intrinsic to each
    good can be measured by the *quantum* of value embedded in the
    monetary unit.

But Menger refuted any idea of measure, seeing that valuations of
goods on a monetary basis are not measures, and such measurement
cannot be done anyway. Valuations are instead monetary balances,
offered or demanded. Conversely, exchanges do not require any preliminary measurement: 'A proper theory of price cannot, therefore,
aim at explaining that supposed "equivalence" between two quantities of goods, which does not exist in any case' (Menger 1925, VII,
Introduction, p. 236, our translation).

Menger further refuted the notion of one unique market price for
each good, because goods do not have fixed relative quantities existing
prior to exchange relations, even in a given space and time. On the contrary, prices are formed in the transacting process between actors: 'In
the description of price formation in isolated exchange, we saw that in
each particular there is a certain range of indeterminacy within which
price formation can take place without the exchange losing its economic
character, and that the extent of this range depends upon the nature of
the particular exchange situation' (Menger 1871 [1950], p. 199).

Menger was rightly concerned with economic transactions involving
amounts of money and implied subjective values, and he developed an
institutional approach to relative prices. His insights paved the way for
considering the whole set of terms and conditions involved in exchange

transactions and trading structures, including knowledge, default penalties and accounting systems. His ingenuity should be set in the context of monetary theory between the last decades of the nineteenth and the first decades of the twentieth century. During the nineteenth century, it was usual to separate the theory of value and distribution from the analysis of the nature and functions of money. At that time,

> Prices (including rates of income) remained primarily exchange ratios, which money reduced to absolute figures without affecting them in anything except for *clothing them* with a monetary garb. Or, in other words, the model of the economic process was in all essentials a *barter model*, the working of which inflations and deflations might disturb but which is logically complete and autonomous. (Schumpeter 1954, p. 1088, italics added)

At the end of the century, however, it had become increasingly clear that money, and the related activities of the banking and financial system, can affect the economic system; this raises the question of defining money, at least at the normative level, in order to leave real processes unaltered, that is, still based on the hypothesis of barter made away from time and space (Schumpeter 1954, p. 1088). This conception of the economic process called for the identification of *neutral money*, conceptually defined by Wicksell, who pioneered the new monetary theory.[2]

> In itself, this concept [of neutral money] expresses nothing but the established belief in the possibility of pure 'real' analysis. But it also suggests recognition of the fact that money *need* not be neutral. So its creation induced a hunt for the conditions in which money is neutral. And this point led to the discovery that no such conditions can be formulated, that is, that there is no such thing as neutral money or money that is a mere veil spread over the phenomena that really matter – an interesting case of a concept rendering valuable service by proving unworkable. (Schumpeter 1954, pp. 1088–1089, emphasis in original)

According to Schumpeter, the imagined notion of the permanent economic value of money is definitely lost, in theory as well as in practice. Relative prices cannot be stable, and cannot vary except for 'real' economic reasons. Changes in values of goods are therefore fundamentally connected to changes in the value of money. Following this line of reasoning, the general economic equilibrium developed by Walras constitutes an early theoretical attempt to integrate money into a peculiar theory of value and distribution, in particular with a fundamental distinction between *money* and *numéraire*:

> Walras, anticipated of course by all the authors who – like A. Smith and Malthus – had used labor as a standard of value, introduced the useful fashion of keeping distinct the numéraire – a commodity whose unit is used in order to express prices and values but whose own value remains unaffected by this role – and monnaie – the commodity that actually serves as means of exchange and whose value is consequently affected because its monetary role absorbs part of its supply. (Schumpeter 1954, p. 1087)

This notion of *numéraire* allows Walras to keep intact the monetary role of a 'measure of values' as a *standard* for the intrinsic value of exchanged goods, just as the notion of labor did in classical economics; this neoclassical analysis emphasizes the independence of relative prices[3] from the influence of money.[4] This Walrasian model is intended to be a static approach to money,[5] and is in line with Irving Fisher's approach. It is no accident, then, that both Fisher and Walras argued against money creation by banking and financial institutions,[6] and believed in the theoretical possibility of measuring the general purchasing power of money, which would allow the economic value of money to be determined and thus eliminate its disruptive impact on the 'real' economy.

The dynamic revolution: money as a process

By contrast, the Mengerian approach enabled Schumpeter to criticize the Walrasian conception of the economic and monetary system:

> The Austrian way of emphasizing the behavior or decision of individuals and of defining exchange value of money with respect to individual commodities rather than with respect to price level of one kind or another has its merits, particularly in the analysis of an inflationary process: it tends to replace a simple but inadequate picture[7] by one which is less clear-cut but more realistic and richer in results. (Schumpeter 1954, p. 1090)

Notwithstanding the theoretical novelty of ordinal utility and equilibrium, the basic relationship between money, price and exchange remains problematic from the Walrasian perspective. In particular, whilst claiming to have developed a system based on market exchanges, the Walrasian system actually excludes the exchange process from its framework: no transaction is or can be performed before the market price is fixed. Conversely, price-fixing is assumed to be performed out of the contextual space and time of transactions. This implies that pricing (meaning price formation) is not so much investigated as assumed by the Walrasian system, which therefore is ultimately *without exchanges*.[8] Again, money is a measure of reference rather than a means of payment in an exchange transaction.

The classical and Walrasian (neoclassical) understanding of the economic system is thus fundamentally *static*. However, the Schumpeterian critique has opened the way to a *dynamic* understanding of the economic system. Schumpeter's first step was the reformulation of the Walrasian system in terms of a 'circular flow'. The economic system is then supposed to replicate itself period after period, through a perpetual cycle of inflows and outflows. In this way monetary payments and economic transfers are distinguished and articulated, but still remain symmetrical. In particular, each transaction is constituted by two complementary flows: on one side, one actor purchases a good and pays money for that; on the opposite side, another actor earns money from the transfer of that good. In terms of the Walrasian 'circular flow', money is neutral and every transaction is at the same time real and monetary. According to Marget (1951, p. 114), this representation of the economic system is 'from first to last, a system of *money* flows'. Money operates here as the means of exchange that performs payments related to exchange transactions. It therefore constitutes a general means of exchange, not a permanent measure of values.

Drawing on Marget and Schumpeter therefore, we can speak of money as a monetary process or, preferably, a monetary system.[9] Money is no longer understood as a quantity or a 'veil', but as a *monetary process* that facilitates horizontal transactions between different actors. Monetary payments form a network of monetary (and financial) transactions that ultimately constitute the banking and financial system of the economy. This system performs transactions, and holds debts and credits on behalf of the participants in those transactions. All these monetary events can be seen as the *first order* of the 'accounting system' of the whole economy. Money, in fact, performs two distinct functions. On one side, it operates as a means of payment in exchange transactions. On the other side, it *accounts for the whole of transactions* performed by each actor and between actors, both situated in a particular context of space and time.

Based on this horizontal web of monetary and financial transactions, financial statements constitute the *second order* of the accounting process of the economic organization or system. Basically, accounting can be understood here as the *imputation device* that articulates inflows and outflows relative to a given economic organization defined as an accounting entity (Stauss 1944). Accounting performs vertical economic co-ordination, connecting separate transactions which are differently located in space and time.

Like the monetary system foreshadowed by general equilibrium theory, the accounting system starts with transactions between the accounting entity and its world, constituted by the various stakeholders in the economic organization. In fact, the flow of these transactions does not establish the accounting system as a complete, overarching activity. Accountants cannot consider only monetary transactions to account for the economy of organizations. Even though actual monetary transfers are accomplished, they are not necessarily market exchanges at market prices. The reductionist connection between money, price and market exchanges is thus cut off. Rather, the basic performance of accounting systems consists of accounting recognition which considers the economic impact – on the accounting entity – of various generating events. First, this recognition is vertical in relation to the horizontal web of related transactions, because it is no longer based on actual cash transfers: the impact of a generating event is accountable even though it has not generated a cash movement. Consequently, the application of accounting techniques introduces non-cash recognition – quantified on a monetary basis – of events located beyond the current period or place in time and space. Various techniques such as depreciation, amortization, provision, impairment and revaluation are therefore seen as 'accounting imputation'.

The place and role of the accounting system

The question of imputation is central to the development of the accounting system. Leading accounting theorists stress the disconnection between this system and the neoclassical approach. In particular, Ijiri (1967, pp. 59–64) showed the problems with the linear logical chain – connecting cost, product and selling price – adopted by marginal economic analysis. Very simple logical chains that involve joint sub-products actually prevent such straightforward imputation of final revenues to initial costs. Anthony (1960) further extends this line of critique to the underlying optimizing principle, which he aims at replacing with the 'satisficing principle' introduced by H. Simon.

Therefore, as claimed by Menger and Schumpeter among others, the marginal analysis does not account for the monetary and economic process generated by the economic organization, chiefly because of its narrow equilibrium approach to unfolding economic dynamics (Shubik 1993). This approach does not fit, either theoretically nor heuristically, the working of the accounting system, as stressed by Shubik (1978, p. 686): '[I]t must be stressed that the type of monetary model constructed here can be most easily formulated by monetizing all assets every period thereby simplifying the concept of income far more than do current accounting practices'. To be sure, accounting does not provide an abstract definition of business income(s) for the economic organization, but rather a method which rests upon general principles of reference. We argue here that the pure logic of accounting implied by this method does not fit the equilibrium approach adopted by neoclassical economic theory.

Whether it is stationary or instantaneous, equilibrium makes cost and price (which are understood respectively as monetary outflow and inflow related to production and sale) simultaneous. Every 'period' of reference for these flows (whether day, quarter, or year) is then made independent by analytical machinery:

> in static theory, [economic analysis] treat[s] the single period as a closed system, the working of which can be examined without reference to anything that goes on outside it (in the temporal sense). (Hicks 1965, p. 32)

> One may make a simple *pro forma* change of notation which treats goods in different time periods as different goods. (Shubik 1993, p. 229)

Being concerned with time-flow, duration and hazard involved by the ongoing process of production and sale, accounting imputation argues against this simplistic view. This implies that accounting provides a specific notion of business income that is potentially fruitful for economic theory and analysis. Accounting focuses on the ongoing monetary and economic process generated by the economic organization as an accounting entity. At least three main features of the accounting system do not fit the equilibrium approach:

(a) Concerning the monetary and financial dimension, the accounting system is not based upon actual cash flow and cash funds, but includes cash-equivalent debts and credits;

(b) Concerning the economic dimension, accounting imputation defines the representation of the economic and monetary process generated by the accountable economic organization over space and time;

(c) Concerning the institutional dimension, this specific representation constitutes the basis for institutional regulations – related to dividend distribution, taxation and maintenance of corporate shareholders' equity and other regulatory reserves – assuring the continuity of the accounting entity and the fulfilment of its obligations over time, and generally making its activity *accountable* to governing and supervisory bodies.

Furthermore, an equilibrium approach involves the logical and heuristic identity of exchange, price and the market of reference, since it defines a simultaneous system of monetary market exchanges. Accordingly, every monetary transfer should involve a market exchange, which is in turn performed on a market of reference. The accounting system does not take into account virtual exchanges, but actual transactions between the accounting entity and its world. These transactions are located in space and time. Therefore, prices are considered either as actual monetary (or financial, cash-equivalent) transfers, or external values of reference – the being preferred by historical cost accounting, whilst the second is preferred by marked-to-market (fair value) accounting that assumes that active markets provide such reference external to the entity's process of becoming. In sum, the price system is limited to a logic of (relative) market prices, whilst the accounting system accounts for the inner dynamics of the economic organization that, through the actual performance of the accounting system, remains distinct from the external markets for factors or products.

This theoretical distinction is erased by economic analysis. The equilibrium approach seeks to isolate periods by the simultaneous imputation of all and only monetary outflows and inflows. This logic assumes that:

(a) All costs (expenses) are monetary and are paid out during the period (or moment) of reference;

(b) All the revenues (products), supposed to be generated by these costs, are also monetary, and are cashed in during the same period or moment.

The equilibrium view depends on this *Walrasian vice*. If the monetary outflow is not directly a 'cost' (for instance salaries),[10] it must be an asset, whose value derives directly from the actualization of the future cash flows (revenues) that it produces individually, in line with actuarial techniques. Accordingly, if markets are perfect and the entrepreneur maximizes the monetary profit of production and sale (null at equilibrium), capital trans-actions related to assets[11] have no impact on the costs of the productive processes that have employed those assets. Only the price (i.e., the mon-etary flow) paid for their use during the period is accounted for, in order to calculate the revenue generated by those productions. The revenue price of each product *separately from other products* must be entirely determined by the sum of cost prices (rent, salary and interest) at the actual moment of their payment. The resulting profit, defined as the difference between simultaneous revenue and cost, is then null.

Whatever accounting model is used, static or dynamic, an equilibrium approach cannot grasp the pure logic of accounting imputation. According to the dynamic accounting perspective that uses a flow method, all logi-cal separation between the cost invested in the asset and its revenue is lost by the equilibrium approach: it would be hard to account for the net result of the sum invested to acquire the asset.[12] Following Pantaleoni (1897, p. 171), the accounting entity constitutes a bridge between costs and revenue-prices, but no one should forget the ditches between them. The static accounting perspective that uses a stock method aims to deter-mine the net worth that the accounting entity has been entrusted with, and this must distinguish the initial endowment from the resulting change. Therefore, whatever purpose is intended – the representation of the dynamic income or the static rent – accounting imputation departs from the monetary process.[13] Accountants know that the entity's cash dimension (comprising its cash flows and cash funds) is insufficient to represent the economic process of production and sale, generating the economic performance of the entity's activity. Therefore, they design a specific device to recognize, classify and allocate monetary (and finan-cial) outflows and inflows according to the activity and the period of reference.[14] Contrary to the equilibrium assumptions mentioned above:

(a) Not all accounting costs are directly derived from monetary out-flows (for instance provisions, amortizations, depreciations, revalu-ation at current values); nor are they paid in the same period as their potential benefits;[15]
(b) Accounting revenues must be imputed to the period of reference whenever they are cashed in, credited (because of delayed pay-ment), or valued at expected levels; they are not therefore paid in the same period as related costs.

Concerning the outflow side, accounting imputation means distin-guishing monetary outflows (expenditures) that pass directly through the income statement as expenses, from outflows that are capitalized as assets in the balance sheet.[16] Concerning inflow, it means distinguishing between revenues (products) and capital endowments (obligations claimed by third parties and advances on uncertain future revenues). Together with these monetary imputations, some non-monetary imputations are performed – including provisions, amortization charges, depreciation charges, revaluations at current values and deferment of accrued incomes.

In sum, whilst the circular flow connects means of exchange and means of payment (all flows of payment are equivalent exchanges), the accounting system recognizes entity flows related to transactions, operations and other generating events, and classifies them according to two basic distinctions:

(a) Concerning outflows, it disentangles expenses from financial investments that acquire assets;
(b) Concerning inflows, it disentangles revenues (incomes) from financial endowments.

This conceptual framework provides the basic distinction between monetary and non-monetary accounting elements that characterize the balance sheet (see Table 1).

Table 1 Accounting representation of functional capital committed to and exploited by an economic organization (entity)

Balance Sheet at the end of the Period			
Assets		**Liabilities**	
1. Monetary assets	*(cash, cash-equivalent, commercial credits)*	3. Monetary debts	*(payables, commercial debts)*
2a. Invested Costs	*(immobilizations, overheads)*	4a. Advances on revenues	*(debt financing, deferred incomes)*
2b. Investments	*(commitments to other entities)*	4b. Conferred endowments	*(net commitments from financiers)*
5. Accumulated negative balance		5. Accumulated positive balance	*(accumulated balance between costs and revenues, including the net result of the current period)*

Accordingly, the accounting system integrates non-monetary classes. It adopts money as a symbol, that is, a mode of representation *quantified on monetary basis*.[17] In particular, it articulates two distinct monetary functions. On one side, money is the means to effect the payments that perform the transaction process; on the other side, money is the mode of accounting for the economic organization of the accounting entity in relation to space and time.[18] These functions are complementary in the functional representation of the economic organization by the accounting system. They are also combined in the economic and monetary process generated by that economic organization as an entity over space and time.

The performance of the accounting system frames and shapes the behaviour of stakeholders in the economic organization, and further defines the second-order structure of the entity relative to the first order of transactions. It participates therefore in the 'institutional structure of production' (in Coase's terms). This implies that, contrary to the surviving classical idea of proprietor-entrepreneur, this structure is not reduced to property rights alone (Biondi, 2006).

In sum, the equilibrium approach tries to exclude the vertical dimension by reducing the entity's dynamics to market cash flows. The monetary and economic process of the accounting entity is replaced by a series of monetary inflows and outflows that are simultaneously independent and coupled.[19] Though this representation has been expanded, equilibrium is always founded on the entity's *treasury*, which distinguishes the values of properties or possessions on the asset side from the property rights or claims on the liability side, both statically evaluated at a particular moment in time.[20] The flow of time is just an intermittent series of solitary moments; furthermore, the entity's functional capital cannot be distinguished from individual wealth (capital = wealth), and corresponds to the net worth of its proprietor. By contrast, the accounting system performs an entity-specific accounting imputation. The entity's functional capital is distinguished by the net worth (or patrimonial) of proprietors. The accounting system focuses on the interactions of the accounting entity with its world, in order to represent the monetary and economic *process* generated by that entity over space and time.

Implication: there is no such thing as capital

This articulation of monetary and non-monetary elements by the accounting system derives from the application of accounting imputation, *whatever accounting model is adopted*. Theoretically speaking, this implies a functional representation of capital committed to the economic organization. This representation overcomes the material or patrimonial concept of capital that was a heritage of classical economics. The classical notion of the proprietor-entrepreneur implies a confusion between the asset side and the liability side of the balance sheet that contrasts with the accounting representation (Anthony 1983, p. 219). Accordingly, whether physical or financial, capital is no longer understood as the ultimate source of income. Income is defined by the whole of revenues and expenses that pertain to the income statement that complements the balance sheet in the accounting representation. Non-monetary accounting classes relate fundamentally to the determination of income and to the accounting representation – on a monetary basis – of the overarching managed organization. This entity involves complex co-ordination over space and time that implies a financial and economic core generating business income specific to that entity. The accounting representation shapes this economic and monetary process, exposing cost allocation performed through invested costs and immobilizations (class 2), and the productive employment of financial commitments (class 4). This process implies that no accumulation of capital is possible, because invested capital (class 4) is not a permanent feature of the entity, but affected by the hazards and transformations relating to the entity's process of becoming. The ultimate purpose and scope of the entity is no longer the reproduction and accumulation of new capital from past capital (nor the production of capital-wealth for its proprietor), but the 'remuneration' of various stakeholders that commit resources into the enterprise process.

The classical English *static* notion is overcome by this *dynamic* accounting and economic conceptual framework. The concept of 'King Midas's touch' paralyses both business profit and money interest: both are initiated by money capital that its proprietor gives out for lending (entity borrowing) or investment (entity shareholders' equity). From this perspective, money interest pays for the use of proprietor's money that is borrowed and progressively refunded over time, whilst the accounting system maintains the proprietor's money capital, increased by net earnings and refunded only at the end of the capital venture, at liquidation. By contrast, the dynamic concept understands both business profit and money interest as dynamically generated by the common source of business income to the firm as an enterprise entity. Following Schumpeter, they are no longer rents or quasi-rents on owned capital, but remunerations paid out by business revenues generated by the business enterprise that liabilities and equities have been jointly financing over time. The ownership of invested money is irrelevant in the case of money interest, because the bank system's collective action creates money *endogenously*, without connection to an existing base of capital, money or gold. Reserves and capital requirements become part of the second order of the financial system. They are neither defined at the level of each transaction, nor reduced to the quantity (or value) of money, but reconsidered at the level of every whole of transactions (pertaining to one entity) or whole of entities (central banking and government) as regulatory devices to assure the systemic properties of these wholes over space and time. Furthermore, the equity financing of the business enterprise no longer implies the ownership of its assets. The entity's business activity is functionally and institutionally separated from its shareholders, who no longer act as owners of it, but as special sources of financing. Finally, both the financing system and the enterprise system involve collective dimensions that constitute a second order of the architecture of the socio-economic system. They add a second floor to the ground floor of exchanges and decisions made by individual actors. Money and accounting can be understood as complementary institutional structures of economy and society.

Neglected paths in the history of economic thought

This pure logic of accounting relates to some neglected paths of the dialectic evolution of institutional and marginalist economic approaches. Dynamic accounting theories – which have best captured this special contribution of accounting to economic theory – have drawn upon the continental European tradition of economic studies, chiefly concerned with institutions, epistemological foundations, theories of value *and* money and the theory of redistribution. In particular, the marginalist heresy of C. Menger – which influenced J. A. Schumpeter, F. von Hayek and M. Pantaleoni – has surely also influenced leading dynamic accounting theorists such as E. Schmalenbach and G. Zappa (Biondi 2002, 2005a, 2005b, 2008a).

At the beginning of the twentieth century, the strong challenge to equilibrium economics has paved the way for accounting theories that called themselves *'dynamic'*.[21] Starting from an interpretation of the economic system in terms of circular flow – [22] shared with Schumpeter (1926) – [23] these theories have tried to both understand and design the role of accounting in the general process of production and distribution of resources. Dynamic accounting theorizing is at ease with overheads allocation and irreversible immobilizations that feature the temporal economic process, that is, an economic process fundamentally shaped by the flow of time. This theory quite clearly understands that proprietorship and ownership no longer capture business economic dynamics and the related accounting representation of business enterprise entity. Rather, it stresses the significance of immobilizations and investments related to the ideas of temporal potential and becoming; of the production potential delivered by working means of production; of the logical priority of dynamic business income over static net worth. According to Schmalenbach (1926, part D, §4, p. 85, our translation),[24]

> The economic function of business-making is not to be or become wealthy (*reich*); and whoever goes on counting (*zählen*) his worth (*Vormögen*) makes unproductive work (*unproducktive Arbeit*).
> Nonetheless, income (*Erfolg*) should be accounted for and kept being accounted (*messen*). For the economic function of business-making is to produce, transport, store and sell goods (*Güter*) until the last man, and to do all this economically so that the means (*Stoff*) of such endeavor do not wear out in the process.

The dynamic accounting focus is then on the economic and monetary process generated by the business enterprise over time. The accounting system is expected to represent and frame this process, and the business entity's role in the general process of production and distribution of resources. It accounts for financial and economic flows in and out of the entity and provides for their imputation (*Zurechnung*) according to the intended use of the related resource and the period of reference. By disentangling financial and economic operations, this approach stresses the continued solidarity generated by the business entity over space and time. In particular, a dynamic balance sheet captures both the liaison between treasury movements and the economic result of that entity, and the dynamic action of financing bank credit (as distinguished by commercial credit) that is explicitly recognized by E. Walb and G. Zappa.[25] It was beneficial that between the beginning of twentieth century and the Second World War, the relationship between economic organization, money and accounting was increasingly recognized by accounting and economics (Biondi and Zambon 2011).

The dynamic interpretation of the accounting system: the case of the business entity

Drawing upon this dynamic spirit, we can come back to the accounting scheme of functional capital (Table 1). Its major distinction between monetary (1 and 3) and non monetary (2, 4, 5) classes relates specifically to the logical distinction between transactions between money and wares (which are usually commercial transactions: classes 1 and 3) and the entity-specific and dynamic allocation of money-to-money (usually related to financial endowments and investments: classes 1 and 4), and, generally speaking, to the method of accounting imputation which determines the business income generated by the economic organization (class 5).

Let us take the example of the business firm.[26] Concerning the first type of money-to-wares interaction, the lucrative economic organization does *demand money* against its offer of products, whilst potential consumers satisfy their need by *offering money* in exchange for the requested products. Concerning the second type of money-to-money interaction, the monetary endowment becomes a temporary means of financing and investing, which allows the economic organization to co-ordinate its ongoing activities over time and space.

These two distinct types of accounting elements correspond to two distinct monetary functions: money as a means of performing payments, and money as a way of *accounting for* (representing) imputations and allocations of past, present and future flows. On this basis, the accounting system specific to every entity is located behind the context (the space and time) of transactions (and related payments), since its unfolding and purposive performance constitutes a second logical order relative to the first order of those transactions. This two-order structure introduces then a theoretical distinction between the entity and the markets of reference for factors or products (Richard 1996, p. 62). The accounting system may theoretically explain and practically determine the business income generated by the entity. In this way, the accounting system further accounts for the active impact of the enterprise entity on the system of monetary transactions. In the balance sheet, the specific economic role of the entity is represented by some non-monetary classes (2, 4, 5). These classes relate to the specific economic and monetary process generated by the entity, and represent

(a) invested costs related to monetary outflows whose potential benefits are expected to last in future periods (class 2);
(b) advanced revenues that refer to free or costly advances of future revenues (from commercial sales, in the case of business firms) that are still uncertain;[27] this class comprises shareholders' equity endowments (class 4b) as well as financing bank credit (class 4a);
(c) last but not least, the business income to the firm (class 5), that is not distributed to shareholders and may be distributed to other stakeholders, or maintained for entity purposes.

Class 2 refers to the accounting method that matches some expenditures to the future (invested cost), because they only relate to future revenues that are not yet accrued. This imputation enables accounting for the full cost of products, as does the imputation of fixed and common costs to several products. This involves an economic solidarity between several (potential) paying buyers, and joins enterprise productions (organizational activities) over space and time. From the accounting perspective, however, the logical distinction between costs and revenues is maintained. This reduction of product cost concerns only the production side of the economic organization, and does not imply any spontaneous or mechanical reduction of selling prices paid by each buyer, contrary to the misunderstanding entailed by the equilibrium approach. The latter prices refer instead to the dynamics of revenues, which in turn refer to the interaction – monetary, economic and social – between consumers and business entities.[28]

Classes 4a and 4b relate to the inter-temporal link allowing the entity to disburse today what will be surely cashed-in only tomorrow. Whether used to pay for tangible, intangible or financial investments, these expenditures are expected to maintain and reinforce the economic generation of business income, for instance by financing entrepreneurial innovations, or technological and organizational development. They confer a current purchasing power to the entity's management that is based upon the future. This monetary dynamic is a mode of coordinating economic activity over time and space.

Class 5 concerns the part of business income that is not yet distributed to any stakeholder, nor expended or invested to sustain the entity's activity. This used to be thought of as a residual destined for self-financing, according to a simplistic alignment of accounting classes and available cash funds. The two-order accounting representation excludes this correspondence, because nothing guarantees that accounting items correspond directly to available cash flows or funds, nor to available financial (cash-equivalent) flows or funds.

In sum, the accounting system is an integral part of the entity system, and constitutes a representation – quantified on a monetary basis – of both the outer monetary transactions (monetary classes) and the inner dynamic combinations *specific to the entity* (non-monetary classes). The latter classes are not numbers or measures, but algorithms or strategies that show the active impact of entities on the functioning of economy and society.[29]

The application of the accounting system makes the dynamics of the economic organization irreducible to exchanges alone, contrary to the misrepresentation entailed by the price system, which is dominated only by monetary market exchanges (actual or potential). This interpretation of the accounting system identifies

(a) the inner economic activity that is specific to the entity and constitutes the non-market field of its economic co-ordination (characterized by productive immobilizations or overheads);
(b) an entity-specific type of transaction and combination (related to financing and investing), both having a dynamic nature which departs from the conceptual framework provided by stationary or static equilibrium.

Some links exist between this accounting view and economic theories that do not adopt the usual equilibrium framework. Following up on the traditional references provided above, class 4 corresponds to the special bank credit that is supposed to finance innovation and novel productive combination in Schumpeter (1926, German edn, p. 147; English edn, p. 101, our translation):

> It is perfectly clear that purchasing power (*Kaufkraft*) is created (*geschaffen*) to which (...) no new goods (*Güter*) correspond before.[30]
> From this it further follows that in real life the total credit (*die Summe des Kredits*) must be greater than it could be if there were only fully covered credit. The credit construction (*Kreditgebäude*) projects not only beyond the existing monetary basis (*Geldbasis*),[31] but also beyond the existing goods basis (*Güterbasis*).

Financing bank credit that pays for the fundamental working of enterprises (*Gründungskredit*), and serves entrepreneurial functions, also fits the non-monetary class of liabilities. On one side, monetary classes 1–3 correspond to commercial credits and debts that are cash-equivalent, and are called by Schumpeter (1926) 'working credit' (*Betriebskredit*).[32] On the other side, non-monetary classes 2, 4 and 5 introduce another kind of credit-debt. These classes do not correspond to market transactions and prevent any actuarial equivalence between current monetary flow and debt (future monetary flow). To these classes the *Gründungskredit* belongs, according to Schumpeter (1926), that is, the credit for financing entrepreneurial functions.

Furthermore, non-monetary class 2 fits irreversible immobilizations introduced by Pantaleoni (1909),[33] as well as the more recent notion of 'specific investments'. In fact, contrary to property rights theorizing, these investments are not specific to the asset owned by the stakeholder that commits it to the joint venture. No stakeholder may then run away with the asset and the asset-specific investment. Specificity implies here a degree or threshold of irreversibility of that investment, which is framed by the dynamics of the whole entity over time and space. Whilst the appropriable notion of specificity adopts the reductionism of methodological individualism, the concept of entity-specificity adopts a comprehensive understanding of the economic organization led by a dynamic holistic perspective.

The dynamic interpretation of the accounting system: the case of the non-business entity

The logical introduction of a second-order accounting structure based on first-order business transactions can be replicated to construct a second-order accounting structure for non-business entities (Biondi 2008b, 2009). The latter may then take into account non-business transactions such as taxation and grants (donations), allowing a further theoretical step beyond the biased reduction of each monetary transfer to a market price. Monetary transfers (payments) may then correspond to commercial, fiscal, or giving relationships. Following Perroux (1966, p. 406), within a universe that admits the enterprise entity and its specific income, it is further necessary to rehabilitate the 'gift'.[34]

Business entities are expected to look after revenues from operations, and gains from investments. The representation of revenues is then determined by aggregating the payments received, or to be received, from a particular set of commercial transactions. Concerning revenue recognition, accounting may then follow the traditional realization principle (Anthony 1978, p. 122; Sunder 1997, p. 194) which fits the dynamic accounting view, or the fair value approach that results in estimating future revenues at the recognition date (Ijiri 2005), the latter fitting the static accounting view. According to an operational understanding of the economics of business entities, and independently of the adopted accounting recognition method, commercial revenues:

(a) Involve the eventual transfer of a good or service in exchange for an actual, promised or expected monetary charge (a transfer of cash or an entitlement to receive cash);

(b) Imply a profit motive, that is, the seeking of a satisfactory (reasonable) business income; accordingly, revenues should 'recover' at least the resources utilized by the generating activity (dynamic view and cost basis) or invested in the related good or service (static view and value basis);

(c) Incorporate in pricing a judgement about the utility of the purchased item based on the voluntary nature of the exchange under competitive conditions;

(d) Depend on prices which reflect the client's *willingness* to pay;

(e) Complete the financial relationship between the client and the business entity. Nothing further is charged to the client, who in turn has no control or influence over the utilization of the revenues realized by the transaction. Generally speaking, once the transaction is concluded, the client does not maintain any link with or obligation to the economic and financial system of the business enterprise.

Neither a static nor a dynamic view of business accounting is suitable for non-business entities, if their nature and role as *non-lucrative* human activities have to be maintained. In fact, what is the performance of a non-lucrative activity? The performance of a business enterprise, with limitations, is represented by the stream of net revenues (incomes) generated, which is allocated and distributed according to various arrangements and conditions. This stream constitutes the business income to the firm. In contrast, the performance of a non-business entity involves direct satisfaction of social and collective needs; consequently there is no need for revenues or incomes to be generated or distributed. Only the cost side is relevant to their economic accounting. Its non-lucrative activity can be accomplished either by transferring and redistributing resources or by the direct performance of activities (including supply of goods and services) without commercial transactions (in particular, without reference to market prices). Non-business activities involve some 'non-business transfer of goods and services' (this is the usual economic jargon). These operating inflows to non-business entities are not revenues, especially because such inflows do not relate to market exchanges or to prices fixed by these market transactions:[35]

(a) The operating inflows are a transfer and are not measured at the equivalent price of a market transaction;

(b) The non-business activity does not imply any profit motive;

(c) The transfer does not imply any evaluation, even crude, of the value of the generating activity;

(d) The transfer is not based on the *willingness* to pay of the beneficiaries, but on their *capacity* to pay;

(e) The transfer does not conclude the financial relationship between the beneficiaries and the entity, since they are still subject to the future implications of the relationship (for instance, the tax levy by the state).

Through both (public and private) grants and operating transfers, citizens confer resources to the state (or to the non-business organization) in order to support activities having a special economic nature and purporting to directly satisfy social and collective needs. Even though the accounting lexicon used by business and non-business entities is often the same, the resources conferred to non-business entities are not 'revenues' but 'contributing sources' which are required to both cover expenses (resources utilized), and finance the resources acquired for performing certain non-business activities.

This special economy of spending and redistributing requires a special system of accounting representation. In particular, both grants and operating transfers should be considered as 'contributions' (and sources of financing). The business accounting system determines and controls the ongoing recovery by revenues of either the costs or the values of the resources mobilized (investments made), since ultimately the absorption of resources must be recovered by commercial revenues or capital gains. In contrast, there is no need for recovering contributions that are granted (voluntary or compulsory) in order to sustain non-business activities. Therefore, the usual accounting representation for business enterprises must be adapted to give an appropriate accounting representation of a non-business entity. Business accounting determines incomes that must recover investments made in order to seek for those incomes. This is why traditional accounting first determines revenues and then matches expenses (costs) against such revenues. In contrast, non-business accounting first determines expenses, that is, the resources mobilized and utilized during the period. These expenses are then matched against different kinds of contributions, since incurred expenses must be covered and financed by available contributions.

This *reversed matching* changes the meaning of accrual basis when non-business accounting is concerned. Expenses no longer represent absorbed costs or values that must be recovered to generate incomes, but rather resources required by the non-lucrative activities that have been performed during the period. Regarding the accounting scheme of functional capital (Table), accounting classes need some special interpretation in the context of non-business entities. The monetary classes are cash and cash-equivalent rights and obligations, but do not correspond to the transaction process of any commercial sale. The non-monetary classes belong to the non-business process of allocating costs through periods, in order to have them split between current and future periods (intergenerational equity). In particular:

(a) Class 2a represents unpaid costs that will be passed through the income statement to be paid in the future;
(b) Class 4b represents financial endowments (public or private grants) that must not be refunded (recovered) in any sense, but are conferred *free* to sustain the entity's activity;
(c) Class 5 can temporarily exist and be positive (negative) if resources have been acquired in excess (in deficit) to pay for or to finance current expenses or investments; however, it cannot be distributed in any way.

From this perspective, public policies of deficit spending and consequent public borrowing perform a special economic function within the economic system. They awaken 'sleeping' financial capital by creating supplementary consumption from the cash holdings (savings) kept by families and firms. The state creates a special economy of consumption based on continued financial borrowing, where its financial liabilities as an entity play a peculiar role as capitals that are going to be spent (functionally speaking, a sinking of capital). In this context, an accounting loss determined on an accrual basis means that the current consumption (determined by expenses of the period) has been bigger than current contributions (determined by net sovereign revenues of the period). This consumption has been permitted by the sinking withdrawal of available financial capital. For the individual lender, this withdrawal is a lending that will be charged with interest and recovered, but for the whole system it acts as a consumption of that 'sleeping capital'. From this perspective, public borrowing by the state depends as much on its solvency as an entity as on its sustainability under the actual financial and economic conditions of the whole financial and economic system. Reduction of deficit-spending implies reducing consumption of sleeping capital (which ought to be awakened in another way), and consequently less redistribution of wealth.

Concluding remarks

Socio-economic scholars are accustomed to considering money either as a thing or as a sign. In either case, money is statically assumed to be the general means allowing or facilitating generalized exchanges, that is, the market. The whole economy is therefore reduced to an aggregation of isolated exchanges at market prices of reference, where prices are supposed to be measures of value.

However, neglected paths in the history of economic thought have suggested a dynamic understanding of money: money may be understood through its functions, including that of means of exchange. Money is then jointly understood as a means of payment and a mode of accounting. It is clear that this view also reshapes the way in which money performs its function as a means of exchange. Whilst the payment function surely relates to actual transactions and payments in a given space and time (context), the accounting function intriguingly enters the realm of socio-economic entities that become over space and time.

From this perspective accounting systems, which perform the accounting function of money, not only take into account isolated transactions and payments located in time and space but, by their very functioning, also constitute the institutional condition for an economic system to overcome that horizontal network of transactions and payments. This vertical dimension of accounting systems appears both in the ways they take into account debt-credit relations, and by the application of accruals and other accounting techniques that are concerned with space and time, such as depreciation, amortization, provision, impairment and revaluation. Accounting systems constitute thus a second-order institutional structure of the economic system relative to the first-order of transactions and payments. If, on one hand, this accounting structure relies on the conception of money as a unit of account, on the other hand it expands such a conception far beyond the notion of a mere unit of denomination for prices and financial rights. Accounting systems embody a specific logic, and perform a specific form, of economic calculation. They play the double functional role, of money as means of payment and mode of accounting, in a co-coordinated way. Therefore, the joint understanding of money and accounting may lead to a better understanding of the economic organization of the economic system and its institutional structure, in relation to the extension of space and the flow of time.

Notes

I am grateful to Martin Shubik (Yale University) for his insightful comments. The usual disclaimer applies.

1. Cf. the chapters by Amato and Fantacci in this volume.
2. On the origin of this expression, cf. Patinkin-Steiger (1989); Klausinger (1990).
3. Schumpeter (1954) considers the terms 'theory of value', 'exchange ratios' and 'relative prices' as virtually equivalents in the economic theory of the period between 1870 and 1914 (see p. 909, footnote 1).
4. Cf. also Tobin (1985, p. 35b). Nogaro (1906, especially pp. 687–690) develops relevant critiques of the representation of the monetary and economic process driven by the distinction between numéraire and money.
5. Cf. Schumpeter (1954, p. 1082); cf. also Schumpeter (1917), Schumpeter (1970) and N. De Vecchi (1983).
6. Cf. Schumpeter (1954, p. 1079).
7. That is, the concept of neutral money.
8. This is also true for the axiomatization developed by Arrow and Debreu that investigates the existence of a price system, not the process of price formation. Shubik (1993) discusses accounting systems and strategic market games as ways to avoid this logical trap.
9. The relationship between the economic organization as an entity and its accounting system relates to the question of the institutional nature of money as a monetary system, already claimed by Berle (1963, p. 27): 'Liquidity in the long run depends on the functioning of the banking and currency system; and in the twentieth century, banking and currency systems are peculiarly and typically the province and prerogative of the modern state'. For recent developments, cf. Aglietta and Orléan (1998) who provide further references. See also the posthumous work of Schumpeter 1970 and Schumpeter 1917.
10. In terms of accounting, this is an expense, which is a monetary outflow imputed directly as a charge of the period.
11. That is, capital transactions which provide the financial endowments (financing) that are employed to acquire the resource (investment) that is capitalized as an asset by the accounting system.
12. Any allocation of flows between balance sheet and income statement becomes problematic on an equilibrium basis; cf. also Shwayder, K. (1967).
13. Here, by analogy with the equilibrium approach, the sequence of strictly monetary entries and exits. This implies abstracting away from real processes (flow of goods and services) that underline the accounting representation, as well as from financial dynamics constituted by cash-equivalent debts and credits.
14. Furthermore, accounting recognition may not refer to a strictly monetary flow, but to the variation of cash or credit, since the design of the accounting system defines also the time and conditions of recognition itself.
15. Gordon, L. A. and W. A. Stark (1989, p. 429 and equation 16) showed that the reduction of accruals (accounting costs and revenues) to cash flows amounts to the elimination all effects of accounting imputation.
16. Among others, through the distinction between 'spesa' and 'costo' (in Italian), 'expenditure', 'expense' and 'cost' (in English), and 'dépense', 'charge' and 'coût' (in French).

17. Cf. Zappa, G. (1937), but also Raby (1959); Littleton, A. C. (1961 [1936], *Symbols of Reality*, pp. 226–227).
18. For a conceptual history of these monetary functions, cf. Fantacci (2005).
19. Cf. also Littleton (1961 [1936], p. 12; collected in 1961, p. 197) who explained this error with the erroneous interpretation of double book-keeping.
20. This evaluation is supposed to align, at least at the time of the preparation of financial statements, financial evaluation based on discounting and market evaluation at the current or exit price.
21. At that time, economic research was looking for endogenous economic factors or conditions able to put the economy out of equilibrium, such as innovating entrepreneurs, opportunistic individuals, imputation of overheads, or allocation of costs among direct and general expenses. Economic dynamics was understood in terms of cycles and levels of prices, which were not mere informational labels, but monetary transfers. On equilibrium economics, cf. Montesano (1972), Donzelli (1986), De Vroey (2001), Frydman (2001).
22. The stationary interpretation of equilibrium, including Walrasian economics, contrasts with an instantaneous interpretation and appears to dominate that time. Moore (1906, p. 213), for instance, distinguishes three method of investigation adopting equilibrium: 'the common form of *coeteris paribus* of the older economists, the static state or statical method of the more recent deductive economists, or the system of simultaneous equations of the mathematical economists'.
23. This work (first published in 1912) theoretically explains the notion of financing bank credit adopted by dynamic accounting theories at the same time. As shown in Biondi (2008a), Schumpeter was aware of the implications of this notion for economic theory and accounting practice.
24. Cf. also English edn (1959, pp. 30–31), and Schmalenbach (1933).
25. Miller (1947) mentioned the special attention paid by the Italian school of business economics (*Economia aziendale*) promoted by G. Zappa to credit economy and dynamics.
26. This example focuses on the accounting system for industrial firms, and does not address the cases of agricultural, financial or commercial firms. Non-business firms will be treated in the next section.
27. Or, alternatively, the deferment of accrued revenues to future periods.
28. This interaction has its own conventions and institutions (including from the accounting viewpoint) related to products and to their quality, duration and standardization, as well as to the policies of price-fixing, including multiple and discriminatory pricing.
29. This concept further applies to the macro-economic accounting of central banking that co-ordinates all the banks.
30. That is, without pre-existing goods.
31. That is, the current monetary basis or, according to the monetary theory of that time, the gold standard.
32. Cf. Schumpeter (1926), German edn, p. 153; English edn, p. 103.
33. To be sure, in both cases, accounting classes comprise other kinds of items, but mentioned items may be distinguished in them.
34. Cf. also Biondi (2002), Chapter 15.
35. The letters correspond to the five characteristics of revenues defined for business enterprises above.

References

Aglietta, M. and Orléan, A. (dir.) (1998) *La monnaie souveraine* (Paris: Editions Odile Jacob).

Anthony, N. R. (1960) 'The Trouble with Profit Maximization', Chapter 12, in Biondi, Y. et al. (2007) *The Firm as an Entity: Implications for Economics, Accounting, and Law* (New York and London: Routledge), pp. 201–215.

Anthony, N. R. (1978) *Financial Accounting in Non-business Organizations. An Exploratory Study of Conceptual Issues*, Research Report (Norwalk, CT: Financial Accounting Standards Board).

Anthony N. R. (1983) *Tell It Like It Was: A Conceptual Framework for Financial Accounting* (USA: Richard D. Irwin Inc.).

Berle, A. A., Jr (1963) *The American Economic Republic* (New York: Harcourt Inc.).

Biondi, Y. (2002) *Gino Zappa e la rivoluzione del reddito. Azienda, moneta e contabilità nella nascente economia aziendale* (Gino Zappa and the Business Income to the Firm. Enterprise Entity, Money and Accounting at the Foundations of Italian Business Economics) (Padua: CEDAM).

Biondi, Y. (2005a) 'L'impresa nella dinamica economica: Gino Zappa lettore degli *Erotemi* di Maffeo Pantaleoni' (The Enterprise Entity and the Economic Dynamics: G. Zappa, Reader of *Erotemi* by M. Pantaleoni), *Pensiero Economico Italiano*, 13, 2005 (2), 179–215.

Biondi, Y. (2005b) 'G. Zappa, T. Veblen, J. R. Commons e l'impresa come istituzione economica' (Zappa, Veblen, Commons and the Enterprise Entity as an Economic Institution), *Storia del Pensiero Economico*, 2005 (1), 93–120.

Biondi, Y. (2006) 'Accounting and the Economic Analysis of the Firm as an Entity', chapter 4, in Dietrich Michael (ed.) *The Economics of the Firm: Analysis, Evolution and History* (New york and London: Routledge), 65–87.

Biondi, Y. (2008a) 'Schumpeter's Economic Theory and the Dynamic Accounting View of the Firm: Neglected Pages from the *Theory of Economic Development*', *Economy and Society*, 37 (4), November 2008, 525–547.

Biondi, Y. (2008b) 'De Charybde de la comptabilité de caisse en Scylla de la comptabilité patrimoniale', *Revue de la régulation*, 3 (4), 2e semestre. http://regulation.revues.org/index5003.html.

Biondi, Y. (2009) 'Should Business and Non-Business Accounting Be Different? A Comparative Perspective Applied to the New French Governmental Accounting Standards', EGPA Annual Conference, Rotterdam, 3–6 September 2008; 12th Biennial CIGAR Conference Paper, University of Modena, Italy, 28–29 May. http://ssrn.com/abstract=1414751.

Biondi, Y. and Stefano, Z. (2011) *Accounting and Business Economics: Insights from National Traditions* (New York and London: Routledge), forthcoming.

Biondi, Y. et al. (eds) (2007) *The Firm as an Entity: Implications for Economics, Accounting, and Law* (New York and London: Routledge).

Coase, H. R. (1990) 'Accounting and the Theory of the Firm', in Y. Biondi et al. (eds) *The Firm as an Entity: Implications for Economics, Accounting, and Law* (New York and London: Routledge 2007), *quoted*.

De Vecchi, N. (1983) (cur) *La teoria austriaca del capitale e dell'interesse. Fondamenti e discussione*, Antology of works by Böhm-Bawerk, J.B. Clark, J.A. Schumpeter e C. Menger, with an introduction by the editor: "La scienza del capitale fra tradizione e irrequietezza", pp. 3–69, Roma : Istituto della Enciclopedia Italiana Treccani 1983.

De Vroey, M. (2001) 'Equilibrium and Disequilibrium in Walrasian Economics', *Journal of the History of Economic Thought*, 24 (4), December, 405–426.

Donzelli, F. (1986) *Il concetto di equilibrio nella teoria economica neoclassica* (Rome: NIS).

Fantacci, L. (2005) *La moneta. Storia di un'istituzione mancata* (Venice: Marsilio).

Frydman, R. (2001) 'L'équilibre économique: intentions individuelles et réalisation sociale', Chapter 1 in J. Cartelier and R. Frydman (eds) *L'économie hors d'équilibre* (Paris: Economica 2001), 15–39.

Gordon L. A. and Stark A. W. (1989) Accounting and Economic Rates of Return : A Note on Depreciation and Other Accruals, *Journal of Business Finance and Accounting*, 16 (3), summer 1989, 425–432.

Hicks, J. R. (1965) Capital and Growth (NY-Oxford: Oxford University Press).

Ijiri, Y. (1967) *The Foundations of Accounting Measurement: A Mathematical, Economic and Behavioral Inquiry* (Englewood Cliffs, NJ: Prentice-Hall).

Ijiri, Y. (2005) 'US Accounting Standards and their Environment: A Dualistic Study of their 75 Years of Transition', *Journal of Accounting and Public Policy*, 24, 255–279.

Klausinger, H. (1990) 'The Early Use of the Term "Veil of Money" in Schumpeter's Monetary Writings – A Comment on Patinkin and Steiger', *Scandinavian Journal of Economics*, 92, 617–621.

Littleton A. C. (1961) Essays on Accountancy, in C. A. Moyer (ed.) 'Part One – On Accounting History'; 'Part Two – On Accounting Theory' (Urbana, IL: University of Illinois Press).

Marget W. A. (1951) 'The Monetary Aspects of the Schumpeterian System', in 'Schumpeter, Social Scientist', *Review of Economics and Statistics*, 33 (2), May, 112–121.

Menger, C. (1871) *Grundsätze der Volkswirtschaftslehre*, English translation: *Principles of Economics* (1950), 1st edn, F. Knight (ed.) (Illinois: The Free Press). Italian translation: *Principii fondamentali d'economia* (1907), 1st edn (Rome: Giornale degli Economisti); *Principi di Economia politica* (1923) (Torino: UTET); *Principii fondamentali di Economia politica* (1925), 2nd edn, preface by Maffeo Pantaleoni (Bari: Laterza).

Menger C. (1892) 'La monnaie mesure de valeur', *Revue d'économie politique*, 6, 159–175.

Miller, S. H. (1947) 'Review of U. Caprara's La Banca: Principii di Economia delle Aziende di Credito', *American Economic Review*, 37 (5), December, 981–984.

Montesano, A. (1972) 'La nozione di economia dinamica', *Giornale degli Economisti*, nuova serie, 31 (3/4), March/April, 185–227.

Moore, L. H. (1906) 'Paradoxes of Competition', *Quarterly Journal of Economics*, 20 (2), February, 211–230.

Nogaro, B. (1906) 'Contribution à une théorie réaliste de la monnaie', *Revue d'économie politique*, 20, 681–724.

Pantaleoni, M. (1897) Du caractère logique des differences d'opinion qui separent les économistes, conference read at University of Geneva on 23 october 1897, Geneva 1897. Italian Translation : Del carattere delle divergenze di opinione esistenti fra economisti, *Giornale degli Economisti*, s.2, a.8, vol.15, 1897, II : December, pp. 501–530. Collected in Pantaleoni Maffeo (1925), *Erotemi di economia*, deux vol., Laterza, Bari 1925, vol I: pp. 157–187.

Pantaleoni, M. (1909) Di alcuni fenomeni di dinamica economica, *Giornale degli Economisti*, s. 2, a. 20, vol. 39, 1909, II, september, pp. 211–254. Collected in Pantaleoni, M. (1925), *Erotemi di economia*, deux vol., Laterza, Bari 1925, vol II: pp. 75–127. English translation: International Economic Papers, vol. 5, MacMillan, London 1956.

Patinkin, Don and Steiger, Otto (1989) 'In Search of the "Veil of Money" and the "Neutrality of Money": A Note on the Origin of Terms', *Scandinavian Journal of Economics*, 91 (1), 131–146.

Perroux, F. (1966) *L'économie du XX° siècle* (Paris: PUF).

Raby, L. W. (1959) 'The Two Faces of Accounting', *The Accounting Review*, 34 (3), July, 452–461.

Richard, J. (1996) *Comptabilités et pratiques comptables* (Paris: Dalloz).

Schmalenbach, E. (1926) Grundlagen dynamischer Bilanzlehre, *Zeitschrift fuer Handelwissenschaftliche Forschung*, Leipzig, Iᵉ édition (1919), 13, 1–60, 65–101. IIᵉ édition (1920), supplement. IVᵉ édition (1926): *Dynamische Bilanz* (Koln and Opladen: Westdeutscher Verlag).

Schmalenbach, E. (1933) 'Business Economics and Changes in German Business Conditions', *Harvard Business Review*, 11 (4), July, 490–497.

Schumpeter, J. A. (1917) Das Sozialprodukt und die Rechenpfennige. Glossen und Beitraege zur Geldtheorie von heute, *Archiv für Sozialwissenschaft und Sozialpolitik*, 44. Band, 1917/18. English translation: 'Money and the Social Product', in *International Economic Papers*, 6, 1956.

Schumpeter, J. A. (1926) *Theorie der wirtschaftlichen Entwicklung*, Iᵉ édition, 1912; IIᵉ édition, 1926 (Leipzig: Duncker & Humblot).

Schumpeter, J. A. (1954) *History of Economic Analysis* (London: George Allen & Unwin).

Schumpeter, J. A. (1970, posthume) *Das Wesen des Geldes*, Mann, F. K. (ed.) (Goettingen: Vandenhoeck & Ruprecht).

Shubik, M. (1978) 'A Dynamic Economy with Fiat Money without Banking but with Ownership Claims to Production Goods', in *Hommage à F. Perroux* (Grenoble: P.U. Grenoble), 675–688.

Shubik, M. (1993) 'Accounting in Its Relationship to General Equilibrium Theory', in Y. Biondi et al. (eds) *The Firm as an Entity: Implications for Economics, Accounting, and Law* (New York and London: Routledge 2007), *quoted*, 73–81.

Shwayder, K. (1967) 'A Critique of Economic Income as an Accounting Concept', *Abacus*, 3 (1), August 1967, pp. 23–35.

Stauss, H. J. (1944) 'The Entrepreneur: The Firm', in Y. Biondi et al. (eds) *The Firm as an Entity: Implications for Economics, Accounting, and Law* (New York and London: Routledge 2007), *quoted*.

Sunder, S. (1997) *Theory of Accounting and Control* (Cincinnati, OH: South-Western College Publishing).

Tobin, J. (1985) 'Neoclassical Theory in America: J. B. Clark and I. Fisher', Centennial Essays (Dec., 1985), *The American Economic Review*, 75 (6), 28–38.

Walb, E. (1926) *Die Erfolgsrechnung privater und öffentlicher Betriebe* (Berlin and Vienna: Industrieverlag Spaeth & Linde).

Zappa, G. (1937) *Il reddito d'impresa* (Milan: Giuffrè). First complete edition, 1929 (Rome: ALI).

4

Silence Is Gold: Some Preliminary Notes on Money, Speech and Calculation

Massimo Amato

What does 'institution' mean? When it is a matter of meaning, language is at stake. This is why it is important to look at the phenomenon of institution, using a long-standing parallel not often considered: the parallel between speech and money.

In order to orient our understanding, I will give a preliminary hint. 'Institution' as such should not be represented as a process of interaction between individual or collective subjects interested in stipulating a contract. Rather it ought to be thought of as a *poetic act*, that is, an act of creation based on law, according to which a contract can be made, stipulated and enforced.

This is a theme that the social sciences tend to neglect, but it is absolutely crucial philosophically. Perhaps the most concrete concept of money cannot avoid abstract questions, which may prove crucial for our understanding of money and calculation.

English, as well as Italian and many other languages, has the adage *speech is silver, silence is golden*, which encapsulates the core theme of this chapter. In fact, this saying depicts both the relationship between both language and silence, and the relationship between language and money. Indeed, since gold and silver have always been the monetary metals *par excellence*, the reference to them in the adage signals a relationship, indeed an affinity, between language and money – an ancient and well-known parallel.

But the saying also evokes a relationship which we usually overlook, between money and language on one hand, and silence on the other. *Silence* is golden. So, if it the adage is understood as an analogy rather than a simple metaphor, it means that gold has an essential relationship with silence.

What should be said about gold as a monetary metal, and a sign of wealth? How can the idea of a gold-silence which emerges from the popular saying – that is, the idea of a word whose value comes from *not* being spent – connect with gold as a metal identified with money, 'putting on it', as Locke says, 'an imaginary value'? Gold is one commodity among many, but it has been given primary importance as a measure for the exchange value of all other commodities. This is surprising, perhaps even more so over the last 35 years, given that since 1973 gold has officially ceased to have any monetary *meaning*. Gold is no longer the measure of anything. Does the abolition of the role of gold in exchange imply the abolition of 'silence', too? What does silence mean in the world of exchange? Could it be abolished with the same apparent lack of consequence which seems to characterize the abolition of gold?

Such questions generate a more puzzling one: what language does money speak today? We could say it has become a mere sign, without inherent value, used only for the communication of value. Money is now just an instrument for the generalized calculation of values in a globalized market. It is a 'signifier' without a 'signified', whose worth is no longer significant, being measured only by the logistics of the exchanges it makes possible.

The end of the identification of money with gold means the relegation of money and its signifying power into the domain of calculation. But if economic calculation proper, that is accountancy, still needs a measure which neither coincides with nor substitutes for that which it measures, money still has a role. In today's globalized financial markets, money is both an object and an instrument of calculation, and apparently has no identity outside the world of financial calculation which it sustains. On a practical level, look at monetary instruments produced by recent financial innovations, such as derivatives. On the theoretical level, notice that 'auto-referentiality' is the main characteristic of money: money is what is *accepted* as money.

If money is now purely 'auto-referential' and 'performative', having no role beyond the calculations it makes possible, then what language does this kind of money speak? I will leave to the end the question of the relationship between calculation and measure – a question which constitutes one of the crucial issues raised in this book. But in order to reach our 'concluding remarks', we must take into account the relationships implied by the proverb we started with: the relationship between money and speech, speech and silence, and, finally, money and silence.

To do this, I will use interpretative resources which connect with the ontological, rather than the economic, meaning of money – that is, its nature, its structure, and indeed its own economy.

I described gold as monetary metal, that is, a metal which by convention has been brought into a privileged relationship with money, and which, during the whole period of the gold standard, has been identified with a specific *weight*. Where does this identification come from? The usual explanation is based on the notion of an intrinsic value of gold. Gold is the commodity with the highest and, above all, most stable value: so gold can represent the 'phenomenic value' of money. This is the assumption, but the economic history of money shows the opposite. Gold and silver have a value only because they are monetary metals, and not vice versa. The fall in the quotations of silver after the demonetizations during the second half of nineteenth century provides irrefutable evidence of this. If we push the argument to the limit, we could say that beyond their monetary use, silver and gold are only *decorative* metals – good for the glory of God and men but beyond that, valueless.

Perhaps (this is a hypothesis) we should turn the current perspective upside down, and say that 'precious' metals actually had a monetary and linguistic use precisely because they *are* worth nothing in themselves: because they are indicators of a *constitutive* silence and nothingness. They therefore embody nothingness, rendering it in some way *perceivable* – gold even more than silver. Silver is what we currently spend, and the money that circulates is currency (it is not by chance that the French language calls currency *l'argent*), gold has been from the very beginning the silent and *unsounded* reserve for that circulation. In gold, it is silence and *soundlessness* that *speak*.

Support for such a hypothesis comes from the etymology of the English and German words for gold. Gold, in fact, comes from the same root of *yellow*, German *gelb*. So the trait that language itself seems to have highlighted for gold is luminosity. What is important in gold is the light it gives off, and not the weight it possesses. Gold *lights up*. It is what it is without any need to describe its 'weight', that is, its mining cost and utility. But what does this identification of gold with light really mean? If we go further with the etymology, we find that gold, as well as yellow, derives from an Indo-European root which means 'bright, shimmering, blank' (*glänzend, schimmernd, blank*). Initially, gold is identified neither by its characteristics as a physical entity, nor from the effect of light on its material body (yellow as a reflection of light), but rather starting with light itself. It is pure refulgence. It means something immaterial, something like a vacuum, a *blankness*. Gold is not originally identifiable with density and weight, precisely because it constitutes the dimension for their manifestation. Gold has originally neither body nor weight, because gold itself determines the characteristics of substantiality and heaviness. Even before illuminating, gold presents itself as the context for the manifestation of light. Before being scientifically classifiable as a 'heavy metal', gold is designed by language itself as the pure element of lightness, in the sense of *weightlessness*. Gold is *light*. It is something lightening (German *lichtend* and *sich lichtend*), not in the sense of an enlightenment or an illumination, but instead in the sense of a something which *lightens* a burden, that is which gives relief and freedom. Being light, and lightening in this second sense, gold seems to offer the possibility of an equilibrium (in German *Gleich-gewicht*) between things which reside in the lightened space of *comparability* which it opens. Heraclitus seems to say exactly that in his fragment DK 90, 'All things are exchanged for fire and fire for all things, even as wares for gold, and gold for wares.' This is only what we can extract, rather crudely, from the etymology – that is, from our understanding of the original sense of the word; but it may be inadequate if an original meaning, destined to be overtaken by human cultural evolution, becomes redundant.

However, let us put aside for a moment the etymology and try to pick up the thread of our argument. Let us start from the affinity – commonly acknowledged, even today – between money and speech. Even here we have to acknowledge a transformation of meaning, in the form of a passage from a mythical affinity to a rational one. Describing an ancient myth of the Dogons, the anthropologist Marcel Griaule tells us the following story:

> 'The double bowl', Ogotemmêli said, 'symbolizes the twins: they have equal height, equal size, equal word'. And as each of the two bowls is equal to the other, so the twins are interchangeable one with the other. 'That is why', he added, 'commerce has begun with them'. He insisted on this idea of equality, which gives birth to exchange: 'the twins have the right word, the same word. They have the same value. They are the same thing. The man who sells and the man who buys, they too are the same thing. They are twins' [...] 'The value of things has been fixed in cowries by the seventh Nommo, the lord of speech [...] The seventh Nommo recommended to put the wares one in front of the other. The word of exchange had to be uttered in front of them. As if it were the wares themselves which were speaking.

They spoke through the mouth of their owners; they understood each other about their own exchange [...] To have cowries is to have words'.[1]

Speech and money come from a divine institution. It is in the name of the god of name and speech that speech and money share the same origin, because they have something in common – exchange.

Herodotus refers to the same immemorial, though not yet civilized, humanity when he tells us the story of 'silent commerce':

The Carthaginians also report that there is a region in Libya, and men dwelling beyond the Pillars of Heracles; when they come there, they unload their cargo; then, having laid it *in order* along the shoreline [i.e., the water's edge], they go aboard their ships and light a smoking fire. When the inhabitants of the land see the smoke, they come to the sea, and lay down gold *in face of* the wares. After that, they leave and go back to their land withdrawing from the wares. Then the Carthaginians, after having disembarked, inspect carefully [the *correspondence* between wares and gold]; if the gold *seems* to them a *worthy compensation* for the wares, they proceed to the exchange [of gold for wares]; but if [the correspondence] does not seem worthy to them, they go back aboard and *wait* on their ships. Hence the inhabitants of the land come back and lay more gold, until they manage to persuade them. Yet, neither party commits injustice against the other: neither do the Carthaginians touch the gold before it has arrived for them to equal the worth of the wares, nor do the others touch the wares before those receive the gold.

Here we face, indeed, a *silent exchange*, where speech and money as means of communication seem to play no role. In any case, it must be emphasized that the silence in which this exchange takes place is a *ritual* silence, that is, a *prescriptive* silence, a silence which precedes and sustains each act of exchange, and prescribes the need to *abstain* from performing exchange until all the conditions for it are in place.

Yet the divine origin of words and the prescriptive role of silence are exactly what the modern world puts aside with gross contempt. Even when silence reigns, as with the 'brief encounters' which characterize automatized exchanges on the global financial market, it seems the opposite of prescription or rituality: a silenced silence, as it were.

Locke affirms that language, facilitating the communication of positive ideas, has to do with silence and nothingness, but in a 'privative' way:

> Besides these names which stand for ideas, there be other words which men make use of, not to signify any idea, but the want or absence of some ideas, [...] such as are *nihil* in Latin, and in English, ignorance and barrenness. All which negative or privative words cannot be said properly to belong to, or signify no ideas: for then they would be perfectly insignificant sounds; but they relate to positive ideas, and signify their absence.

Locke continues:

> Indeed, we have negative names, which stand not directly for positive ideas, but for their absence, such as insipid, silence, *nihil*, etc.; which words denote positive ideas, v.g. taste, sound, being, with a signification of their absence.[2]

The modern and rational formulation of the relationship between speech and money, founded on English empiricism, seemingly wants to silence any mythical or mystical element. For Hume, the relationship between speech and money is only an analogy between two of the many conventions by which civilized life is organized, starting with the primary convention regarding the status of property and promise:

> This convention [of property] *is not of the nature of a promise*: for even promises themselves, as we shall see afterwards, arise from human conventions... In like manner are languages gradually establish'd by human conventions without any promise. In like manner do gold and silver become the common measures of exchange, and are esteem'd sufficient payment for what is of a hundred times their value.[3]

The promise itself, that is, the place where speech encounters explicitly and ritually the dimension of sacredness and of juridicity (Roman law develops as a law of oath, *jus jurandum*) has been completely put aside. This opens the way to a purely evolutionary interpretation of convention, as we find in von Hayek:

> But the superstition that it is necessary for government (usually called the 'state' to make it sound better) to declare what is to be money, as if it had created the money which could not exist without it, probably originated in the naïve belief that such a tool as money must have been 'invented' and given to us by some original inventor.

This belief has been wholly displaced by our understanding of the spontaneous generation of such undesigned institutions by a process of social evolution of which money has since become the prime paradigm (law, language and morals being the other main instances).[4]

In fact, when language is thought of as a convention, what is primarily silenced is silence itself. And it is not a mere casualty, in either sense of the word. The other side of this reduction to silence is the very possibility of representing language and money *as mere means of communication*, arising not from an act of establishment but from a process of pure interaction. This appears to be presupposed by the technological, and hence essentially anti-mythical (and therefore anti-linguistic, since the Greek word 'mythos' means simply 'word'), approach to language and money.

It remains open to question whether the relationship that speech and money have with silence can be reduced to the simple terms of a binary opposition, even when what is at stake appears to be the communicative function of money and speech. In fact, in order to function as means of communication, money and speech must be capable of signifying something *other* than themselves. This process of signification seems to involve a substantial diminution of what makes it work: they circulate as signs, but money and words do not have any substance of their own.

This, referring to money, is what Keynes seems to highlight in an important passage of his *Tract on Monetary Reform*: 'It is not easy, it seems, for men to apprehend that their money is a mere intermediary, without significance in itself ...'. Money is a mere intermediary, Keynes says. And being an intermediary, it has no significance in itself, that is, no meaning of its own. This *meaninglessness* of money is strongly tied by Keynes to its *capacity to disappear*. His sentence continues as follows, '... money is a mere intermediary, without significance in itself, which flows from one hand to another, is received and is dispensed, and disappears when its work is done from the sum of a nation's wealth'.[5]

Only money which can properly disappear, having duly accomplished its work, is properly *meaningless*. We could say that its *meaningfulness*, that is, according to the Oxford English dictionary, its specific quality and capability of 'communicating something that is not explicitly or directly expressed', coincides, during the course of its circulation, with its *meaninglessness*, provided that it is *constructed* so as to disappear. The insignificance of money is not a natural, but an institutional, insignificance.

This is why money institutionally identified with a quantity of gold is not, to Keynes's eyes, consonant with its institutional meaning. The root of Keynes's criticism of the gold standard perhaps lies here. Strangely enough, the gold standard, that is, the very convention which aims to *establish* money as just a means of communication, makes it difficult to apprehend money as a mere intermediary, and even more difficult to understand that its role as an intermediary implies a disappearance – that is, a *return to silence* – as a structural condition for the peculiar meaningfulness of money.

We could say that where gold is charged with the duty of defining, in absolute and unconditional terms, the very being of money, the status of money itself becomes troubled. There is a void, a silence, which is peculiar to money simply in order for it to do its work. But this void is totally filled by its substance, identified by its quantity and its weight. Silence is hindered by the cumbersome presence of something that, at least originally, should be a guarantee of that void and silence.

Perhaps if we start from here, we can revisit the etymological remarks made previously, and grasp the strong affinity of money with speech, and with silence. Indeed, if gold is silence, in the sense that it was never originally a substance (a thing), what is the proper substance of money?

An answer to this question, originating with Keynes, can be found in a text by Kant, in paragraph 31 of his *Metaphysik der Sitten*, published in 1795. To the question 'What is money?' (*Was ist Geld?*), Kant answers as follows:

> Money is a thing, the use of which is possible only by its cession. This is a good *nominal* definition [...], *namely* it is sufficient to distinguish objects of the will of this kind from all other objects. But it gives us no clue as to its feasibility.[6]

It is only through its cession (ceding, or surrendering) that money is properly used. The verb used by Kant to indicate the act involved in 'cession' is *veräußern*. The *proper use* of money is its *Veräußerung*. This, for Kant, is a good *nominal* definition of money: 'nominal' not only in the sense that it leaves out of consideration the material content of the thing defined, but also, and more significantly, in the sense that it identifies the substance of money with *a name* and *a capability of nominating*. In its cession, that is, when it is properly used, money is divested of all material traits. It does not depend on the material it is made of. Whatever it is made from, and however it is embodied or made visible, its *incorporation* or *establishment* must allow the use of money in the form of a *Veräußerung*. Through the *Veräußerung*, money becomes what it is: purely a name. The *Veräußerung* makes clear, indeed calls forth, the *proper nature* of money, by dissociating it from any material substance. Precisely because it is now *lightened*, that is, delivered from any weight, money can *compare*, that is, assign the right or equal weight (*ein gleich gewicht*) to the items being exchanged by means of it. Money can silently bring equilibrium (*gleichgewicht*). In the very moment in which it ceases to be a mere name, and starts to sound (with its 'clinking clanking sound'), flowing from one hand to another, money contributes to the achievement of a standstill: of a silence, of a peace, of an appeasement, of a *payment*. Money is in this sense the instrument of clearing and of the *appeasement of the debtor-creditor relationship*. In order to be safely and clearly obtained, equilibrium presupposes that the items to be weighed can be submitted to the light and lightening dimension of measure. It is this lightness that money takes upon itself, when it is money proper.

If considered in all its implications, the *Veräußerung* which Kant calls into play allows us to see where the linguistic aspect of money lies. *The word itself* tells us quite directly. The term *Veräußerung* is very close to *Äußerung*, which literally means *utterance*. Therefore *Veräußerung* describes the way in which money is *uttered*, that is, the way in which it becomes a word: in fact, a word *entrusted to circulation* – literally, and against all conventional interpretation, a *circulating promise*. We must then ask ourselves: how should we understand think utterance itself? In the *Oxford English dictionary,* under the etymology of the word stem 'to utter', we read

> Partly from out *adv.* or *v.* (with shortening of the vowel as in utter *adv.*), partly ad. MDu. *uteren* (also *uyteren*, Du. *uiteren*, WFris. *uterje*) to drive away, announce, speak, show, make known, or MLG. *üteren*, *ütern* to turn out, sell, speak, demonstrate, etc. (LG. *ütern*), = MHG. *ûᶻeren*, *ûᶻern*, *iuᶻern* (G. *äussern* to speak, declare, ϯbring forth)

The verb is therefore originally related to exchange in its broader sense, and not just to the vocal pronunciation of words. Something is put *outside*, that is, into an *already opened* domain, so that other people, who have access to the same space, can perceive it, receive it, accept it. Originally the verb is less specialized than in its present meaning. Or rather, its primary meanings do not have its current linguistic sense.

Among the meanings historically attested, even if now obsolete, we can find:

> To put (goods, wares, et cetera) forth or upon the market; to issue, offer, or expose for sale or barter; to dispose of by way of trade; to vend, sell.
>
> To give currency to (money, coin, notes, et cetera); to put into circulation; *esp.* to pass or circulate (base coin, forged notes, et cetera) as legal tender (ex: 'Last night I saw a proof-piece of seven-shilling pieces... I know they were not uttered, but could you get me one from the Mint?')
>
> To issue by way of publication; to *publish*.
>
> To produce or yield; to send out, supply, or furnish.
>
> To show, display; *to bring to light*.
>
> To send forth as a sound; to give out in an audible voice; to give vent or expression to (joy, et cetera); to burst out with (a cry, yell, et cetera).
>
> To give utterance to (words, speech, a sentence, et cetera); to speak, say, or pronounce.
>
> To give expression to (a subject, theme, one's thoughts, et cetera); to express, describe, or report in words; to speak of or about (ex: 'Flowers utter their beauty and their fragrance, as much as birds utter their songs').
>
> To disclose or reveal (something unknown, secret, or hidden); to make manifest; to declare, divulge.

These original meanings explain how the further specialization of the verb, that is, the pronunciation of sounding words, has become established. The verb itself points towards a pure movement of exit, or rather a movement of *entry* in an already opened and public space: a space which is *free* for all those who have access to it. Something is entered into a space of common perceivability, and in this sense it appears in it and is available for a *perception* (either for listening, or for appropriation and exchange).

The thing uttered must then pass through an already opened space. From this perspective, the coincidence with another signification of utter – from French *outrer*, to go beyond, cross, traverse – is perhaps not accidental. The movement of appearing brings the possibility of springing out into a tacitly unfolded and hence accessible dimension. The verb points towards a movement of exit which presupposes a previous movement of opening. That which has *previously* opened up differs from all things that can appear and be perceived, listened or exchanged, within it. The space which has previously opened itself is thus a space of comparability, that is, a space of possible measurement. *Previously* opened means in relation to all that will appear and sound in it: tacitly, silently. The space of possible comparison has to do with a definite and particular silence.

Perhaps we have taken some important steps forward in our interpretation, but it is impossible to avoid the most immediate objection. All that has been said until now can be drawn from a *strongly interpretative* approach to etymology. But what can we understand about utterance from linguistics, the science of language?

Utterance has become a 'terminus tecnicus' of linguistics. Thinking of language as communication, linguistics has to describe language and speech regardless of their materiality. Utterance is for linguistics the 'smallest institutional unit of language activity'. This is why utterance can be applied to linguistic actors, meaning speakers and receivers: that is, as actors in a linguistic communication exchange.

But such an exchange cannot do without silence as an element of mediation. We can read this technical definition of utterance: 'An utterance is any stretch of talk, by one person, before and after which there is silence on the part of the person'.[7] The first and last 'thing' that the speaker has in common with the receiver is silence. This silence does not merely tether the linguistic act of a subject, but, *being shared by the recipient*, it constitutes the very medium in which not only a linguistic act but also, and more importantly, a linguistic exchange become possible. Silence not only delimits but defines linguistic exchange, and not only linguistic exchange. Exchange *as such* occurs in the context of silence. That is why, contrary to all conventional assumptions, the silent commerce described by Herodotus is a profoundly linguistic exchange, and in this sense even a profoundly monetary one, even if there are neither words being uttered nor coins passing from hand to hand.

'Silence' opens up so that a word can resound in it and be not only primarily perceived, but also secondarily understood. The word, being *understood* by the recipient, actually *shows* the thing indicated, so that the thing itself which is nominated can *appear* to the recipient. If this holds true, then silence is not the simple opposite of word, nor its mere absence. The expression of an uttered word is not the opposite of silence, but lies in a primary relationship with it. In this sense silence is the dimension of the linguistic exchange, the medium for the encounter between the nominating word and the thing nominated. In the same way, money is not the opposite of wares, but the dimension and the medium for the encounter between things exchanged, for their passage from one hand to another.

This is what we can draw from a comparison between money and speech in their relationship to silence. But in monetary as well as in linguistic matters, things seem to be very different, at least in the conventional way of representing money and speech.

The gold standard, together with modern economic thought, has produced a conflation of money in its role as a measure with its function as a means of exchange, thus assigning to money *one* eminent function, that of a store of value. To *assign* this function to money, however, is to *deprive* it of the real possibility of disappearing, and hence to end its essential silence. The identification between measure and means of exchange, and hence the characterization of money as a store of value, far from ceasing with the recent demonetization of gold, is becoming sharper.

The same has been done, in theory and practice, with the technological approach to language. The representation of word and language as the unity of signified and signifier, which Saussure compared to the two sides of the same sheet of paper (we could say: the two sides of the same coin), corresponds to the identification of the unit of account with the means of exchange.

These two identifications result in an implosion. The relationship between the conceptuality of the signified and the materiality of the signifier becomes a purely conventional relationship. In the same sense, the identification between the materiality of gold and the conceptuality of money appears as the consequence of an evolutionary convention. Here we find again, after this brief excursion, the positions of Hume and Hayek, which I quoted above.

The analogy between money and speech remains even today, but it is divested of its very substance, that is, deprived of any reference to silence. Silence, however, now appears to be just the opposite of speech and money, but the *opening* of a dimension and a measure *in view of exchange*. This opening is not natural, nor purely conventional. Aristotle speaks of name and money, *ónoma* and *nómisma*,[8] as entities that do not come into being by nature, nor by convention, but, as he says in his treatises on language and on money: *katà synthèke*. There are very good reasons for rejecting the customary translation of *synthèke* as 'convention'. I have explored this question in a detailed work, which I will briefly summarize here. By *synthèke* we understand an activity which *puts together* those 'things' which, if they are not properly put together, are not properly what they are, that is, are not *stable*. So, being an activity which makes a relationship *stable* and *meaningful, synthèke* actually means *establishment.*

The factor which allows us to understand the deep analogy between money and speech is therefore not convention, but what we should call *establishment.* So the question that now arises is: how and where does establishment occur?

It has been pointed out that the representation of speech as unity of signified and signifier tends to be seen in binary terms. In this view there would be only two elements, signified and signifier. In reality, the terms of this relationship *stay together* as a result of a *putting together,* a *synthèke,* the establishment of a relationship between signified and signifier, in which a signifier can legitimately signify a signified, that is, the signifier can signify the signified according to a previously established *legality.* The ontological structure of money and speech is not a binary but a ternary structure, because the very structure of exchange itself, being essentially different from barter, is a ternary structure.

As I have observed, money cannot emerge from the complication of binary relations of exchange. This is not the way an instrument of multilateral and simultaneous comparison, what we might call a *numéraire,* can emerge. A numéraire is not simply a number, the *number one,* but a principle of enumeration, a *unit* of account. And for there to be a unit of account, something must have been previously – and as we have seen, *tacitly* – opened, in order for what must be *compared* in exchange to enter into a relationship of comparison controlled by measure. What must be first established is not measure itself, but the dimension in which the *relationship* between measure and measured can properly occur.

This is what Keynes emphasizes from the very beginning of his *Treatise on Money.* Establishing money does not mean constructing an abstract unit of measurement, but rather *producing* and *enacting* the *relationship* between measurement and what is to be measured. As far as money is concerned, what has to be enacted is the relationship between money as a unit of account and money as a means of payment – in Keynes's terms, the relationship between 'money' and 'money of account'. This relationship presupposes a distinction between its elements, but also a unity brought into being by a law of articulation:

> Money itself, namely that by delivery of which debt contracts and price contracts are *discharged,* and in the shape of which a store of general purchasing power is *held,* derives its character from its relationship to the money of account [...] Something which is merely used as a convenient medium of exchange on the spot may approach

to being money, inasmuch as it may represent a means of holding general purchasing power. But if this is all, we have scarcely emerged from the stage of barter. Money proper in the full sense of the term can only exist in relation to a money of account. Perhaps we may elucidate the distinction between *money* and *money of account* by saying that the money of account is the *description* or *title* and the money is the *thing* which answers to the description. Now if the same thing always answered to the same description, the distinction would have no practical interest. But if the thing can change, whilst the description remains the same, then the distinction can be highly significant. The difference is like that between the king of England (whoever he may be) and King George. A contract to pay ten years hence a weight of gold equal to the weight of the king of England is not the same thing as a contract to pay a weight of gold equal to the weight of the individual who is now King George, it is for the State to declare, when the time comes, who the king of England is [...] The State, therefore, comes first of all as the authority of law which enforces the payment of the thing which corresponds to the name or description in the contract. But it comes in doubly when, in addition, it claims the right to determine and declare *what thing* corresponds to the name, and to vary its declaration from time to time – when, that is to say, it claims the right to re-edit the dictionary.[9]

The state, for Keynes, does not correspond to a specific political form. It is not necessarily 'the Leviathan', and even less necessarily an interventionist state, nor a chartalist State à la Knapp. 'State' here means nothing but the *authority* which has the *competence* to decide the correspondence, not just between a signified and a signifier, but between a thing and *its* name, in view of the proper meaning of monetary exchange, which is not the exchange of money *for* money, but the exchange of goods, and the payment of debts, *through* money. What is at stake with the establishment of money is an exchange which has to find, when the time comes, a standstill, an equilibrium, an appeasement. In the economy of Keynes's discourse, the state is nothing but the competence to establish money as an instituted *tertium* in view of the process of exchange and the equilibrium of exchanges. As for 're-editing the dictionary', it establishes signification *in view of sense*, and *drawing from sense*.

The institutions of speech and money are political, precisely and solely because they answer to the demands of sense. What is at stake in the institution of money and its linguisticity is the possibility of a sense which can be shared – a *common sense*. Common sense is often opposed to the purportedly abstract speculation of philosophy – for instance the anti-metaphysical metaphysics which is British empiricism. Yet common sense, if only to produce conventions and contracts, must have a prior relationship with *law* and *legality*.

So the *tertium* itself, in money as in linguistic matters, is establishment. It is the *trait d'union*, the line of separation and union, which is present even in silent commerce, in the form of a shore*line*. This establishing trait differs from the relationships between all entities which take place in the space opened by establishment itself.

We can now return to the initial question that we left partially unanswered: what kind of language does money speak today? The answer we gave, namely that money speaks the language of calculation, can now be expanded. Language itself, or rather what remains of language after its radical binarization, is now a calculation process.

Reduced to a means of communication, money and speech can legitimately appear as objects of a calculation. The main characteristic of this calculation – logic reduced to mere logistics – is, however, the fact that it demands to be performed as a total calculation, that is, a calculation capable of calculating its own conditions of possibility.

Notes

1. Griaule (1975). Translated from the Italian edition (Dio d'acqua, pp. 240–242, passim).
2. J. Locke, *An Essay Concerning Human Understanding, Book III: Of Words*, Chapter 1, 'Of Words or Language in General'.
3. D. Hume, *A Treatise of Human Nature: Book III, Of Morals, Part I, Of Virtue and Vice in General*, Section II, 'Of the Origin of Justice and Property'.
4. Von Hayek (1990, pp. 37–38) ('The Mystique of Legal Tender').
5. Keynes (1923, p. 124).
6. 'Geld ist eine Sache, deren Gebrauch nur dadurch möglich ist, daß man sie veräußert. Dies ist eine gute Namenerklärung desselben (nach Achenwall), nämlich hinreichend zur Unterscheidung dieser Art Gegenstände der Willkür von allen andern; aber sie gibt uns keinen Aufschluß über die Möglichkeit einer solchen Sache'.
7. Harris (1951, p. 14).
8. Respectively in *Perì Hermenèias*, and in *Nicomachean Ethics*.
9. Keynes (1930, pp. 3–4, italics in original).

References

Griaule, M. (1975) *Conversations with Ogotemmêli: An Introduction to Dogon Religious Ideas* (Oxford: Oxford University Press).

Harris, Z. S. (1951) *Methods in Structural Linguistics* (Chicago: University of Chicago Press).

Hume, D. (2003) *A Treatise of Human Nature, Dover Philosophical Classics* (New York: Dover Publications), pp. 348–349.

Keynes, J. M. (1923) 'A Tract on Monetary Reform', in *The Collected Writings*, vol. 4 (London: Macmillan, 1971–1989).

Keynes, J. M. (1930) 'A Treatise on Money', in *The Collected Writings*, vol. 5 (London: Macmillan, 1971–1989).

Locke, J. (1849) *An Essay Concerning Human Understanding* (Chicago: William Tegg), pp. 75, 289.

Von Hayek, F. (1990) *Denationalisation of Money – The Argument Refined* (London: Institute for Economic Affairs).

5
What Kind of Calculation Is Implied in the Money Rate of Interest?

Luca Fantacci

> It is the money that counts, and money makes money, but what makes money make money?
>
> H. Miller

The rate of interest is implicitly called into question by the title of this book, concerning the relationship between money and calculation. Even before extending beyond the sphere of economic relationships, the scope of calculation has been broadened within that sphere, to include money itself. Since the beginning of the modern era, in fact, money started to be, not merely the instrument of a calculation directed towards the exchange of goods, but itself the object of calculation and exchange. The rate of interest was first sanctioned by law in the sixteenth century as the legitimate price of money.

The legitimization of the rate of interest represents a historical turning point for the concept of money, in its relation to commodities, credit, time and sovereignty.

- Interest makes money a commodity. To assign a price to money, in the form of a rate of interest, implies a radical transformation in the meaning of money. From the moment it has a price, money becomes a commodity. This is a fact which all theories and histories have to reckon with, if they want to give account of how money actually works in the modern economy (even if they assume that money proper cannot be a commodity). However, this leaves open not only the question of the legitimacy of considering and treating money as a commodity, but also the question of the peculiarity of money with respect to other commodities, even when it is treated as a commodity itself.

- Interest makes money and credit interchangeable. Interest may also be defined as the money paid for the forbearance of a debt. Interest therefore provides a quantitative measure of the difference between credit and money: it is the charge for a temporary exchange of money against a credit. With the establishment of interest on loans, money and credit are interchangeable, according to a fixed ratio for a specified period of time.
- Interest affects the way in which economic life unfolds in time. It provides a quantitative measure for the comparison of money values through time. Being always positive, it systematically values the present above the future, and the near future above the distant future. More importantly, it allows comparisons over indefinitely long time-periods, thus transcending any expiration, any bottom line, or any account closure.
- Interest implies a change in monetary sovereignty. Monetary sovereignty always concerns the form of the relation between money and credit. Pre-modern monetary authorities defined by decree the value of coins as legal tender for the payment of debts in terms of an abstract unit of account. A modern monetary authority fixes, with the bank rate, the money to be paid, not for the payment, but for the forbearance of the debt. The exercise of pre-modern monetary sovereignty is intended to allow the closing of debt/credit relations. The exercise of modern monetary sovereignty allows the indefinite postponement of payments and the increase of imbalance.

All these issues certainly deserve deeper consideration. However, the main object of this paper is to investigate not the consequences of the legitimization and generalization of interest on loans, but the assumptions on which they rest. The question is not what is implied *by* the rate of interest, in terms of a change in the status of money, but rather what is implied *in* the rate of interest, in terms of a particular form of calculation. My hypothesis is, in fact, that interest is not merely a matter of fact, nor merely a matter of ethics or law, but a matter of peculiar logic, underlying both the economic practice and its legal sanctioning. Hence the question that gives the title to this paper: What kind of calculation is implied in the money rate of interest?

In order to address this question, I shall go back, not to the period when the institutional foundations of the modern practice of interest were laid but to a period when, since they appeared to falter, the soundness of those foundations was brought into question. I am referring to the interwar period, and in particular to the writings and activities of John Maynard Keynes. A crisis is always an occasion to investigate not only the contingent factors that make it happen, but also the structural factors that make it possible. For Keynes, the interwar crisis was indeed an occasion to question the assumptions on which both economic theory and practice rested.

The two sides of Keynes's criticism, however intertwined, are not to be confused: on one side, there were the faults of the economic – particularly the monetary – system that Keynes held responsible for the severe and persistent imbalances of the time; on the other, there were the shortcomings of the prevailing economic and monetary theory, which failed to give account of those imbalances. The issue at stake was, therefore, not merely theoretical, but institutional. According to Keynes, if the assumptions of contemporary economic *theory* had proved inadequate to explain what was happening in practice, it was not just a matter of correcting the theory, since the assumptions of contemporary economic *practice* had proved equally inadequate to assure the proper functioning of the economy. Keynes dug deep into the foundations of the economic system, and arrived at re-opening the case against the legitimacy of the rate of interest, partially rehabilitating usury laws (Keynes 1936, pp. 351–353) – and he did so explicitly, not on moral but on scientific grounds.

The relevance of Keynes's thought for the argument of my inquiry follows from various circumstances:

(a) In his analysis of the current economic situation, Keynes identified the rate of interest, and specifically the high level of the long-term rate of interest, as the principal cause of the depression afflicting the British economy since the early twenties, and the world economy throughout the thirties.

(b) Consequently the rate of interest, and the difficulty for the monetary authority to regulate the prevailing market rate through conventional bank rate policies, came to play a crucial role in his theoretical account of economic imbalances. His understanding of the rate of interest as the price of money lent, and not merely of money saved, is the main point of departure from the classical theory and the main explanation provided in the *General Theory* for the possible difference, in nature and in level, between savings and investments.

(c) Keynes's theory of the rate of interest is grounded on his theory of probability. Having defined the rate of interest as a 'liquidity

premium', Keynes repeatedly suggested that it should be understood in the light of a concept that he introduced in his *Treatise on
Probability*, namely the 'weight of arguments'. This is the point most
directly related to the question that guides this paper. As I will try
to show, following Keynes's scant remarks on this issue, the rate of
interest is not the result of a calculation of probability, but rather
reflects the degree of confidence in that calculation.

(d) Keynes discussed the flaws of the classical theory, but also the institutional flaws of 'money as we know it'. My last step will therefore
be to enquire, in the light of Keynes's analysis, what makes money
the object of that peculiar form of calculation that is embodied in
the rate of interest.

The points briefly outlined above will be developed in the following
sections.

I

The rate of interest is the price of money. More precisely, it is the price
paid for the use of money for a certain time. In still other terms, it is
the price paid for the anticipation of a sum of money. Like all other
prices, it is traditionally represented by economic theory as the point
of intersection between a supply and a demand, where the demand is
expressed by those who need the money to finance an economic activity, and who expect to pay the interest from the proceeds of that activity, and the supply is provided by those who have accumulated money,
by refraining from expenditure. Like all market prices, the interest rate
is assumed to settle at a level where demand equals supply, so as to
clear the market. Following this line of reasoning, the classical theory
described the market rate of interest as the clearing price for savings and
investments.

According to this theory, the rate of interest appeared as a remuneration for the thrift of the savers, paid by the proceeds of the activities,
innovations and progress that were made possible by the anticipation of
money to the investors. It was on this basis that, following Locke (1692)
and Bentham (1787), the classical economists advocated a liberalization
of interest on loans. This was seen as the best way to ensure an adequate
incentive for the activity of saving, as a source of finance for economic
growth and development. The idea, gradually disseminating common
thought and practice, was eventually erected into an economic principle that appeared to reconcile personal and collective interests. Saving,

no longer identified with the hideous vice of avarice, became a virtue, public and private; and interest, once banned under the infamous name of usury, became its legitimate reward.

It was this ostensible reconciliation between God and mammon that attracted Keynes's attention ever since his *Tract on Monetary Reform* (Keynes 1923, p. 6). His concern was not ethical, but practical: the rate of interest appeared to be too high to allow the investments required for the attainment of full employment; this peculiar market price ceased to balance supply and demand; savings were no longer matched by investments. The excess of savings called for scientific explanation, not for moral contempt. The shortcoming to be accounted for was at once empirical and theoretical: Why did the market rate of interest fail to bring into equilibrium savings and investments? And why did the classical theory fail to foresee this possibility?

Keynes identified the excessive level of the long-term rate of interest as the principal cause of low investment, worldwide depression and chronic underemployment. He formalized this view in his *Treatise on Money* (Keynes 1930), and propounded it in a number of articles, testimonies before government advisory bodies, public conferences and letters to statesmen throughout the thirties.[1] The level of the interest rate apparently reflected the operation of market forces: the price of money was high, because there was a large demand with respect to supply. However, as Keynes's analysis of the situation highlighted, the demand for money was inflated by 'distressed' borrowers, who needed the money not for investments but to repay wartime debts, whereas the supply of money was restricted by the fact that it was accumulated, without being lent, by governments and central banks building up reserves to defend their currencies, and by private banks and individuals withholding liquid stocks in the expectation of decreasing prices and rising interest rates. In other words, not all borrowers were willing to invest, and not all savers were willing to lend. Hence, the market rate of interest did in fact balance the demand and supply of loans, without however equalizing investments and savings. And it was doomed to remain at too high a level to perform its traditional task of transforming the results of individual thrift into the conditions of collective prosperity – despite the expansionist policies carried out, though belatedly, on the part of monetary authorities, by lowering the bank rate and increasing the money supply.

The assumptions on which the nineteenth century had built its economy and growth were thus called into question. The possibility that had been disregarded, and that now came to the fore as an imposing reality, was that money saved was not in fact lent, but simply withheld from circulation, with the prospect of benefiting from more favourable conditions of expenditure or investment in the future. Economic theory had veiled this possibility by conceiving the rate of interest as the remuneration for saving, thus implicitly assuming that all money not spent was automatically lent. Since this assumption had to be abandoned, the theory of interest required a radical revision.

II

Keynes's contribution to the understanding of the rate of interest may be summarized in these terms: interest is not a compensation for the decision not to spend money, but for the decision not to hoard it. This is clearly stated by Keynes in the *General Theory*, in Chapter 13, specifically dedicated to 'The General Theory of the Rate of Interest'. The statement is preceded by the locution that Keynes uses to mark something evident but usually overlooked:

> It should be obvious that the rate of interest cannot be a return to saving or waiting as such. For if a man hoards his savings in cash, he earns no interest, though he saves just as much as before. On the contrary, the mere definition of the rate of interest tells us in so many words that the rate of interest is the reward for parting with liquidity for a specified period. (Keynes 1936, p. 167)

Keynes defines the rate of interest as a 'liquidity premium', that is, a price for money demanded and supplied as liquidity: a price earned, not for the merit of saving, but for the decision to lend; a price paid, not for the opportunity of investing money, but for the opportunity of borrowing it, regardless of the purpose.

Consequently, the market rate of interest does not balance savings and investments, but supply and demand of loans. The supply of loans is not identically equal to savings. The amount of money offered to borrowers is not simply the result of the decision not to spend, but depends on the further decision, on the part of those who have saved, to actually lend the money thus accumulated. This second decision becomes crucial in determining the supply of loans, as long as one acknowledges the possibility that money be kept, without being either spent or lent. In other words, the difference between savings and supply of loans, and hence the difference between savings and investments, depends on the possibility of holding idle money balances. This demand for money plays a crucial role in the *General Theory*, under the heading of 'liquidity preference'.

This expression seems to refer to a subjective, psychological attitude, which attaches particular importance to holding wealth in the form of money rather than in any other form. Indeed, what Keynes describes as 'liquidity preference' is a sort of Midas complex, which however affects not primarily individuals but rather the economic system as a whole. In fact, money can be demanded as a preferred form of holding one's wealth only if its function as a store of value is institutionally sanctioned. Money can be saved, without being lent, only if there is the possibility of saving money as such. There can be a liquidity preference only if there is liquidity.

What is liquidity? Whence does money derive its liquidity? What gives money this peculiar quality that allows it to be exchanged at a premium with all other forms of asset? Keynes addresses this issue in Chapter 17 of the *General Theory*, on 'The Essential Properties of Interest and Money', where he sets out 'to enquire wherein the peculiarity of money lies as distinct from other assets' in order to identify the source of the money rate of interest. Keynes identifies the superior liquidity of money as its main distinguishing feature, and describes it in the following terms:

> the power of disposal over an asset during a period may offer a potential convenience or security, which is not equal for assets of different kinds, though the assets themselves are of equal initial value...The amount (measured in terms of itself) which [people] are willing to pay for the potential convenience or security given by this power of disposal..., we shall call its liquidity-premium. (Keynes 1936, p. 226)

Money is liquidity, that is, power of disposal. The rate of interest is a liquidity premium, that is, a price to pay in order to benefit from this power of disposal, and to compensate the owner of the money for surrendering this power, for a specified period of time. According to Keynes's definition, not only money but all assets have a power of disposal, a certain degree of liquidity: 'capital equipments will differ from one another [...] in the rapidity with which the wealth embodied in them can become "liquid", in the sense of producing output, the proceeds of which can be re-embodied if desired in quite a different form' (Keynes 1936, p. 240). In the light of this passage, liquidity is seen quite literally as the property of a fluid, which has no independent shape and is capable of assuming different forms. Liquidity is interchangeability, and money is liquidity *par excellence.* What distinguishes money is its having the highest degree of liquidity, compared to all other assets and commodities, since it can be transformed immediately into any form of wealth, whereas other assets need first to be 'liquidated' and, in the process of being liquidated, may result in a loss for their holders. The rate of interest is a compensation for the owner of money who agrees to exchange it temporarily for a credit, thus surrendering liquidity, together with the 'convenience and security' that it affords, and accepting exposure to a possible loss.

III

Stated in these terms, the rate of interest appears to be the result of a probability calculus on prospective profits and losses. More precisely, the rate of interest appears to be determined by the intersection of two calculations: from the perspective of the lender, it would have to reflect the possibility of the loss involved in agreeing to temporarily hold a credit instead of cash; from the perspective of the borrower, it would have to reflect the expected yield of the investments made possible by the money anticipated, that is, by the temporary command over its power of disposal. This probability calculus helps to determine the level of the rate of interest on a specific asset.

However, according to Keynes this is only one component, and not an essential but rather an additional component, of the rate of interest. It is what Keynes calls the *risk premium* and is only present when the asset received in exchange for a certain amount of money involves a risk, that is, a positive probability of not being exchanged back into an equivalent sum of money. But the rate of interest may be positive also on risk-free assets. A positive money rate of interest does not necessarily depend on risk. This is the reason why Keynes defines the rate of interest not as a risk premium, but as a liquidity premium: a compensation for parting with money, even if there is no calculable risk of not having it returned.

How are we to understand this liquidity premium, how does it differ from risk premium? In the *General Theory*, Keynes provides only the hint of an answer: 'The liquidity premium, it will be observed, is partly similar to the risk premium, but partly different; – the difference corresponding to the difference between the best estimates we can make of probabilities and the confidence with which we make them' (Keynes 1936, p. 240).

In two footnotes to the *General Theory*, and in a letter to his student, Hugh Townshend, Keynes gives further indications that may help to elucidate this point. He suggests interpreting 'liquidity premium' in the light of a concept introduced in his *Treatise on Probability*, namely the 'weight of arguments'. It is nothing more than a series of hints, which, however, taken together, provide sufficient evidence of the fact that, according to Keynes, the nature of the interest rate ultimately depends on the logic of probability, as expounded in the *Treatise*. In the letter to Townshend, Keynes writes

> I am rather inclined to associate risk premium with probability strictly speaking, and liquidity premium with what in my Treatise on Probability I called 'weight'. (Keynes 1938, p. 293)

The weight of arguments refers not to the probability of an estimate, but to the confidence with which that probability is assessed: 'The weight, to speak metaphorically, measures the *sum* of the favourable and unfavourable evidence, the probability measures the *difference*' (Keynes 1921, p. 84). Hence, 'the "weight" and the "probability" of an argument are independent properties' (ibid. p. 83).

To associate the rate of interest, as liquidity premium, with the weight of arguments, means to understand it not as a compensation for a possible loss or as a participation in a possible profit, but as a remuneration, which is independent of profits and losses and of their degree of probability, and which is paid to the lender of money for the very fact of surrendering the absolute certainty associated with money: 'A liquidity premium … is a payment, not for the expectation of increased tangible income at the end of the period, but for an increased sense of comfort and confidence during the period' (Keynes 1938, p. 294).

The rate of interest is not intended to compensate the lender of money for the risk, that is, for the calculable probability of losing it, but to compensate him also for the uncertainty, that is, for the incalculable possibility of losing it. But what exactly does it mean to say that money gives to its owner an absolute certainty, which is shared by no other asset? And what is it that gives money this peculiar trait? 'What makes money make money?'

IV

Keynes shares with classical and neoclassical economists the idea that in equilibrium money should not exist, just as he shares with them the idea that in equilibrium unemployment should not exist. The difference is that the non-existence of money and unemployment are not for him states assumed from the beginning by hypothesis, but states which may eventually arise as one of the possible outcomes of the interplay of economic forces. 'Moreover', as he observes, 'the characteristics of the special case assumed by the classical theory happen not to be those of the economic society in which we actually live' (Keynes 1936, p. 3). This statement applies both to full employment and to the disappearance of money – and it may be applied equally to the economic society in which we live today.

The two characteristics of economic equilibrium that Keynes considers desirable, but not at all certain, are not associated by chance. They stand and fall together. More precisely, one is the condition for the other: unemployment arises because money is held as an asset, in preference to other forms of wealth. 'Unemployment develops, that is to say, because people want the moon' (Keynes 1936, p. 235).

This is how Keynes condenses the *General Theory* in a formula. The argument is developed more broadly in the whole of Chapter 17, from which the previous quote is taken. That chapter is dedicated to illustrating, as the title suggests, 'the essential properties of interest and money', and is intended to show how the theory of employment (or rather of unemployment) presented by Keynes in the previous chapters crucially depends upon those properties. The intention is explicit from the very first lines of the chapter:

> It seems, then, that the *rate of interest on money* plays a peculiar part in setting a limit to the level of employment, since it sets a standard to which the marginal efficiency of a capital-asset must attain if it is to be newly produced. That this should be so, is, at first sight, most perplexing. It is natural to enquire wherein the peculiarity of money lies as distinct from other assets, whether it is only money which has a rate of interest, and what would happen in a non-monetary economy. Until we have answered these questions, the full significance of our theory will not be clear. (Keynes 1936, p. 222, emphasis in original)

The questions are: What does money provide for its owner? What are the particular merits of money as an asset? Why is money demanded at all as an asset, in preference to other assets? What makes money a desirable store of value given that, unlike to most other assets, it yields apparently nothing to its owner, and is completely 'barren' (Keynes 1937a, p. 115)? Why is money preferred to other assets, such as to entail compensation for parting with it? So 'what makes money make money?' What particular service of money is remunerated by the rate of interest?

One does not have to wait until Chapter 17 to find a first answer to this question. Already in Chapter 13, entitled 'The General Theory of Interest', Keynes introduces the concept of liquidity-preference, defining it as the function that expresses the demand for money in relation to the rate of interest. After having underlined that 'this is where and how the quantity of money enters into the economic scheme', Keynes appropriately stops to consider the factors that concur to determine the existence of such a relation: 'At this point, however, let us turn back and consider *why such a thing as liquidity-preference exists*' (Keynes 1936, p. 168; my emphasis). It is worth noting that, since the liquidity-preference is defined as 'a potentiality or functional tendency' (ibid.), the question concerns not the existence of a demand for money but the existence of a relation between the demand for money and the remuneration for its use. In other terms, the question is not why money is demanded, but why this demand has a price: *why such a thing as the rate of interest exists*.

This is where Keynes, building on the traditional distinction between the use of money as a means of payment and the use of money as a store of value, introduces his celebrated distinction between the three motives for liquidity-preference:

(a) The transactions-motive, i.e. the need of cash for the current transaction of personal and business exchanges;
(b) The precautionary-motive, i.e. the desire for security as to the future cash equivalent of a certain proportion of total resources;
(c) The speculative-motive, i.e. the object of securing profit from knowing better than the market what the future will bring forth (Keynes 1936, p. 170).

However, if the intention is not simply to explain why money is demanded, but why the demand for money varies with the rate of interest (i.e., 'why such a thing as liquidity-preference exists'), we cannot be satisfied with just recognizing that money is indeed capable of satisfying these three motives, but we must explain why, to satisfy them, it may be preferable to hold money rather than interest-bearing loans.

Before reviewing the determinants of the liquidity-preference, it is worth underlining and explaining what is, in fact, a major point of departure of the *General Theory* from the classical (and neoclassical) theories of the rate of interest. Keynes assumes that the market rate of interest is stabilized at the level that equates the demand and supply of money (Keynes 1937a, p. 117) and not at the level that equates the demand and supply of loans. The latter would seem more appropriate given that the rate of interest is the price of loans and not of money – in Keynes's words, 'the reward for parting with liquidity for a specified period' (Keynes 1936, p. 167). However, this approach would require the schedule of the demand for loans in relation to the rate of interest to remain fixed when the schedule of the supply of loans shifts – and, as Keynes argues, this is not the case. In fact, both schedules depend, *inter alia*, on the level of income; yet a shift in either schedule will cause a change in the rate of interest, and hence a change in the level of income, which will determine in turn a shift in the other schedule. It is impossible, therefore, to determine the positions of the demand and supply curves for loans unless the level of income or the level of the rate of interest are determined from outside this scheme by the interaction of independent variables (Keynes 1936, pp. 179–184).

To illustrate this idea Keynes went so far as to use a graph, the only one in the whole *General Theory*, which shows that a shift of the demand curve (from X_1 to X_2) will cause the supply curve to shift (from Y_1) to another position, which it is impossible to determine unless the rate of interest (r_1 or r_2) is determined by some other source.

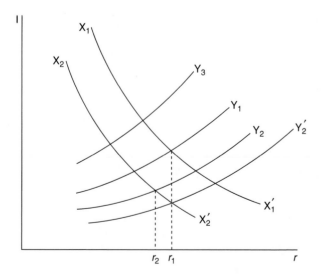

In order to overcome the indeterminacy, and to have an alternative, independent source for the level of the rate of interest, Keynes looks at the rate of interest from a different perspective, as the factor which adjusts at the margin the demand for money and the supply of money, since the latter are in fact independent.

As a consequence of this approach, the schedule of the demand for money in relation to the rate of interest, that is, of the liquidity-preference, acquires a crucial role in the *General Theory*, for it explains the existence and the actual level of the rate of interest, and hence the constraints imposed on the efficiency of every capital good, if it has to be newly produced. Let us then consider in succession the factors that Keynes mentions as possible determinants of the liquidity-preference.

(a) At first glance, it seems quite obvious that a certain quantity of money is required as ready cash to face the current expenses of individuals and businesses, that is, for the purpose of transactions. However, on further consideration, the use of money as a medium of exchange can be seen as the function in which money may be more easily and expediently substituted by some form of credit. Indeed, if it were always possible to purchase goods by contracting a debt (e.g., by signing a bill of trade or by drawing on an overdraft facility from a clearing centre), there would be no need for money, other than as a convenient unit of account to denominate those debts. This is what Keynes implies when, discussing 'the psychological and business incentives to liquidity' in Chapter 13, he states that 'there is no necessity to hold idle cash to bridge over intervals if it can be obtained without difficulty at the moment when it is actually required' (Keynes 1936, p. 196).

This is also what Keynes aimed at when he designed the Clearing Union as a system capable of providing 'a quantum of international currency [...] governed by the actual current requirements of world commerce' (Keynes 1943a, p. 168). In fact, the Clearing Union would have allowed for the settlement of international transactions without issuing an international medium of exchange, but simply by providing overdraft facilities denominated in a unit of account (*bancor*) for the centralized recording and multilateral compensation of all debts and credits arising from international trade. In other words, the Clearing Union would have been an international payments system without an international medium of exchange. In Keynes's words: 'The C.U., if it were fully successful, would deal with the quantity of international money by making any significant quantity unnecessary' (Keynes 1943b, p. 31).

Therefore, insofar as alternative methods of payment are available, transactions are not a good reason to hold cash. In practice, the relevance of the transactions-motive in explaining the demand for money will depend on how widespread, cheap and reliable various forms of overdraft may be. As long as we are considering the demand for money as a means of payment, and as long as a banking system provides an alternative form of payment to cash, the rate of interest cannot exceed the costs of running the banking system (and hence it will not be, strictly speaking, a rate of interest, but a charge, which need not be proportional either to the amount or to the time-span of the anticipation provided). No one will be willing to borrow money, for the purpose of carrying out current transactions, if the same transactions can be performed by some form of draft or overdraft at a lower price.[2]

Hence, there is no necessary relation between the quantity of money required as a means of exchange in transactions and the level of the rate of interest. As R. Wray has shown, Keynes insisted particularly in his defence of the *General Theory* 'that an increased demand for money *need not* raise interest rates *so long as* banks accommodate' (Wray 2006, p. 187, emphasis in original). Expenditure, either on consumption or on investments, is not constrained by the amount of money (saving) previously accumulated by individuals or businesses, but by the amount of credit (finance) provided by the banking system. 'Unless the banking system is prepared to augment the supply of money, lack of finance may prove an important obstacle to more than a certain amount of investment decisions being on the tapis at the same time. But "finance" has nothing to do with saving' (Keynes 1937b, p. 209). Thus, as long as banks conversely accommodate the demand for money for transactions, adjusting to the scale of economic activity, interest rates are not affected.[3]

(b) The precautionary-motive for liquidity is commonly described in terms of a demand for money in view of *un*expected purchases, as opposed to the expected purchases that are supposed to drive the transactions-motive. Indeed, this is what Keynes seems to imply when he describes it as a further motive for holding cash 'to provide for contingencies requiring *sudden* expenditure and for *unforeseen* opportunities of advantageous purchases' (Keynes 1936, p. 196, emphasis added).

However, it is easy to observe that the remarks in the previous section concerning the transactions-motive are quite independent from the fact that the transactions involved are actually expected or unexpected. In either case, the presence of a clearing system will make the holding of money superfluous. And where instead there are no similar facilities, variations in the rate of interest will affect the amount of money demanded for expected purchases (e.g., a fall in the rate of interest will induce expectations of higher purchases), but there will be no reason for them to affect the amount of money demanded for unexpected purchases. Therefore, if the precautionary-motive is intended in this sense, it can add nothing to the explanation of the existence of the liquidity-preference.

Yet perhaps this is not what Keynes intends. Let us read again more carefully the previous quote, which is the only passage in the whole *General Theory* that might seem to legitimize the common interpretation of the precautionary-motive. There is no reason to believe that the 'unforeseen opportunities of advantageous purchases' must be understood as purchases *of goods*. In fact, the same passage continues by describing, as a further element of the precautionary-motive, the desire 'to hold an asset of which the value is fixed in terms of money to meet a subsequent liability fixed in terms of money'. So Keynes could be referring to the purchase, not of goods, but of assets. This is even more consistent with the definition of the precautionary-motive that I quoted above ('the desire for security as to the future cash equivalent of a certain proportion of total resources'), and with the considerations that Keynes develops immediately after that passage, where indeed he assumes that there is a market for debts and that, in deciding how much money to hold for future transactions, individuals and businesses have to weigh that decision against the alternative option of purchasing a long-term debt and subsequently turning it into cash. In other words, what Keynes appears to be implicitly assuming here is that there are no clearing facilities and that therefore the purchasing power to face future expenses, be they expected or unexpected, must be hoarded in advance either in the form of money or in the form of *debts purchased on the market* (i.e., bonds).

Now in this scenario, the expectation of expenses does make a difference. In the case of expected disbursements, it is always convenient to hold wealth in the form of bonds (expiring on the date of the expected disbursement) rather than cash, as long as the rate of interest on those bonds is positive, and regardless of its actual level. If instead, as it were, unexpected disbursements are expected, that is, if there is uncertainty as to the timing of the actual disbursements, the latter may fall due before the maturity of the bond. In this case, the bond will have to be discounted at the rate of interest prevailing at that moment on the market, and it may happen that this discount exceeds the one at which the bond was originally bought, thus leaving the purchaser of the bond with a net loss, which could have been avoided if the money had been simply held in the form of cash. Therefore, there will be an incentive to hold money as a store of wealth in the face of future unpredictable contingencies if there is uncertainty as to the future rate of interest (Keynes 1936, pp. 168–169). Hence, even interpreting in this sense the precautionary-motive, it is easy to show that, as long as the rate at which debts are remunerated and discounted is not negative, there will be no incentive at all to hold cash, even as a precaution for unexpected disbursements, unless there is uncertainty concerning the future level of such a rate.

It is worth noting, incidentally, that this motive for holding money applies equally well to the case in which expenses are in fact predicted, but bonds are not available for the exact date of payment, which is in practice what will typically occur in organized bond markets. On such markets, bonds for fixed maturities are sold and bought: the set of maturities is discrete, whereas the exchange of bonds against money is continuous. For this reason it is not relevant, even in this case, to distinguish between expected and unexpected contingencies that require ready cash: in both cases, the bonds held as a store of wealth will have to be liquidated on the market at an unknown discount. What is relevant is not the uncertainty of the actual moment of liquidation, but the uncertainty of the prevailing rate of interest in the market at any given moment in the future.

This leads us to the most important implication of these remarks for our enquiry into the reasons 'why such a thing as liquidity-preference exists'. Since the precautionary-motive for liquidity, however defined, has been shown to depend on the *uncertainty* as to the future rate of interest rather than on the *level* of the rate of interest, it may help to explain why money is demanded (liquidity) but it contributes nothing to explaining why the demand for money should vary according to the *level* of the rate of interest (liquidity-preference). Hence, the precautionary-motive is even less relevant than the transactions-motive in providing an explanation for the existence of, and the variations in, the rate of interest.

(c) This leaves us with the speculative-motive. Our previous considerations about the precautionary-motive have led us to consider the holding of money as an alternative to the holding of bonds. One reason to hold money rather than bonds is to avoid *unexpected* depreciations of the bonds due to *unexpected* variations of the rate of interest: this is the precautionary-motive. However, there may be another reason for an individual or a business to hold money rather than bonds, namely the *expectation* of a rise in the rate of interest, and hence of a depreciation of the bonds: this is the speculative-motive.

It is quite obvious that the demand for money due to the speculative-motive will be very responsive to actual variations in the rate of interest: every rise in the latter will induce more and more individuals and businesses (the 'bulls') to exchange money for bonds in the expectation that the future rate of interest will fall below the actual rate, and hence that the price of their bonds will rise. At the same time, the number of those who expect the rate of interest to rise still further and who therefore have an incentive to sell bonds (the 'bears') will decrease. The demand and supply of money against bonds due to the speculative motive will respond immediately and significantly to any variation of the rate of interest, and the rate of interest will adjust in order to balance the sales of the 'bears' with the purchases of the 'bulls'.

Hence the relationship between the quantity of money and the rate of interest described by the liquidity-preference function appears to depend decisively upon the speculative-motive. This is stated quite explicitly by Keynes when he observes that 'the amount of money required to satisfy the transactions-motive and the precautionary-motive is mainly a resultant of the general activity of the economic system and of the level of the money-income' – and not, it is implied, a result of the variations of the rate of interest. On the contrary, 'it is by playing on the speculative-motive that monetary management (or, in the absence of management, chance changes in the quantity of money) is brought to bear on the economic system' (Keynes 1936, p. 196).

Therefore, the existence of the liquidity-preference – understood not generically as the demand for money balances, but strictly as the functional relationship between the demand for money balances and the rate of interest – seems to depend entirely on the speculative-motive, and not on the combination of three different motives. Moreover, if the liquidity-preference function depends on the speculative-motive, also the level of the market rate of interest and its variations depend on the speculative-motive – that is, on expectations. This amounts to stating that the market rate of interest settles at a certain level only because it is expected to do so. Keynes is again quite explicit in this respect: '*Any* level of interest which is accepted with sufficient conviction as *likely* to be durable *will* be durable' (Keynes 1936, p. 203, emphasis in original).

However upsetting this may sound, it is not necessarily a bad explanation of what actually occurs. Indeed, financial markets often appear to respond to self-fulfilling expectations more than to any fundamental, and even monetary authorities are concerned about influencing expectations at least as much as they are concerned about managing the quantity of money.

However, even assuming that this is an accurate description of the forces that concur to determine the level of the rate of interest, it is not yet an explanation of why such a thing as the rate of interest exists. We cannot be satisfied with a theory of the demand for money that tells us only that a good reason for people to hold on to their money (or to be compensated for parting with it) is that they expect a day, a moment, or an opportunity to come, in which they might be able to make more money out of lending it. Even assuming that the level of the rate of interest is determined by expectations, we must ask why any expectation of a positive rate of interest should arise in the first place.

Once again, the questions are: What makes the payment of an interest on loans at all plausible? Why does the temporary cession of money require compensation? What conveniences does the actual possession of money afford? One is tempted to reply that money is never demanded to be simply held; that those who borrow money do not borrow it to leave it idle, but to use it, for example, to finance new investments; that therefore money is not barren, but may bear fruit in terms of increased productivity and output; and that those who lend money, allowing those fruits to be brought forth, are legitimately entitled to their share.

However, this is not a complete economic explanation of the existence of a positive rate of interest until account is given of the sacrifice that the loan imposes on the lender. For if no such sacrifice were involved in lending, the competition between the holders of money in their search for a willing borrower would necessarily drive their compensation down to zero. Hence, a positive rate of interest may only be explained by providing evidence of the costs that a loan imposes on the lender, in terms of decreased yields or actual losses.

These remarks may serve perhaps to shed light on the reasons why Keynes rehabilitated 'the attitude of the Medieval Church to the rate of interest' (Keynes 1936, p. 351). In fact, usury laws prohibited any rate of interest that was not justified by decreasing yields (*lucrum cessans*) or actual losses (*damnum mergens*). Following the line of Keynes's argument, it appears quite clearly that the ban was not inspired by merely moral intentions and that these concessions were not 'Jesuitical attempts to find a practical escape from a foolish theory' (ibid.). Rather, the scope and limits of the ban were based on the fact that the rate of interest cannot find any logical explanation, let alone juridical legitimization, until account has been given not only of the good reasons why loans are demanded, but also of the good reasons why the demand should be rejected. In other words, the rate of interest cannot convincingly be described as a market price, until account has been given of both the demand and the supply curves.

And in order to explain what determines the supply of loans, as we have seen, we have to explain what determines the demand for money as an asset. This is why, in Chapter 17 of the *General Theory*, Keynes turns – and must turn – to investigate the peculiar properties of money as an asset, as distinct from other assets. It is worth noting that here 'assets' means 'real assets', that is, commodities (both consumption and investment goods), as opposed to financial assets, that is, debts. However remote and exoteric it might seem, this investigation is essential to his theory, and not merely incidental. The whole *General Theory* stands or falls with the possibility of explaining why money is demanded as an asset.

Keynes distinguishes three types of assets, according to the returns that they provide to their owners, merely by the passage of time.

(a) Some produce a return, 'by assisting some process of production or supplying services to a consumer' (Keynes 1936, p. 225). We could call them, for simplicity, investment goods, even though Keynes does not use this expression and includes in this category also durable consumption goods, using the house as an example. The return to the ownership of this kind of asset may be called its *yield*.

(b) Other assets 'suffer some wastage or involve some cost through the mere passage of time', in a material sense, that is, without considering a change in their relative value, and whether they are or are not used to produce a yield. As an example of this category, Keynes mentions wheat. The return to the ownership of this kind of asset is negative and may be called *carrying cost*.

(c) Money does not fit in either of the previous groups: it does not decay nor produce a yield merely by being held. Yet it does offer to its holder a 'potential convenience' or a 'security', consisting in its 'power of disposal', that is, in its capacity to be readily transformed into any other asset of any kind. This property, which money displays pre-eminently but which belongs in lesser degrees also to other assets, may be called *liquidity*.

The three types of assets thus characterized are ideal types. Most assets will in fact share, to a certain degree, the characteristics of various types. Therefore, in general, we may say that 'the total return expected from the ownership of an asset over a period is equal its yield *minus* its carrying cost *plus* its liquidity' (Keynes 1936, p. 226).

It is worth noting that in the passage just quoted Keynes writes 'liquidity-premium' and not 'liquidity'. Yet it seems more appropriate to reserve 'liquidity-premium' to indicate not the return to the holding of the asset, but rather the compensation for parting with it. The confusion between liquidity and liquidity-premium may be explained by the fact that it is only through the latter that the former appears and is measured. In fact, as Keynes himself observes, 'there is, so to speak, *nothing to show* for this [liquidity] at the end of the period in the shape of output; yet it is something for which people are ready to pay something' (Keynes 1936, p. 226, emphasis added). And it is the amount which people are willing to pay that Keynes more strictly defines as the *liquidity-premium*.

Now, one peculiarity of money with respect to other assets is that it corresponds entirely to one of the ideal types: the only form of return that money affords to its owner is liquidity, and it does this more than any other asset; money is characterized pre-eminently and exclusively by liquidity; liquidity is the only quality of money as an asset; money is liquidity. The compensation for parting with money, that is, the rate of interest, is a liquidity-premium.

What makes money even more peculiar is that its distinctive property, namely liquidity, happens to coincide with the only form of return, which appears only if it is made visible and measurable by a transaction. The yield of a grain of wheat used as seed appears in the fields, at the time of harvest, regardless of the fact that it is marketed. The negative return of wheat, stored in a deposit, appears through waste and decay, regardless of the existence of a market for wheat or even storage facilities. By contrast, the return of money occurs only if there is someone willing to pay for it. This is yet another way of stating what we have already observed, that is, that the rate of interest depends entirely upon expectations and upon the possibility of expressing these expectations by negotiating in an organized market for money loans.

Until now, following Keynes, we have simply assumed the existence of such a market. Keynes himself expresses some doubts about its usefulness:

> the question of the desirability of having a highly organized market for dealing with debts presents us with a dilemma. For, in the absence of an organized market, liquidity-preference due to the precautionary-motive would be greatly increased; whereas the existence of an organized market gives an opportunity for wide

fluctuations in liquidity-preference due to the speculative-motive. (Keynes 1936, pp. 170–171)

If it is true, as I have argued above, that the precautionary-motive is entirely due to the need to hedge against unexpected variations in the rate of interest, and that, in turn, all variations in the rate of interest depend on the operation of the speculative-motive, it is quite evident that, at least from the perspective of the economic system as a whole, no true dilemma exists: if there were no money market, there would be no need for one.

This, in turn, implies that the only reason to hold money, the only motive for the demand for money, is the expectation that its temporary cessation may allow the owner to obtain more money in return. Thus money, as an asset, is entirely identified by this possible use. In other words, money is defined as that asset, the loan of which is compensated by the payment of interest. There would be no money 'as we know it' if there were no rate of interest, and hence no money market. The rate of interest, the money market and 'money as we know it' are one and the same thing.

Notes

1. For detailed references to these writings, and an interpretation of the ongoing interest that inspires them, see Fantacci (2005).
2. And it is evident that, although the failure of Keynes's proposal at Bretton Woods has left international trade without a clearing system, national economies can certainly rely today on more widespread, dependable and affordable clearing systems than at the time when Keynes was writing.
3. Wray (2006, pp. 187–189) describes this as a fourth motive for holding money, the 'finance motive', elaborated by Keynes in response to his critics. However, for the purposes of my argument, it is not relevant to distinguish whether money is demanded for consumption or for investment. As long as the latter is intended in real terms as the purchase of investment goods, both components of money demand may be subsumed in the transactions-motive and both are capable of being satisfied through different forms of anticipation by the banking system, and hence are ultimately irrelevant to the explanation of a positive rate of interest.

References

Bentham, J. (1787) *Defense of Usury; Shewing the Impolicy of the Present Legal Restraints on the Terms of Pecuniary Bargains. In a Series of Letters to a Friend* (London: T. Payne), reprinted in W. Stark (ed.) *Jeremy Bentham's Economic Writings*, vol. 1 (London: G. Allen & Unwin, 1952), pp. 121–188.

Fantacci, L. (2005) 'J. M. Keynes: Escaping the Liquidity Trap', *ISE Working Paper*, 2 (Milan: Bocconi University).

Keynes, J. M. (1921) *A Treatise on Probability* (London: Macmillan), reprinted in D. Moggridge (ed.) *The Collected Writings of John Maynard Keynes*, vol. 8 (London and Cambridge: Macmillan and Cambridge University Press, 1973).

Keynes, J. M. (1923) *A Tract on Monetary Reform* (London: Macmillan), reprinted in D. Moggridge (ed.) *The Collected Writings of John Maynard Keynes*, vol. 4 (London and Cambridge: Macmillan and Cambridge University Press, 1971).

Keynes, J. M. (1930) *A Treatise on Money* (London: Macmillan), reprinted in D. Moggridge (ed.) *The Collected Writings of John Maynard Keynes*, vols 5 and 6 (London and Cambridge: Macmillan and Cambridge University Press, 1971).

Keynes, J. M. (1936) *The General Theory of Employment Interest and Money* (London: Macmillan), reprinted in D. Moggridge (ed.) *The Collected Writings of John Maynard Keynes*, vol. 7 (London and Cambridge: Macmillan and Cambridge University Press, 1973).

Keynes, J. M. (1937a) 'The General Theory of Employment', *The Quarterly Journal of Economics*, 51 (2) (Feb. 1937), 209–223, in D. Moggridge (ed.) *The Collected Writings of John Maynard Keynes*, vol. 14 (London and Cambridge: Macmillan and Cambridge University Press, 1973), pp. 109–123.

Keynes, J. M. (1937b) 'Alternative Theories of the Rate of Interest', *The Economic Journal*, 47, June, 241–252, republished in D. Moggridge (ed.) *The Collected Writings of John Maynard Keynes*, vol. 14 (London and Cambridge: Macmillan and Cambridge University Press, 1973), pp. 201–215.

Keynes, J. M. (1938) 'Letter to Hugh Townshend', 7 December, in D. Moggridge (ed.) *The Collected Writings of John Maynard Keynes*, vol. 29 (London and Cambridge: Macmillan and Cambridge University Press, 1979), pp. 293–294.

Keynes, J. M. (1943a) 'Proposals for an International Clearing Union', in D. Moggridge (ed.) *The Collected Writings of John Maynard Keynes*, vol. 25 (London and Cambridge: Macmillan and Cambridge University Press, 1980), pp. 168–195.

Keynes, J. M. (1943b) 'The Objective of International Price Stability', *The Economic Journal*, 53 (210/211), Jun./Sept., 185–187, republished in D. Moggridge (ed.) *The Collected Writings of John Maynard Keynes*, vol. 26 (London and Cambridge: Macmillan and Cambridge University Press, 1980), pp. 30–33.

Locke, J. (1692) *Some Considerations of the Consequences of the Lowering of Interest and Raising the Value of Money. In a Letter to a Member of Parliament* (London: A. & J. Churchill).

Wray, R. (2006) 'Keynes's Approach to Money: An Assessment after Seventy Years', *Atlantic Economic Journal*, 34, 183–193.

6
A Time and a Place for Everything: Foundations of Commodity Money

Dick Bryan and Michael Rafferty

Central bankers' success in containing inflation during the past two decades raises hopes that fiat money can be managed in a responsible way. This has been the case in the United States, and the dollar, despite many challenges to its status, remains the principal international currency.

If the evident recent success of fiat money regimes falters, we may have to go back to seashells or oxen as our medium of exchange. In that unlikely event, I trust, the discount window of the Federal Reserve Bank of New York will have an adequate inventory of oxen.

Former US Federal Reserve Chairman
Alan Greenspan, 2002

No one doubts that oil is a key commodity. What has happened to its price in the past few years? Most will be quick to answer that the price of oil has gone up rapidly – indeed, to record levels – before falling almost as rapidly. Perhaps, but the actual price movement depends on when and where you stand.

If you asked that question of someone from the nineteenth century, operating under the gold standard, they would say that the price of oil has been remarkably stable. Data show that, over the past 30 years, the prices of oil and gold have moved broadly in parallel. In contemporary markets the answer depends, among other things, on the currency in which the oil price is quoted. It is conventionally quoted in US dollars, reflecting an established dollar hegemony. But the relative price of the US dollar itself fluctuates, and it fluctuates differently between different currencies, different assets and different commodities. With the dollar volatile, and the more so due to the global financial crisis, the 'lived' price of oil depends on the currency in which it is quoted. But then, what is the lived price? Is it the spot price, or a future price determined in oil derivative (futures and options) markets? And is the currency conversion a spot exchange rate or a derivative one?

The apparent problem, highlighted by the volatility of the US dollar, is that in a globalized economy there can be no single and predictable measure of money's value, and no agreed monetary standard by which to benchmark prices. It all depends on where you stand and when you stand there. This is something of a new experience, at least since we had a developed notion of globalized financial markets, and it challenges our understanding of what elevates a particular expression of money to be the monetary reference point – the standard or benchmark.[1]

In this paper we seek to return focus to the materiality of money and finance and the changes to money (and the monetary system) itself that have been critical in the current era: in particular the processes of securitization and the growth of financial derivatives. This focus is not to diminish the importance of cultural and sociological issues in money and finance: what is accepted as money can never be reduced to technical attributes, and the role (technical and sociological) of different forms of money remains contested. Nor is it to diminish the need for regulatory reforms in the management of the global financial system. But our agenda does assert the significance of the changing form of money itself – its materiality – in understanding contemporary global money and, by implication, the history of money. Here, we are reminded of Charles Kindleberger's observation that '(a)s a unit of account, money is a creature of the state; as a medium of exchange, despite the legal tender question, it is what markets use' (1984, p. 38). We know that in an era of rapid financial innovation, 'what markets use' cannot have a permanent answer. Money itself will be constantly evolving, and sometimes in ways that challenge existing accounts of money.

Our analysis, focusing on 'what markets use' and the implicit tensions that may arise between what the state provides and what markets use, is no doubt contentious. It is designed explicitly to wrest control of theoretical debate away from those who take the effective exclusivity of state money as the premise of their analysis. The governor of the Bank of England, Mervyn King, observed that monetary practice is now ahead of monetary theory (2005), and the gap can be seen to have widened markedly as ad hoc monetary policy has driven responses to the global financial crisis. Periods of financial volatility may remind us of the fragility of finance, but are also surely the times to look for new understandings, and observing what is happening in global financial markets seems a sensible place to start.

Moreover, the global financial crisis has revealed that the contentious dimension of money is its legitimacy not so much as a means of exchange, but as a store of value. Money as means of exchange is undoubtedly dominated by state money, but storing value involves more and more diverse monetary (and near-monetary) forms, and this dimension rests on competitive as well as state foundations. The height of the financial crisis occurred when the inter-bank market crashed or, as is popularly conceived, when liquidity dried up: when banks refused to trade with each other in what is generally presumed to have been a highly liquid market. That crisis was at the interface between storing value and liquidity (or its 'fungibility'). This situation revealed that the critical liquidity in financial markets is not simply a matter of converting to cash (state money) but also the liquidity of (non-state) means of storing value.

Framing a materialist question of money

Much has been written about the theory of money, but most of has been within a single currency, with a single state, a single legal system and a single culture of monetary trust. The additional question is: what should we observe about money as it operates beyond the jurisdiction of nation states? Currently, we know that exchange rates seem beyond prediction, even beyond retrospective explanation. It is argued that economic growth has been funded predominantly by debt and that the scale of financial growth is out of proportion to the 'real' economy; that finance has acquired a new autonomy. It is debated (again) whether the dollar will remain strong long-term or the era of dollar hegemony is coming to an end.

These are all important questions, but they are receiving focus almost to the exclusion of a consideration of the materiality of money and finance. It is as if the issue of materiality is now absent, and financial volatility is to be understood as a process of smoke and mirrors, deception and distortion. In the context of the global financial crisis, there has been a preoccupation with the dramas of crisis conceived in corruption and the opacity of market processes, and this has often been at the expense of understanding longer-term developments in the mechanisms of financial innovation.

Part of the problem may be that the dominant conception of money has long been embedded in functionalism: the various 'functions of money' that are taken to *define* money. Reference here is to the four conventional functions of money: medium of exchange, store of value, standard of deferred payment and unit of account. This functionalist foundation sees that financial volatility as interpreted in terms of *dys*functionality (and 'crisis'), rather than as an expression of the process of change within money and the monetary system itself. Alternatively, questions of materialism cause us to focus on the concept of money itself, and to downplay issues of dysfunctionality and crisis.

Further, the prominent debates over money (the critiques of the orthodoxy) are complicit with this functionalist interpretation precisely because of a consensus that money has been disembodied of materiality. The starting point in popular debate is that money must be understood as fiat money, in which the money thing lacks value ('it is only paper', for example). Accordingly, the materiality of money is seen as a non-question, or one of mere historical interest.

Starting with fiat money and functionalist definitions of money also sets up some restrictive agendas. There are three complementary restrictions.

First, there is the question of whether, for something to fulfil the criteria of 'money', it must perform all four functional roles, or just some roles, and in the latter case, which one/s is/are privileged. With minor exceptions, state money is privileged as unit of account and the means of exchange. But is a virtual state-money monopoly over the unit of account and the role of means of exchange sufficient to exclude other forms from being 'money'? Conversely, on an international scale, each nation-state's money is not a recognized unit of account or means of exchange: Japanese yen, for example, cannot generally be used in shops in the United Kingdom. By contrast, it could be said that in this context, some derivative products which have expression in multiple currencies are more liquid than cash!

The problem can be posed simply: are the four functions of money a definition of money, or an ideal type of money's roles, from which particular monies will vary: and if the latter, we need a concept not of money with an absolute definition, but of 'moneyness' or liquidity, where the benchmark of liquidity is not closeness to cash (one particular form of money) but readiness of convertibility to another, preferred form of money. In other words, liquidity is always context-specific so moneyness can be expected to be constantly evolving.

We see recognition of this point in two developments in monetary policy. The first has been the new attempts to measure the money supply that accept the inherent instability in what is used as money. Within money supply measurement, the concept of 'divisia money' attempts to absorb the changing context-specific nature of money back into a national aggregation approach to money (Hancock 2005). The second development has been the abandoning of money-supply targeting in monetary policy and, more recently, by the downgrading of the use money supply measurement. As the then Federal Reserve Chairman Alan Greenspan noted in congressional testimony in 2000,

> the monetary aggregates as we measure them are getting increasingly complex and difficult to integrate into a set of forecasts. The problem we have is not that money is unimportant, but how we define it...our problem is not that we do not believe in sound money; we do...The difficulty is in defining what part of our liquidity structure is truly money. We have had trouble ferreting out proxies for that for a number of years. And the standard we employ is whether it gives us a good forward indicator of the direction of finance and the economy. Regrettably none of those that we have been able to develop...have done that...and as a consequence of that we have downgraded the use of the monetary aggregates for monetary policy purposes until we are able to find a more stable proxy for what we believe is the underlying money in the economy.[2]

Secondly, within the dominant theories, it is the nation state that issues money.[3] In some versions, this is an issue of popular trust in the state; in others it is the state's capacity to determine what is paid in taxes that ultimately determines the dominance of state money. That debate itself is not our concern. But the effect of its parameters (what in another context has been referred to as 'economic methodological nationalism' (Gore 1996) is that money, by its attachment to the state, is inherently always national money. Beyond the nation, the value (and acceptance) of state fiat money, which is beyond the capacity of the nation state to enforce, is a moot point. At that international level, analysis must revert to largely descriptive observation of the operation of foreign exchange markets, and an acceptance that they reliably convert between different state monies, and/or to various proposals for inter-state regulation of the global interaction of national monies.

Thirdly, there is a widespread consensus that fiat money is a logical development of capitalism, both because of the impracticalities of metallic money and because money has evolved into 'credit money': the social relation of credit and debt. It is the social-ness of credit that then forms the foundation of a sociology of capitalist money.[4] Our concern here is not to deny the dominance of credit, or the possibility of seeing all transactions as 'claims', but to emphasize that there is so much more to say about money than that it is 'credit'. After all, 'the credit system' is the way Marx talked in *Capital* about money in capitalism and, 150 years on, there is scope for observing something different – not just refinements within the credit system, but other monetary developments too.

But the problem, which defines the conventional wisdom as conventional, is that credit is taken as the *defining characteristic* of capitalist money, not just a particular form of money. And here, too, there is an implicit premise of a single money of account within each political unit: the assumption that the social dimensions of claims are immune from the contestability of the value of money itself. At least the issue of contestability is additional, not integral to the theory of money, for contestability is an expression of dysfunctionality: a challenge to, not an attribute of, money. As a result, at the global level, this dominant approach slides from a theory to a vision, based on inter-state co-operation, with appropriate institutional support to achieve precisely what is contested.

But the *current* global financial order, full of uncertainty and fracture rather than co-operation and co-ordination, is where theories of money need to be analytically tested. In this context, these dominant theories of money remain relatively silent about global financial developments. Global foreign exchange and derivative markets are turning over each day the equivalent of many trillion US dollars in currency and interest-rate products, and only a small fraction of these markets involve what fiat money theorists would accept as money. In effect, the process of commensuration of different (national) fiat monies occurs through a process not based on state decree, but on competitive pricing in highly liquid derivative markets. These markets, by definition, must exist 'outside' fiat money, for if they didn't they could not perform the commensuration role.

But once we recognize that derivative markets play a role in commensurating different fiat monies through exchange-rate and interest-rate derivatives, we cannot stop there. These markets commensurate not just different fiat monies through space and time, but all sorts of different financial assets, including those that crashed in the global financial crisis. Hence these other derivative markets, no less than exchange rates and interest rates, are part of the diverse processes of value commensuration.

Yet these other forms of derivative, and especially those that crashed, are readily dismissed as sites of 'speculation'. Our proposition is that any theory of money must confront what this activity means for an understanding of money; not dismiss it as (non-monetary) 'speculation', which will go away after the current crisis.

So what is the materiality of money that we find in financial derivatives? Derivative and securities markets do not replace money as we currently know it (state-issued money; credit). They are not taking over the four functions of money. But they create new types of money, especially for use by capital, by highlighting the different *attributes* of money. They deconstruct any particular form of money (a particular currency, with a particular interest rate, over a particular time period) into its various constituent attributes (or risk exposures, as some approaches would frame them). They then commodify these attributes individually, and in a range of combinations, by pricing them and trading them. As such, they commodify money: they break it (and non-monetary assets) down into a spectrum of products. They give money a materiality not in terms of what it (symbolically) represents, but in terms of what it, itself, is and does.

In subsequent sections, we build on this materialist interpretation of contemporary global money. We start from the premise that if we go outside the confines of the fiat/claim approach to money and look for a materiality of global money in financial derivatives (and securities), we can find it. This is, no doubt, a controversial proposition. Further, and perhaps just as controversially, if we then read the last hundred or so years of international money backwards, we can see this (evolving) materiality continually coming into focus, albeit not always in welcome or expected ways.

Securities and derivatives: new commodity money?

Financial derivative markets do not exist so as to be sites of money creation. They have evolved as markets for risk transference, and, as the global financial crisis made stark, they are also sites for uncertainty transference: a dimension which restricts the treatment of such markets as subject to 'scientific' calculation (McKenzie 2006).[5] As a corollary, they are also sites for speculation about risks and uncertainties.

These markets commodify risk. The issue here is not just that they are part of the commodification of everything and the incorporation of all social processes into the profit-making nexus. That much is taken as given. The issue is that when risk becomes a commodity in its own right, it is separated from its connection to the underlying object of risk. The commodified risk of the change in price of a barrel of oil (oil futures and options) is traded without the necessity of trading the barrel of oil itself. A mortgage-backed security trades exposure to the performance of a mortgage (strictly, borrowers' repayments and the associated risks of ongoing repayment); it does not trade the mortgage itself.

The point is critical (albeit often ignored) because this separation of risk from the object of risk is what makes these markets so liquid: it is so much easier to transfer the ownership of an exposure than the ownership of the underlying asset. Further, because different risk exposures are being traded in highly liquid markets, they are being priced relative to each other. These risk exposures therefore offer fluid markets of commensuration, in which the commensuration of fiat monies via exchange-rate and interest-rate derivatives are just elements (albeit quantitatively by far the most important). As well as these purely financial risks, we see default risk being priced relative to equity prices, and hurricane risk priced relative to house-price or beef-price movements. More broadly, these markets are sites of global liquidity.

But is liquidity a sufficient criterion for the attribution of 'moneyness'? Framed differently, in what sense are financial derivatives money? There are several ways of answering this question, though none should be interpreted as a proposition that derivatives are replacing state fiat money: indeed they are complementing and extending it, especially globally. Here is the case for financial derivatives being considered as money.

(a) To engage the conventional, functionalist definition of money first of all, derivatives fulfil some key money functions – though, of course, not all. They are not used as means of exchange, and for some definitions this function is the litmus test of money. But derivatives are critically a store of value and a standard of deferred payment in a multi-currency, multi-interest-rate world. In this context they also compensate, as it were, for the fact that there is no universal unit of account. Interest-rate and currency futures, for example, store value globally in a way that cash cannot. Cash cannot preserve value if it is involved in currency conversions. Foreign-exchange futures lock in a rate of conversion, and so store value over time at an agreed rate. And as there are no 'true' relative currency values, all that can be stored is determined by contractual agreement. The same can be said of interest derivatives. If we think of the money being stored not as cash, but as a line of credit, it faces interest-rate variability. At what interest rate is its value said to be 'stored' over time? There is no formal answer. Interest-rate derivatives are a means to store (a chosen proportion[6] of) deferred payment. Oil in 90 days; yen in 3 hours – this is the stuff of derivatives. What makes derivatives distinctive in these money functions is that most of the storage is of very large values and for very short periods. This fact confirms simply that derivatives are money for capital (not so much for households) in a volatile financial world.

(b) If we invoke a concept of 'moneyness', rather than of money as an absolute category, claims to moneyness do not have to involve reference to an idealized concept of fulfilling all functional forms of money in the one 'money'. But there are limits here. Many objects store value (e.g., works of art), but they are not sensibly thought of as money. What gives derivatives their moneyness is their liquidity, where liquidity is defined not simply by their ease of conversion to cash (for that would serve uncritically to privilege state money as the benchmark of moneyness), but by their ease of conversion to other money forms and functions, among which means of exchange is but one. Derivative markets certainly store value and provide systems of deferred payment, but their liquidity is also critical to their moneyness. The ease of closing out a position, of converting equity into debt, of pricing one risk relative to another, are all dimensions of liquidity and hence of moneyness.

But we should note that having moneyness does not entail generating monetary stability. Research by Akthar (1983), the Bank for International Settlements (1994) and Vrolijk (1997) have all found evidence that derivatives have created instability in the measurement of monetary aggregates, and in the concept of money more generally. More recently, Savona and Maccario (1998) and Savona, Maccario and Oldani (2000) extend this proposition. They argue that the monetary nature of derivatives is verified by their empirical impact on interest rates, and that the neglect of this relation distorts national monetary aggregates as an object of monetary policy.

(c) Historically, we have seen derivatives and securities being held as a direct alternative to, and for the same reasons as, more conventional notions of money. Once we think of diversification as a standard risk-management strategy, a conventional practice will be to diversify currency holdings. But the practice will also be to diversify the way in which wealth is held within a currency – not just treasury bonds or deposits in AAA-rated banks, but perhaps also the holding of AAA-rated mortgage-backed securities, which, until the crash, were rated as highly and were giving better rates of return than treasury paper and trading bank deposits. The fact that their credit rating was categorically wrong does not deny the monetary motive with which they were widely held, though it points to clear fragilities in these monetary forms. (It can also be noted in this context that the first, decisive response by central banks to the liquidity crisis in 2008 was to convert mortgage-backed securities into cash: a statement that these securities had indeed been used by the markets as benchmark liquidity assets.)

So in what sense can we say that derivatives are 'money'? The above arguments amount to privileging the role of liquidity in storing value (risk-adjusted competitiveness in value-storing instruments) over the role of a state-endorsed means of exchange. To deny the former monetary dimension and just privilege the latter seems to us to rely on a circular argument: if you define money in terms of the state, then the question of any 'moneyness' of derivatives is nonsensical. But, we contend, over time the definitional association of money with the state must be challenged – not so as to dissociate money from the state (for political legitimacy is always critical), but to open up possibilities that the relation between money and the state may be changing. Our point, to reiterate, is not that derivatives are replacing the state's money; only that, in Kindleberger's terms, what markets use must be brought into the money fold. To exclude derivatives in order to protect old definitions is an insufficient rationale.

Our analysis now has an open and difficult issue: if derivatives have attributes of money, but they are not state money, what sort of money are they? In what sense are these derivatives to be considered commodities, and hence commodity money?

They certainly challenge our concept of what a commodity is; but standard commodities are not money-like (we will return to gold shortly). Here are some possible ways of framing derivatives as commodities:

(a) Derivatives pertaining to exchange rates and interest rates are bought and sold in huge quantities, creating the appearance of a commodity market. But this is a flawed verification of commodity money. After all, when at the airport we go to the foreign-exchange counter and convert euros into British pounds, the pound in this transaction appears as a commodity. But we would not say that the pound is therefore commodity money. So we do not pursue this path to commodity status. But nor do we need to.

(b) Derivatives, as the name implies, are derived from something else. The etymology of the term is associated with the value of a derivative being determined from the value of the underlying asset (e.g., the future price of wheat deriving from the current price of wheat). But in their evolved, more elaborate and current usage derivatives are associated with the decomposition of an underlying asset into a spectrum of attributes, with the attributes themselves being commodified and priced. There are no longer implications of causality in price determination: indeed, the evidence is more of a reversal in price determination.

As Das has observed, there has been a change in what we understand financial derivatives to be doing. This change comes in the wake of 'a progressive re-definition of risk in financial markets... The concept of financial derivative is increasingly becoming one of the *trading of attributes of assets*' (2005, pp. 2–3, emphasis added). Derivatives in relation to money (currency and interest rates) express the commodification of attributes of money; most particularly, the attribute of variability in money's value.

(c) Derivatives are like insurance contracts – more precisely, insurance contracts are like derivatives. Think of car insurance: it is really a series of call options. A modest annual payment gives you the right, but not the obligation, to obtain mechanical and panel repairs on your car should a certain event happen (a crash) and those repairs are to a value significantly in excess of the insurance premium. We would think of an insurance contract as a commodity, and its 'value' is determined not by reference to the cost of writing the contract (any more than a derivative can be valued by the cost of its own manufacture), but to the cost of repairs it sets in motion should the option be exercised.[7] So it is with the value of a derivative: it is what the derivative is able to set in motion that defines its use value, and the fact that this capacity for conversion can be traded defines it as an exchange value (i.e., as a commodity).

To build toward the proposition that derivatives are commodities in themselves, and commodity money in particular, we must combine the emphases of these second and third propositions. If we adopt simply the second proposition, it could be argued that derivatives are not themselves money, any more than the future price of wheat is itself wheat.

But money is different from wheat (financial derivatives are different from commodity derivatives), for the financial derivative has no use value apart from prices (relative values). We are, by analogy with wheat, thereby framing financial derivatives in terms of the future price of a relative price. An interest rate derivative, for example, is the price over time of the inter-temporal price of a unit of value. These money derivatives cannot be disentangled from money itself, as can wheat from the price of wheat.[8]

What makes derivatives a form of commodity money is what the derivatives *do* as commodities (the insurance-like attribute).[9] What they do is compute and convert. They translate across different asset forms, different time horizons and different places: they commensurate. They are not a rigid form of equivalence – they reconcile within the ongoing existence of volatility. With a world of unknown (unknowable) 'real' (or 'fundamental') values, derivatives are products which create equivalence out of perceptions of the real, and risks that derive from its unknowability.

A brief comparison with gold

To frame financial derivatives as a form of commodity money suggests a very different notion of commodity money from that associated with gold. Indeed it is clear to see, when the issue of commodity money is addressed, how universal is the presumption that the money commodity must be a physical commodity, even though in advanced capitalist countries around 80 per cent of produced commodities are services. When we move away from the notion that commodity money must be a physical commodity, many of the supposed critiques of commodity money lose significance.

In essence, there are four 'standard' critiques of commodity money (understood as gold). Let us see how each applies to financial derivatives (in italics).

(a) Inappropriate quantity:
   Gold is limited in supply (but supply can be subject to sudden growth, such as with the discovery of new deposits), and supply does not grow in proportion to the value of output.
   For derivatives, quantity (and turnover) may be extremely high, but there is a counterparty on each side of a contract and what matters is price, not quantity. (And for this reason, the growing turnover of derivatives is not inflationary.)

(b) Physical limitations:

Gold as money requires periodic verification of its weight and quality associated with the potential for gold 'clipping' and other forms of currency debasement. It also has portability problems. *Derivatives inherently involve a process of continual verification of the value of one form of money in terms of other forms of money, and all in terms of other asset prices. The concern about verification in derivative markets, as we have seen with asset-backed securities and other collateralized debt obligations, is that insufficiently regulated markets permit market-deceiving behaviour. But these concerns are not money-specific.*

(c) Dual values:

Gold's value as money and its value as a commodity may not be the same – indeed, if gold's industrial value is greater than its monetary value, currency will be melted back into metal.

Derivatives have no use other than in commensurating value. They are pricing contracts par excellence. They may be subject to speculation (as may all assets), and derivatives may exert impacts on prices, but this is not inconsistent with their role of commensuration. There is no equivalent notion of derivatives being 'melted down'.

(d) Simplicity:

Gold is limited to fairly simple (and pre-capitalist) monetary functions, and for this reason is to be seen as historically superseded by capitalist development and associated financial complexity. Here is the conventional wisdom that the impracticalities of gold see it replaced by fiat money. *Derivatives are not constrained by any notions of simplicity – indeed their most notable characteristic is financial innovation, and their ability to express highly complex relations.*

Conversely, the supposed virtue of gold was that it is 'real' – it is scarce, prized and has value in its alternative, industrial use. This is, perhaps, the ultimate concern about derivatives as commodity money – there is nothing 'real'. These derivatives are just bits of paper that disappear at expiry; they become valueless. But the critique remains rhetorical, for 'realness' can hardly be found in chartalist (token) money. Derivatives are entirely creatures of circulation – they stay in circulation, and have no expression outside of circulation. That is precisely their 'reality' – they exist to commensurate, and when each contract's particular act of commensuration has been enacted, they 'die', to be replaced with new contracts, having slightly different terms. Yet the *system* of contracts, the macro process of commensuration, is perpetuated (perhaps until some idealized time when money's value is completely stationary, in which case they would have little or no functional role as money).

This makes derivatives distinctly capitalist products: capitalist money rather that money within capitalism (Bryan and Rafferty 2006b). It is indeed a very different notion of commodity money than that associated with the nineteenth century and gold. It is predicated on flexibility and complexity of money; not rigidity and simplicity.

Reading the history of money backwards

Turning from the current era of enormous global derivatives and securities markets, back one chapter in global financial history, we need to ask why financial derivatives only came into prominence *when* they did. There is a technological history here of computer development and mathematical tools for the pricing of risk (the Black-Scholes model). But central also is that the ideology of floating exchange rates, and the argument that they would gravitate to purchasing power parity (PPP), failed to materialize: exchange rates proved beyond explanation in terms of PPP models.

This has been commonly treated as a failure of laissez-faire economic theory, but it was actually a failure of a particular interpretation of the materiality of money. After all, an emphasis on PPP, from David Hume to Milton Friedman, has always been couched in terms of the quantity theory of money: the idea that money is (or should be) a veil that simply expresses the 'real' economy in monetary units. The foundation of PPP is that relative currency values will reflect the material world: relative productivity performances of different countries, with PPP values thereby serving to equate exports and imports (generating trade according to comparative advantage, not exchange-rate advantage). But the materiality of monetarism was a displaced materialism: it was to be found in what money represented (money as superstructure, perhaps); not what money actually is. Read this way, therefore, floating exchange rates were one material foundation of money which gave way to another, which addressed directly the failures of the former.

And if we turn back another chapter, to the circumstances generating the termination of the Bretton Woods Agreement, we see the clash between a cultural/ideological foundation of money and a material foundation. What makes this termination of such eternal fascination is the multiple layers to the clash. One layer (the simplest) is that the attempt within the exchange-rate formula of the Bretton Woods Agreement to reconcile the ideological and cultural with the material proved unsustainable. The US dollar (the ideological foundation) could not sustain its rate of conversion to the material (gold). But beneath this apparent failure lay a deeper story of the inability of a national currency to serve both national and global roles with equal effect: the contradiction first identified by Robert Triffin in 1960.

And going back one chapter further, to the late 1930s and early 1940s, we see the debates leading up to the Bretton Woods Agreement. At this time, some economics and business intellectuals, including Benjamin Graham, the so-called 'Dean of Wall Street'[10] (the father of 'value investing' – that is, investing according to the fundamental value of company assets; an innately materialist framework), along with the anti-statist economists (leading them Hayek and Friedman, re-affirmed by John Hicks in the mid-1960s), were calling for a commodity reserve currency. They wanted financial markets backed by a physical hoard of storable agricultural and mineral commodities as the anchor for the post-war financial system.[11]

Further back still, we come to a global financial system based on metallic money – gold and silver. But our focus here is not on gold as the archetypal commodity money. Indeed, in many ways gold and financial derivatives are complete opposites: one is physical, the other computational; one is valued for its scarcity in production, the other produced at will and valued for its liquidity in circulation. We focus instead on understanding the demise of this commodity money in historical context.

As Barry Eichengreen (1998) explains so succinctly, the automatic domestic price adjustments that were integral to the operation of the gold standard were not compatible with the emerging role of the modern, regulatory nation-state. The new expectations of social welfare and state economic management that came with active trade unionism, working-class political representation and the end of the war were not consistent with the domestic price flexibility required by the gold standard.

We should note also that this period of the rise of nation-state monetary policy *contra* the gold standard was the time when Georg Knapp (1924) developed his theory of chartalist money, involving the attachment of money to the state (via the taxation condition): a theory that was readily adopted by Keynes, and which remains a foundation proposition in current money theory (Ingham 2004). The historical observation warrants noting because it points to the possibility of a particular, historically-specific change in money being elevated beyond its histori-cal context and seen as the basis of a 'general theory' of money.

It points, moreover, to the issue of policy as a driver of theory. Chartalist money was the theory of money that privileged the state as both the supplier and manager of money. Keynes, adopting Knapp's insight, had opposed both the gold standard (which he described as a 'juggernaut'[12]) and the late-1930s proposal of Graham, Hayek and Friedman for a com-modity foundation to post-war money (Keynes 1938), essentially on the grounds of the need for national policy autonomy (including of money) if states are to create full employment. Chartalist money suited the Keynesian national policy agenda, just as the concept of a national economy did his macro-economics and its policy agenda. It remains the case today that a policy focus on the capacity of nation-states to man-age full employment will readily adopt the Knapp/Keynes position on the nature of money, for it is the one conceived to affirm nation-state policy capacity.[13]

However, currently, in 'realeconomik', we see the breakdown of national barriers to capital mobility, and the development of globally-integrated financial markets. We see a return of elements of Keynes's 'juggernaut'. It is popularly called 'globalization' and 'neo-liberalism'. It does not comply with the Keynesian policy vision; nor, we must con-jecture, with the Keynesian money vision. Perhaps then, reading his-tory backwards, it is not surprising that we observe the recent rise of commodity money – and with the same (reverse) historical rationale as was applied to the gold standard. As the state has withdrawn from the Keynesian policy agenda of fixed exchange rates and capital con-trols, and we have seen a decline in interest-rate stability, we have seen the emergence of commodity money in the form of monetary products (financial derivatives) that are designed to simulate stability – albeit for only short periods. Moreover, as the state has withdrawn from a range of other future guarantees – be they about housing or education or health – so markets have emerged to create products to cover this absence, and they have been commodified (securitized) and sold glo-bally as financial assets.

Conclusion

We return to the issue of oil that started this investigation. Oil, gold, dollars and euros are all different units of measure – all possible anchors of measurement. None can claim analytical privilege, and political privilege is neither permanent nor always official. In the current era, without an official, multi-state-sanctioned anchor (such as the Bretton Woods Agreement or the gold standard), many would invoke the status of the US dollar as the global anchor. For many, that claim rests on the predominance of dollars in global circulation and the utilization of the dollar in so many international financial contracts – though this is, it must be said, a somewhat tautological explanation. But it does bring home the importance of convention in such explanations. For others, there is some material basis: the global position of Wall Street, and the industrial and military might of the US.

Some, such as George Soros (2008), have already announced the end of the dollar era; others have argued that it still has another couple of centuries to run. All are guessing, and such speculation is largely beside the point anyway. While money is what people think money is, and most people think the US dollar is serving as a global currency, the question of other monies and of an anchor is different. In a world of volatility in currency and commodity values, an anchor is more than a popularity contest. And the current challenges to the US dollar make clear that we should not conflate objective measures with popularity.

The reader will note, we hope, that this is the first time the term 'objective' has been used in our analysis. It is situated deliberately, for we can now address the attachment of an anchor to 'objectivity'. The simple point is that *there is no objective measure of the value of one form of money in terms of another.* Gold in the nineteenth century was not 'objective' – it was decreed by states that gold would be the unit of money, and keeping it so involved massive state force. Under Bretton Woods, and until the beginning of the 1970s, state decree continued to substitute for an objective measure. But once that decree was removed, the status of the US dollar has looked increasingly like a matter of convention, and less and less like an anchor.

But in a financial world where there is no objective unit, yet markets require a benchmark, financial derivatives provide a 'web of anchors', a system of computational links across a range of measures – privileging none, but reconciling all. Framed this way, we can see central bank purchases of mortgage-backed securities as forms of monetary intervention.[14]

Financial derivatives form a continuous, floating link between various financial asset forms (futures on oil denominated in euros; gold options denominated in dollar; euro/dollar swaps). Indeed, so diverse are the asset types that are linked by derivatives that there is no real reason to isolate gold, oil and euros as the ordained anchor should the US dollar wilt in status: asset markets of all sorts, linked through highly liquid derivative contracts, themselves become an anchor. It matters not whether these liquid markets push exchange rates or any asset values towards 'fundamental value' – we now know that fundamental value is a measure in the minds of equilibrium-obsessed economists; it matters simply that there are mechanisms to bridge volatility and unpredictability, for just 30 days, 3 days or even 3 hours.

Nor does it matter (at least for our analysis) that this bridging mechanism is fragile, vulnerable to speculation and susceptible to unethical practices (a characteristic that would in any case encompass almost all historical forms of money). What matters is that this picture of derivatives depicts the global financial system as being anchored by commodities, and requiring for asset values an understanding of capital's time and place.

At a global level, where nation-states individually and collectively have been ineffective in stabilizing exchange rates and equalizing interest rates on different currencies, we do now have various types of commodity money in action ... if we choose to see them.

Notes

1. The proposition is not that all monies do defer to a benchmark (Zelizer's [for example, 1994] important work on differences in particular monies and different meanings attached to particular uses of money can be noted here). But in international financial markets, where a range of monies are convertible into each other as specific prices, we can either see money as purely relative values (the room of mirrors), or as having some anchor from which all other monies become relative forms of value.
2. In a separate speech chairman Greenspan (1997) noted that '... as the historic relationship between measured money supply and spending deteriorated, policy-making, seeing no alternative, turned more eclectic and discretionary ...'.
3. There may be a caveat that the state need not be the issuer, but the condition of general acceptance means, in practice, that fiat money is effectively state money. We are here treating Europe and the euro as a single political entity.
4. This issue has been subject to ongoing debate over the past seven years, most notably in the journal *Economy and Society*.
5. For convenience we will use the simple term 'risk', recognizing that in lived experience in financial markets risks and uncertainties are not separable.
6. A forward-rate agreement fully preserves value; options and other derivative products offer degrees of risk management of value variability over time.
7. The difference with financial derivatives is that I can take out a position on you having a crash – there is no ownership dimension here. Framed in that way, we can see how derivatives can be conflated with speculation. But perhaps if I'd lent you the money to buy the car, or we had an agreement that if

you crashed your car you would borrow mine, it is clearer why I might or might not want to take on exposure to your car insurance.

8. In another context, we have referred to derivatives as 'meta-commodities', because they remain in circulation throughout their existence (Bryan and Rafferty 2006a, p. 13).

9. There are parallels here with Marx's view on whether money is productive (Marx 1939, p. 214).

    The question whether money as medium of exchange is productive or not productive is solved just as easily. According to Adam Smith, money is not productive. Of course Ferrier says, for example: 'It creates values, because they would not exist without it'. One has to look not only at 'its *value* as metal, but equally its *property* as money' (emphasis in original). Adam Smith is correct, in so far as it is not the instrument of any particular branch of production; Ferrier is right too because it is an essential aspect of the mode of production resting on exchange value that product and agency of production should be posited in the character of money, and because this characteristic presupposes a money distinct from products; and because the money relation is itself a relation of production if production is looked at in its totality.

10. See Graham and Chatman (1996).

11. The key contributions to this proposal are reprinted in Schwartz (1992).

12. Keynes put it passionately in 'The Economic Consequences of Mr. Churchill':

    We stand midway between two theories of economic society. The one theory maintains that wages should be fixed by reference to what is 'fair' and 'reasonable' as between classes. The other theory – the theory of the economic juggernaut – is that wages should be settled by economic pressure, otherwise called 'hard facts', and that our vast machine should crash along, with regard only to its equilibrium as a whole, and without attention to the chance consequences of the journey to individual groups. The gold standard, with its dependence on pure chance, its faith in the 'automatic adjustments', and its general regardlessness of social detail, is an essential emblem and idol of those who sit in the top tier of the machine. I think that they are immensely rash...in their comfortable belief that nothing really serious ever happens. (Keynes, J. M. [1925/1972], pp. 223–224)

13. This is inherent in post-Keynesian debates centering on the money-supply function, and central to monetary proposals for full employment (e.g., Wray 1999).

14. Indeed, in 2000, a period when US government debt was running down rapidly, and some were wondering if there would be government debt securities on issue, Alan Greenspan (2000) noted: 'I would merely say that monetary policy can be run in a number of different ways...Clearly, if we had to, we could invest in private securities or quasi-private securities'.

References

Akhtar, M. (1983) 'Financial Innovations and Their Implications for Monetary Policy: An International Perspective', *BIS Economic Papers*, 9, December (Basle: BIS).

Bank for International Settlements (1994) *Macroeconomic and Monetary Policy Issues Raised by the Growth of Derivatives Markets* (Hanoun Report) (Basle: BIS).

Bryan, D. and Rafferty, M. (2006a) *Capitalism with Derivatives: A Political Economy of Financial Derivatives, Capital and Class* (London: Palgrave Macmillan).

Bryan, D. and Rafferty, M. (2006b) 'Money in Capitalism or Capitalist Money?', *Historical Materialism*, 14 (1), 75–95.

Das, S. (2005) *Credit Derivatives: CDOs and Structured Credit Products*, 3rd edn (Singapore: John Wiley & Sons Asia).

Eichengreen, B. (1998) *Globalizing Capital: A History of the International Monetary System* (Princeton, NJ: Princeton University Press).

Gore, C. G. (1996) 'Methodological Nationalism and the Misunderstanding of East Asian Industrialization', *The European Journal of Development Research*, 8 (1), 77–122.

Graham, B. and Chatman, E. (1996) *Benjamin Graham, the Memoirs of the Dean of Wall Street* (New York: McGraw-Hill).

Greenspan, A. (1997) *Remarks at the 15th Anniversary Conference of the Center for Economic Policy Research at Stanford University*, Stanford, 5 September. Downloaded from http://www.federalreserve.gov/boarddocs/speeches/1997/19970905.htm. Date accessed: 20 July 2009.

Greenspan, A. (2000) 'The Conduct of Monetary Policy', Testimony *to the US House of Representatives, Committee on Banking and Financial Services* (Washington DC), 17 February. Downloaded from: http://commdocs.house.gov/committees/bank/hba62930.000/hba62930_0.htm. Date accessed: 20 July 2009.

Greenspan, A. (2002) 'The History of Money', *American Numismatic Society Exhibition* (New York: Federal Reserve Bank of New York), 16 January. Downloaded from: http://www.federalreserve.gov/BOARDDOCS/SPEECHES/2002/200201163/default.htm. Date accessed: 20 July 2009.

Hancock, M. (2005) 'Divisia Money', *Bank of England Quarterly Bulletin*, 45 (1), Spring, 39–46.

Hayek, F. A (1978) *Denationalization of Money*, 2nd edn (London: Institute for Economic Affairs).

Ingham, G. (2004) *The Nature of Money* (Cambridge: Polity Press).

Keynes, J. M. (1925) 'The Economic Consequences of Mr. Churchill', reprinted (1972) in D. Moggridge (ed.) *The Collected Works of J. M. Keynes* vol. 13 (London: Macmillan).

Keynes, J. M. (1938) 'The Policy of Government Storage of Foodstuffs and Raw Materials', *The Economic Journal*, September, 48, 449–460.

Kindelberger, C. (1984) *A Financial History of Western Europe* (London: Allen & Unwin).

King, M. (2005) 'Monetary Policy: Practice ahead of Theory', The Mais Lecture 2005, *Bank of England Quaterly Bulletin*, Summer, 45 (2), 226–236.

Knapp, G. (1924) *The State Theory of Money* (London: Macmillan).

Marx, K. (1939) *Grundrisse* (trans. M. Nicolaus) (Harmondsworth: Penguin 1973).

McKenzie, D. (2006) *An Engine, Not a Camera: How Financial Models Shape Markets* (Cambridge, MA: MIT Press).

Savona, P. and Maccario, A. (1998) 'On the Relation between Money and Derivatives and Its Application to the International Money Market', *Open Economies Review*, 9 (1), 637–664.

Savona, P., Maccario, A. and Oldani, C. (2000) 'On Monetary Analysis of Derviatives', *Open Economies Review*, 11 (1), 149–175.

Schwartz, A. (ed.) (1992) *Commodity Monies*, vol. 1 and 2 (Cheltenham, UK: Edward Elgar).

Soros, G. (2008) 'Remarks to the "Who's in Charge?" Forum', *World Economic Forum*, Davos, 23 January. Downloaded from: http://www.weforum.org/en/knowledge/KN_SESS_SUMM_23393?url=/en/knowledge/KN_SESS_SUMM_23393. Date accessed: 16 May 2008.

Triffin, R. (1960) *Gold and the Dollar Crisis* (New Haven, CT: Yale University Press).

Vrolijk, C. (1997) 'Derivatives' Effect on Monetary Policy Transmission', Monetary and Exchange Affairs Department Working Paper, WP/97/121 (Washington, DC: IMF).

Wray, R. (1999) *Understanding Modern Money* (Cheltenham: Edward Elgar).

Zelizer, V. (1994) *The Social Meaning of Money* (New York: Basic Books).

7
Calculating Life and Money as Resources

Luigi Doria

Introduction

The theme of calculation is becoming ever more prominent in the social science debate. This is a theme that is at the core of fundamental lines of modern social thought from Weber to Sombart to Simmel. Yet the issue seems now to be felt with particular intensity (and with renewed scientific attention, mixed with a certain uneasiness and overtones of philosophical interrogation) because of the 'universality' which calculation manifests in late modern societies.

One of the most important phenomena in the current calculative scenario is the fact that calculation tends to enlarge its scope, covering 'objects' – such as emotions, passions, identity, heritage and intellectual labour – which have historically been beyond its reach. *Calculating the incalculable* is a crucial task in contemporary societies and indicates a tendency towards including every dimension of human life in the domain of the measurable.

Scientific reflection, including studies on management, receives this impulse for measuring everything as a peculiarly unconditional demand. It takes the form of a calculative proliferation which resists any limitation, and accepts critiques only insofar as they lead to the proposal of more adequate (or more socialized) measurement.[1]

The wide interdisciplinary debate on the morphology, role and performativity of calculative practices, therefore, goes together with a more or less explicit interrogation of the very meaning and provenience of the imperative to calculate everything.

This chapter addresses the issue of universal calculability, starting with an interrogation of the relationship between calculation and mobilization. Can we assume, as suggested by a wide field of social thought, the unlimited commodification/marketization of life to be the driver and the end of unlimited calculation? Is it possible, in other words, to see the universality and the plasticity of calculation as the outcome of a transformation of social reality into a commodity or, indirectly, of the result of the subjection of social life to the logic of the market? Is it the mobilization of social phenomena in the sphere of commodity circulation that steers the movement of calculation? Or should we see calculation in the light of a different understanding of mobilization?

The hypothesis that I advance in this paper is that the morphology and the meaning of calculation in the social domain needs to be interpreted as constitutively related to a demand for a total and undetermined mobilization. The latter aims at more and more completely transcending any element of distinction, and avoiding any possibility of defining its 'finalization'.

This phenomenon manifests itself in the contemporary socio-economic lexicon by the representation of development as a mobilization of calculable resources. At the core of the linguistic architecture of management and development, we find 'resource' as a ubiquitous key-word for an unlimited catalogue of (human, cultural, territorial, communicative) resources.

I argue that the *unlimited* calculation and mobilization of resources is a movement towards the obliteration of the dimension of *measure*. It is by interrogating this obliteration of limit and measure that I will try to clarify what is at stake in the project of calculating the incalculable.

With this perspective, I will investigate the fact that money itself – whose 'transformation' into a commodity constitutes one of the most decisive events of Western history – has come to be seen as a calculable resource. In the catalogue of resources, money, the entity whose nature is to provide a measure for exchange, sits side by side with another primary resource: man, as human resource.

Introducing resourcification

Commodification and resourcification

A wide corpus of study, which includes Marxist and Foucauldian orientations, interprets the tendency to measure an increasing range of phenomena as related to a general process of commodification of social life. The theme of commodification of life (in its diverse aspects) has been at the core of several social science debates and interconnected with analysis of other major issues, including the hyper-rationalization or hyper-managerialization of social reality.

I will specifically focus on the so-called new sociology of capitalism, and particularly on the argument of Boltanski and Chiapello (2005), who in their analysis of contemporary capitalism and the future of its critique develop a number of theses on the relationship between capitalism, commodification and calculation.

The process of commodification is seen as integral to the capitalistic assimilation of life, on the assumption that capitalism has wrested unprecedented freedom of manoeuvre and commodification (Boltanski and Chiapello, 2005). What Boltanski and Chiapello (2005, p. 445) call 'capitalism's assimilation of the demand for authenticity' develops through the *inscription* of the 'sources of authenticity' (which are constituted, for example, by human beings, tastes, ways of being) in the sphere of commodification and calculation. The process develops through a constant re-assimilation of every authentic difference into that sphere, which continuously transforms sources of authenticity into new (emotional, affective, relational, 'artistic') commodities. What is at stake is an ever more complete *commodification of the authentic*, which transforms all 'personal human qualities' into commodities.

It is in this context that limiting the process of commodification is seen to be a crucial task for the renewal of the *artistic critique*[2] of capitalism. To provide an area protected from marketization is a way of reducing the mechanistic measuring of humanity, and safeguarding its immeasurable authenticity. What is at stake especially is the protection of the unique quality of certain entities (bodies, artworks or cultural artefacts, interpersonal relations, feelings and emotions), which are threatened by the contemporary tendency to measure, codify and commodify what is specifically human about human beings.

But is the power of contemporary calculation related to an increasingly capitalist assimilation of life, with the commodification of human life at its heart? Is the proliferation of measurement in all aspects of human life due to the incursion of market logics from their own sphere of business and commercial life?

As promised, I will focus on some important aspects of the discursive architecture of contemporary society, with this question: Why is the term *resource* commonly used, in the sphere of management and development, as a precise term for nominating diverse beings?

The etymology of the term relates to the Latin verb *surgere*, to rise. Re-source suggests the movement of rising again. With current definitions of the term[3] (which basically refer to a means of supplying some want or deficiency, or to a stock or reserve upon which one can draw), there is a reference to repeatedly rising again. The term 'resource' seems therefore to point to a constant potential to rise again.

My hypothesis is that, just on the basis of a very broad reference to the movement of rising again, 'resource' has become the most convenient term to justify the demand for indeterminate mobilization, becoming more and more unfocused and unrestricted.

Let us come back to the argument about the commodification of life. The critique of the capitalistic assimilation of authenticity – Boltanski and Chiapello argue, referring to Debord and Baudrillard – focuses on 'the destruction of any authentic life force that, however faint, is immediately *encoded* in order to take its place in the commodity circulation of signs' (Boltanski and Chiapello 2005, p. 450; italics in the original text). The reference here is still to the exchange of commodities as an act which affects the temporal structure of the process of calculation and mobilization even if the exchange is disfigured by a continuous unmeasured proliferation of exchanges, blurring the distinction between what *may be and what should not* be commodified.

I propose to regard as a decisive trait of *resourcification* its aim to radically obliterate any form of temporal delimitation and any form of clearing, characteristic of exchange. Moreover, the integrated development of resources overcomes the distinction between economic, social, civic and cultural development. In the sphere of resource, economic, social and political aspects of mobilization are not distinguished. We constantly find, in expert and lay discourses, diverse entities described as *economic*, *social* or *political* resources. But to label a resource economic, social or political means introducing an element of distinction which resourcification tends to obliterate. Thus the mobilization of resources appears to be a 'plastic' movement which does not have temporal or 'spatial' delimitations. I mean that no space outside resourcification exists, at least not in the sense in which a sphere outside the market exists.

Let us try to clarify this point. What are we saying when we say, for instance, that territory is a resource? Are we defining just a commodity, or an opportunity for developing market-oriented processes? Or are we identifying just a factor of production? We refer to the unconditional and plastic involvement of territory in the process of mobilization, an involvement of the totality of its dimensions in a temporally unlimited – and in general terms, undetermined – mobilization. We refer, in other terms, to the fact that all its (natural, cultural, personal, socio-relational) 'components' are taken into account and continuously mobilized in view of the continuous integrated development of territory. This development is a movement which constantly reinforces, 'empowers', the identity of the territory; it takes the shape, and not by chance, as we will see later, of a continuously increasing 'territorial quality'. It is not therefore merely the sum of diverse developmental dimensions, which may appear as 'components' only once the territory, as something to be mobilized in its *totality*, has appeared.

In order to understand the phenomenon we are trying to observe, we must look at the primary resource, which defines the entire process of resourcification: the *human resource*. We need to focus, in particular, on two sides which are intimately related.

Resource and the undetermined mobilization of the human

The term *human resource* is so profoundly natural that it pervades lay and scientific discourses. But what does it mean, beyond its definitions in the field of managerial sciences, where it has become a crucial *terminus tecnicus*?[4]

It refers to the involvement of all human dimensions and capacities (competences, emotions, passions and relations) in a context of mobilization which transcends the traditional limits of working life: the development of human resources continues before and after working life, and beyond the borders of a given job.

It is precisely in the context of *human resource* that the issue of the separation between work and non-work emerges. I am referring to the problem, which is well known to contemporary sociology, of distinguishing between the aspects of individuality involved in the (knowledge-intensive, creative, potentially 'autonomous') spheres of work and the aspects involved in the *cultural, social* and *civic* development of the person.[5]

It is because the *totality* of human dimensions is mobilized in such an *undetermined* way that this is one of the most dense and controversial issues in contemporary social science: the crucial place of human resource in value creation, and the problem of measuring it. The calculation of human resources means the calculation of the most precious resource, and yet the most incalculable one. Incidentally, it is worthwhile noting, in view of the argument that will be developed in the next paragraph, that this calculation tends to take the shape of the measurement of the quality of human resources, quality being a key word of contemporary business management.

This issue, surrounded by an extraordinary proliferation of debates, is critical for contemporary business management. *Human resource management* deals with this problem through a continuous reconfiguration of calculative methods, aiming to include the use of human resources in the accounting procedures of the company. But these calculative attempts do not enable us to overcome the problem. See how the issue is addressed, in a recent contribution by a sociologist of calculation: 'Today, person-nel departments and management are desperately looking for strategies to attach *true* and measurable values to the immaterial resources that are at the core of immaterial labour and capitalism' (Vormbusch 2008, p. 8). These desperate attempts need to be understood in terms of *calculating the incalculable*, as a watchword of contemporary management. 'If man's creativity and sociability are regarded as the origins of value creation, then the very non-calculability of these resources is developing into a fundamental problem for contemporary capitalism' (ibid. p. 8).

The crucial problem outlined above manifests itself in the fact that the numbers continuously produced to measure the self at work appear to be ungrounded. As Vormbusch points out, the *objectivity* of those numbers (the way in which they refer to an external reality) does not appear to be relevant. Calculative technologies seem to exist mainly in their own capacity for (communicative) self-mobilization: 'calculative devices are not so much utilized to pin somebody down to a specific and immutable value, but to induce discussion about how to continuously work on the perfection of the self' (ibid. p. 10).

We will come back to this important issue, which bears on the rela-tionship between calculation, mobilization and the incalculable in the contemporary scenario. Let us just note here that the crucial problem mentioned above does not relate only to business management. As it will be clarified below, it is a problem which concerns the 'management of society' itself – and, in my view, not because of the encroachment of market logics outside the sphere of business.

It is worthwhile emphasizing here that it is precisely with regard to the unlimited and undetermined mobilization of the human that the argument of *immeasurability* has been developed by well-known repre-sentatives of radical thought, such as Negri and Hardt.[6]

The thesis of immeasurability follows from the acknowledgement that today all social life is productive. In a world where everything is a value-generating activity (paid labour as well as social relationships, and the acts of creation and innovation which pervade the contemporary city), and in which the entire life is the time of production, labour is defined as productive activity *outside measure* (Hardt and Negri 2000).

What needs to be considered, according to this line of argument, is the self-valorization of creative production, values, feelings and knowl-edge: an indefinite proliferation of the human, generating an immeas-urable excess of value (Hardt and Negri 2000).

The thesis, as developed in Negri (1999), argues in favour of both the immeasurability and uncontrollability of value. The fact that labour 'finds its value in affect' (ibid. p. 79) leads to the impossibility of measuring the productivity of labour, and requires abandonment of the theory of labour-value. What he calls the 'postmodern political economy' would then, according to Negri (ibid.), acknowledge the impossibility of measuring value, but would try to reactivate forms of biopolitical control on proliferating life. Anyway, all these strategies of control would be unsuccessful, since human self-valorization (which has to do with an 'expansion' of affect, defined as a *Spinozian power to act*) is beyond any measure, any control and any calculation.

I do not intend to discuss here the roots of the argument concerning this immeasurable proliferation of the human.[7] What I want to stress is that, in this line of argument, the thesis of the immeasurability and incalculability of the human goes together with a kind of liberation from the dimension of measure itself. The incalculability of the human seems to abolish the problem of measure.

I will come back to this point later, when I will ask what interpretation of calculation and incalculability is a similar argument based on.

The calculation of quality of life and integrated human development

I have focused in the last paragraph on how the development of human resources, total and undetermined, calls into question the problem of measurability. This problem tends to be addressed by human resource management through a proliferation of ever more sophisticated calculation; and, in a completely different perspective, it lies at the core of the argument about the essential immeasurability of life.

Let us focus now on another important aspect of the contemporary calculative scenario, pertaining to the ever more precise calculation at a social level of all 'features' of human life. How does this calculation develop? Why does it go on? And what kind of mobilization is it related to?

Let us consider a number of calculative experiments which have obvious political relevance, and aim to go beyond measuring gross domestic product. With these measuring processes, the calculation of economic values tends to be complemented by the calculation of total quality of life (happiness, well-being), under the ethical demand for *integrated human development*.

I will specifically refer to a recent report[8] which, by virtue of the reputation of its authors, will probably become a point of reference in the very lively and dense international debate on the issue (Stiglitz, Sen and Fitoussi 2009). The report aims at providing a more complete and adequate measurement of development and progress, starting with the acknowledgment that conventional, market-based measures of income, wealth and consumption are insufficient to assess human well-being.

To measure GDP means measuring in monetary terms the total economic value produced and exchanged in a certain country. The contribution of the various 'factors' (human, natural, social, institutional, cultural) to the generation of economic value is the object of complex calculative operations. Important economic procedures are focused precisely on these forms of calculation, which constantly deal with operational and methodological difficulties concerning the definition of the various factors, the measurement of their interrelations and the production of adequate indicators.

One of the main[9] (and in my view definitely the most important) paths along which the 'evolution' of the processes of measurement moves is the measurement of quality of life. The latter, according to the report, 'includes the full range of factors that make life worth living, including those that are not traded in markets and not captured by monetary measures' (Sen, Stiglitz and Fitoussi 2009, p. 58).

The measurement of quality of life (QoL) develops in two intertwined strands, along this clearly-defined line:

> The information relevant to valuing quality of life goes beyond people's self-reports and perceptions to include measures of their 'functionings' and freedoms. In effect, what really matters are the capabilities of people, that is, the extent of their opportunity set and of their freedom to choose among this set, the life they value. The choice of relevant functionings and capabilities for any quality of life measure is a value judgment, rather than a technical exercise. But while the precise list of the features affecting quality of life inevitably rests on value judgments, there is a consensus that quality of life depends on people's health and education, their everyday activities (which include the right to a decent job and housing), their participation in the political process, the social and natural environment in which they live, and the factors shaping their personal and economic security. Measuring all these features requires both objective and subjective data. (Sen, Stiglitz and Fitoussi 2009, p. 15)

A first calculative aspect, concerning the measurement of objective features,[10] is the deconstruction of QoL into a number of components, which are assumed to be linked by an extremely complex web of interrelations (whose definition and framing represents the main task of measurement).

If the above features may be considered, broadly speaking, as 'indicators' of QoL, they are themselves calculated by being translated into a set of indicators. The definition of indicators (a primary calculative practice in the current socio-economic scenario, surrounded by a plethora of methodological controversies which do not represent a limit to calculation) plays a pivotal role in calculation. But initially, indicators evidently play a crucial role in constructing and representing those entities as *calculable objects*.

The calculation of QoL through the production of indicators concerning its objective features goes together with another calculative avenue, relating to the measurement of 'subjective' perceptions of QoL: what people perceive about the quality of their lives.

> Subjective well-being encompasses different aspects (cognitive evaluations of one's life, happiness, satisfaction, positive emotions such as joy and pride, and negative emotions such as pain and worry): each of them should be measured separately to derive a more comprehensive appreciation of people's lives. (Sen, Stiglitz and Fitoussi 2009, p. 16)

> One intrinsic limitation of all measures of SWB is that reported data cannot be validated against objective measures of the same phenomena, for the simple reason that no obvious external benchmark for these phenomena exists. (Sen, Stiglitz and Fitoussi 2009, p. 150)

> The specific feature of the subjective measures of quality of life discussed here is that what people report about their own conditions has no obvious objective counterpart: we can compare 'perceived' and 'actual' inflation, for example, but only respondents can provide information on their own subjective states and values. Despite this feature, a rich literature on these subjective measures concludes that they help to predict people's behaviour (e.g. workers who report more dissatisfaction in their work are more likely to quit their job), and that they are valid with respect to a range of other information (e.g. people who report themselves as 'happy' tend to smile more and to be rated as happy by people around them; these self-reports are also correlated with electrical readings of the brain). (Sen, Stiglitz and Fitoussi 2009, p. 43)

The calculation of quality of life thus takes the shape of both a calculative 'determination' of life in terms of calculable components, and a calculative treatment of the subjective perceptions of life itself. The latter are supposed to be 'objectivized' through an external rating of the subject's happiness by other subjects and through the contribution of psychological and neurological sciences, to provide a natural objective *validity*. Let us note here that all these calculative paths, which model a continuous interrelation between the subjective and the objective, appear to be put side by side, in terms of their complementarity.

This and other modes of representing the dimensions of social life and their relations may be addressed in the light of the reflection on *qualculation* (on this notion see Cochoy, 2002; Callon and Law, 2005). The report can be seen as the result of those calculative practices which, according to recent sociological thought, involve figuring, classifying, representing, displaying and interrelating social phenomena (see, in particular, Callon and Law, 2005). More precisely, I refer to those particular *qualculative* practices (endowed with a peculiar performative capacity), that are represented by the theories of social sciences[11]

But what is particularly important from our point of view is that, given the subject of the report, the framing and classifying that it proposes constantly point towards a number of radical issues concerning the calculation of social life. Bearing this in mind, we can address another crucial complementarity: measuring quality of life in relation to other forms of measuring 'social progress'.

The report puts three forms of measurement (Classical GDP, QoL and Sustainability) side by side, seeing complementarity between them. From my point of view, however, what is at stake is not just complementarity but the dominance of the measurement of quality of life – a dominance of which there is no explicit mention in the report.

At the core of the transformation of social measurement, there is, as I will discuss later, a fundamental demand to *take into account* life in all its dimensions. This demand proceeds along the privileged way represented by the calculation of human life *in terms of quality*. More precisely, it proceeds by demanding information on quality and thus by transforming quality into something measurable.

What lies at the heart of this process is an assumption confidence (which needs to be constantly confirmed) that total quality of life can be calculated; more precisely, that life can be treated in terms of quality, and *assured* as a knowable object for the living subject, by the provision of information about its quality.[12] This is a phenomenon which, as will become clear, is at the very frontier of the calculation of the human.

On the basis of the assumption referred to above, calculation can proceed towards its 'objective': an ever-increasing quality. We might say that life is calculated as a resource for its own constant improvement; more particularly it is mobilized towards constant improvement in quality.

What is at stake therefore is not bio-political strategy aiming to recon-figure, through the ideological mask of quality, forms of control on human life. What is at stake, rather, is a fundamental pathway through which the calculability of the human proceeds. So what goes under the heading of measurement of quality *precedes* (in a sense that we should try to better understand) any other form of measurement. After all, if a calculable quality of life exists, what is more important for a prop-erly human development than the constant attainment of that quality? And, after all, is it not implied by the measurement of *total* quality of life that the production of economic value can be comfortably framed as one component of a total?

In the programmatic horizon which this calculation opens, the meas-urement of value produced and exchanged is the measurement of only one contribution (no matter how important) to the supreme calculable value, the quality of life itself. We can better understand this point by focusing on the alleged complementarity between the indicators which are used for measuring.

One of the most crucial issues in the report is the relationship between monetary and non-monetary indicators of social progress. But, if the argument I am advancing deserves consideration, the monetary meas-ures already serve a total form of calculation. In the latter, the basic, pre-eminent *measures* are indicators which (whether or not summarized in a single comprehensive indicator)[13] provide information on the improve-ment of life. But another implication is that, in this general framework, money tends to be more and more completely reduced to a calculative operator. The fact that money takes the shape of a mere calculative operator is, as we will see in the next paragraphs, a phenomenon which deserves the highest attention.

Money as a resource

The phenomena I have analysed below point towards the interrogation of the relationship between the calculation of the human and its indetermi-nate mobilization; at the same time, they allow us to catch a glimpse of the relationship between the unconditional demand for calculation and the dimension of *measure*. This relationship is beginning to appear decisive.

We must ask directly: Where is money in respect to this scenario? What does it mean to say that money today is a financial resource? And first of all, what does it mean *for money* to be a resource?

Let us start with the basic phenomenon of the transformation of money into a commodity. Amato (2010) says that money is the *institu-*

tion, which makes the exchange true and meaningful for those who participate in it. It is the condition which *delimits* exchange and makes it possible. It is only by virtue of money, and by virtue of its relationship with the dimension of institution, that exchange and the calculation that it implies can find their own measure.

The reduction of money to money-commodity is therefore the reduction to an exchangeable commodity of the institution which delimits the exchange of commodities. This reduction, which was decisive in Western history and radically transformed the meaning of money, is all about calculation. As a particular commodity, money has come to be increasingly included in the sphere of calculability.

The calculation of interest is indeed the calculation of the price of money as a commodity and determines the relationship between money and time (see Fantacci, Chapter 5 in this volume).

Along the path defined by the transformation of money into a commodity – a transformation which Amato (2010) describes as the effect of an *initial hesitation* in the history of Western humanity with respect to the task of thinking money as an institution – the absorption of money in the regime of calculation must be constantly re-assured.

In this context I address the thinking of Dick Bryan and Michael Rafferty developed in a recent article (2007) and in their contribution to this volume, concerning financial derivatives as money.

According to Bryan and Rafferty, derivatives should be considered with regard to their capacity to compare money and assets in respect to their future and, at the same time, to compare a wide range of physical and financial assets – and different monies – with one other.

Derivatives are thus a calculative technology or a technology of calculative assurance, built on the primary calculative operation which is constituted by the commodification of risk and uncertainty.

Let us specifically focus on financial derivatives. As Bryan and Rafferty point out, 'Derivatives in relation to money (currency and interest rates) express the commodification of attributes of money; most particularly the attributes of variability in money's value' (Bryan and Rafferty, Chapter 6 in this volume). Let us focus on this sentence. Derivatives protect us from variability in the value of money. Hence their 'use value', which is clearly high. But why is it so high? Because, in my view, variability in the value of money is not just an attribute of money among other attributes, and its assurance is not an assurance among other assurances. Money's variability is the variability of the price for a commodity which is not a commodity. In that variability it is peculiarly exposed to the paradoxical trait of the decisive reduction mentioned above.

The security-oriented stabilization which derivatives provide must be interpreted not so much as a stabilization of money markets (until and unless future crises occur), but rather as an assurance of the commodity nature of money, the calculative assurance of the initial hesitation which Amato refers to: a calculative movement that, precisely by aiming at stabilizing money as a commodity, leaves even more exposed, but not necessarily more evident, the abyss on which the reduction of money to commodity resides.

But there is something more. Derivatives are a calculative technology that, according to Bryan and Rafferty, can be understood as a form of money: a form of money based on the unconditional calculative commensurability of everything with everything. They can be considered a form of money *shaped by calculation*: 'So it is with the value of a derivative: it is what the derivative is able to set in motion that defines its use value, and the fact that this capacity for conversion can be traded defines it as an exchange value (i.e., as a commodity).' (ibid.)

In this context the two economists argue that derivatives as money play the role of monetary anchor in the current monetary system. According to them, there is no objective measure of value (in particular, no objective measure of the value of one currency in respect to another). Their argument moves, in the same vein, from the idea that the way in which liquid asset markets are constructed makes 'fundamental values' irrelevant. The only anchor is a calculative technology of commensuration – that is, derivatives: 'Financial derivatives provide a "web of anchors", a system of computational links across a range of measures – privileging none, but reconciling all. Framed this way, we can see central bank purchases of mortgage backed securities as a form of monetary intervention' (ibid.).

This means that the only 'anchor' of the movement of calculation and mobilization of money is calculative process; namely, the process which, by commodifying the variability in money's value, continuously re-presents money as a commodity. The only 'fundamental value' for calculation-mobilization is the continuous development of calculation-mobilization.

In this perspective, the self-empowerment of money is based on the relationship between calculation, mobilization and *measure*. More precisely, the calculation and mobilization of money appears here related to the obliteration of the original relationship between money and measure, to the obliteration of the fact that measure is the essence of money as an institution.

The self-empowering system of derivatives comes about as the result of a peculiar dissociation from exchange. Prices and their variability can be calculatively managed through derivatives without participating in the exchange; without participating in what money as measure fundamentally performs and delimits as a proper political act.

Let us try to summarize. Along the path marked by its reduction to a commodity, money becomes more and more completely a mere calculative operator for exchange.[14] This movement needs to be understood as a movement in which exchange itself become more and more obliterated: its basic relationship with measure, which is at the core of its proper political role, comes to be more and more eroded.

Money *as a resource* does not therefore mean a further evolution of money-commodity. It means instead that, through the increasing erosion of its relationship with the dimension of measure, money becomes increasingly formatted to serve the calculation of exchanges in view of their constant, calculatively secured, development.

Further – and this should not be seen in evolutionary terms, but as something which obeys the same basic demand – economic life tends to be framed in terms of a range of technologies which contribute to the constant increase of the total quality of life.

When we consider the calculation of life and money (and we interrogate the meaning of these calculations) we must always keep in mind the movement aimed at calculatively assuring economic life itself, as a space decisively marked by the meeting between man and money. Against the movement aimed at 'securing' it, though the securing of the *risk* it implies, that space is determined by incalculability; it is a space in which (in the exchange, in credit-debt relationship) the in-securable lies in ambush – possibly not as a danger. It is precisely in this perspective that we must understand, as difficult as it may be, the radical difference between *money as a measure* and money as an operator which calculates – secures – economic life, in view of its constant empowerment.

Resource, calculation, assurance, empowerment

Let us try to summarize the argument so far. What does the relationship between calculation and mobilization of *resources* point towards? It points, in my view, towards a demand for total calculability (a demand for the calculative assurance of every being, including humans themselves) and a demand for an undetermined mobilization of the calculable.

Let us focus on calculation. The demand of calculation typically appears as an *unlimited* calculation, which proceeds by *calculating the incalculable* and particularly by addressing the *incalculable* human.

But how ought we to understand this unlimitability? On the basis of what notion of limit? And what does it have to do with the incalculable? And finally, what is this incalculable?

I advance here a hypothesis: the incalculable does not indicate an attribute we may straightforwardly refer to the human, nor an unavailable property of the human, nor something which merely resists calculation, in the form of a properly human value.

This sounds a bizarre hypothesis. This is precisely the configuration of the incalculable which we are mostly familiar with and which is at the core of the denunciatory argument about the disturbing effect of calculation.

But let us try, so to speak, to reverse the argument.

Is it not precisely through this representation of the incalculable that anything incalculable comes to be constantly assimilated in the movement of calculation? Is it not though this basic representation that *calculating the incalculable* continues to reign as the watchword of the present day?

We should perhaps begin to consider that *calculating the incalculable* is a truly comfortable operation for management today. We should begin to suspect that the value of calculation lies precisely in taking over the incalculable as the most important value: the fact that the most valuable resource is the most incalculable is not a coincidence. This is why the incalculable is not a *limit* to calculation, but lies at the very frontier of its development.

Nothing here speaks of a proper limit to anything. Where is the limit then? What is the limit we refer to when we deal with calculation?

This limit is not something which may be located near or far from calculation, being in its own space external to it. This limit has to do with the possibility which human beings have to relate to what is radically other to them: death and nought. This relationship is radically incalculable, and radically un-assurable. It is precisely through the constantly re-invested oblivion of this dimension that calculation proceeds.

But does this have anything to do with *measure*? We have a clue in the fact that the answer is positive. We feel that when referring to an *unmeasured* calculation, we are not just referring to a calculation which continuously proliferates.

And a fundamental confirmation that yes, we are on the right path comes from the interrogation that Amato (2010) has carried out on money as measure and as institution. The concept of money as an institution is propounded by Amato on the basis of an understanding of the act of institution, the act through which man relates to the radically incalculable: death, want and nought. Economic life is, precisely by virtue of money, the dimension in which man has to do with what, being radically other to man, constitutes, in proper terms, his or her limit.

Although it seems that this kind of philosophical argument leads us far from the analysis of the movement of calculation, it is in this perspective that we need to address the project of *calculating the incalculable* and the uneasiness which this term generates.

To understand calculation in its relationship with the obliteration of limit (measure, the incalculable) means to understand the movement of calculation-mobilization as a response to the demand for not having to do with the dimension of limit.

It is not by chance perhaps that the 'extreme' thesis on the incalculability of man I have mentioned above – a thesis which seems to go together with an abolition of the problem of measure – developed precisely in the context of an understanding of humanity as the subject of a refusal of death. This is how Negri defines 'multitude', the subject of an unlimited human proliferation beyond measure: 'The multitude is the only subject susceptible of launching this creative challenge to death. [...] The multitude's way of being is nothing other than this continuous proliferation of vital experiences which have in common the negation of death, the radical and definitive refusal of that which arrests the process of life' (Negri 2008, pp. 70–71).

Running the risk of being extreme, let me put it this way: when death is conceived as an obstacle to remove, calculation appears as an external menace, a menace to the incalculable proliferation of the human.

When death is something man still has to deal with, the unconditional demand for calculation is not external to anything; it is instead something profoundly human and, at the same time, something carrying the risk of the most radical dehumanization. It is the way in which human beings try not to have anything to do with death and nought. Yet this refusal of the nought is exactly how humanity in the epoch of calculation continues to be in relationship with nought itself.

This calculative reconfirmation of the refusal of the relationship with nought moves along the path marked by an initial hesitation in Western history – and constantly reassures it. This hesitation has to do with the perfecting of calculation; one of the fundamental forms of the latter is the transformation of human existence itself into a calculable entity.

Let us try to move further, following one of the passages of the Heideggerian thought, in which the issue of the *perfection* of calculation, like the perfection of the metaphysical parabola of *ratio*, is addressed in a dizzily illuminating way. The epoch is the epoch in which calculation is taken to perfection, under the authority of the *principle of reason*; the principle whose enunciation by Leibniz represents a pre-eminent moment in the history of metaphysics.

But what does the principle says? And how does its perfection shape the epoch of calculation?

On the basis of the principle and its perfection the I relates to the world as something which is 'securely established as an object (*Gegenstand*), that means, as an Object for a representing subject' (ibid. p. 119). Reasons must be rendered to humans 'who determine objects as objects by way of a representation that judges' (ibid. p. 119). The principle says: 'every thing counts as existing when and only when it has been securely established as a calculable object for cognition' (ibid. p. 120).

The epoch of the perfection of calculation is the epoch in which the fundamental metaphysical demand for the calculative assurance of beings comes to perfection, under the imperative of having all beings as securely calculable for a calculating subject. It is the epoch in which the calculative parabola of Western Ratio comes to perfection, the parabola along which man relates to the world and to his own existence as a calculable object, as an object which can be unconditionally known and communicated.

Modern technology, Heidegger says, pushes, assuming the unqualified validity of the principle of reason, to the greatest possible perfection of the claim of the principle. 'This perfection consists in the completeness of the calculably secure establishing of objects, in the completeness of reckoning with them and with the securing of the calculability of possibilities for reckoning' (ibid. p. 121). It is by heeding the claim of the principle that today 'humanity runs the risk of measuring the greatness of everything grand only according to the reach of the authority of the *principium rationis*'.

In this long quotation, we have run several times into a number of words which refer to the sphere of assurance. The establishing of objects which metaphysics must constantly reinforce is the establishing of objects for a representing subject. This establishing is *calculably secure*. At the very core of calculation there is a demand for assurance, for assuring beings. Heidegger provides another clue: the metaphysical thinker who enunciates the Principle of Reason is the same who invents *life insurance* and the same who theorizes a *lingua rationalis*, which is 'the sort of reckoning that is in the position of giving a full accounting of the relations between word, sign, and thing – and thus for everything that is' (ibid. p. 101).

Life assurance: we suddenly bump into the demand for assurance which I have several times referred to above, when the attempts to calculate life have appeared as something very close to a calculative assurance of life. *Quality assurance* is, after all, a ubiquitous watchword for contemporary management.

As anticipated, calculating the totality of life, by providing information on its quality, should be understood as the path along which our age responds to the demand for holding the human in the dimension of assurance and mobilization.

But there is something else which is related to all this: *securization* as an assurance of money, as an assurance of money as a calculable object and a calculative operator, as an assurance of the obliteration of the dimension of measure which money belongs to.

The calculation of life and the calculation of money appear here as two extremely important phenomena, which need to be understood by looking at how they both conform to a basic demand for calculation and mobilization. In order to better understand this crucial nexus between assurance and mobilization, let us refer again to *The Principle of Reason*.

The epoch of calculation is for Heidegger the atomic age. The principle of reason, in its perfection, leads every form of knowledge to procure energy (an ever higher level of energy) and, *at the same time*, securely establish its calculability. The principle empowers our age (makes it as mighty as it is) and allows the domination of man over the whole earth; this domination progresses through the exploitation of atomic energy and leads the present age of world history to be moulded by atomic energy and its potential unleashing.

The frontier on which natural sciences – which play a leading role in the development of all sciences – respond to the authority of the principle is the domination of the atom, as an unmeasured source of energy. This domination develops through a cycle of calculative exploration, exploitation and securing of energy.

We face here a wide space with temptations of analogical reasoning, which must be handled very carefully.

One tempting analogy comes first to our eyes. The calculation of man, down to his most incalculable 'aspects' (passions, feelings, affects), liberates an impressive power, which requires in turn a huge effort of control and management: the power of a resource endowed with an enormous energy, human resource. And it is precisely by referring to the power handled by physics that *Human Resource Management* describes the most promising employees as *high-potential human resources*.

But we should be wary of free-and-easy analogies. We should instead try to understand the way in which the human sciences respond to the demand for dealing with beings in terms of assurance and mobilization; we should ask how science determines man as a calculable and mobilizable being.

I have once again referred to the crucial relationship between calculation and mobilization.

What appears in the contemporary scenario of management *as calculation for calculation* must be understood as a continuous cycle of assurance for empowerment.[15] This movement has no other law than a demand for empowerment to performance.

But how ought we to conceive this *performance*, whose attainment, at an ever higher level, steers the development of every science? The uneasiness that we experience in dealing with this performance precisely derives from its constitutive attribute of unspecificability, or undeterminability. The uneasiness derives from the fact that performance is nothing other than a movement from *a minus to a plus*.

The calculation of human resources is a movement whose only law is the constant attainment of a *plus* of man. What does it mean to keep the human in the dimension of a minus to a plus? This minus to a plus should not be understood in a merely quantitative sense. A plus of man does not mean a bigger amount of man. It means a man who is *more* man.[16] The way in which this plus provides the direction for the human (the way in which it formats humanity in the dimension of empowerment) must be more and more completely a *human* way. It must be a way proper to the human, but not adapted to it: it must spring, more and more precisely, as an auto-confirmation of the human. The ever-increasable quality of life – what the techno-science of man accepts as its guiding reference – cannot be defined if it does not refer to this plus of man.

A plus of man means a man who auto-confirms himself in his self-empowerment, which means in his will of not having to do with what constitutes his limit, his measure: nought as revealed by mortality, understood as the existential assumption of the relationship between human life and human death. Yet man continues to be in relationship with the nought just through and into the movement of this constantly re-invested refusal.

It is in this context that the techno-science of man ought to be understood as a science of the calculation and empowering mobilization of human resources. This is not an uncertain monstrosity to remove from our eyes; it must rather be understood, with all the sobriety we can manage, as the task on which science is already at work.

From this perspective, the scientific treatment of man cannot be properly addressed, as is often done with a denunciatory stance, as a

quantification of the human; neither can it be understood as an econo-
mization of life – in other terms, as a reduction of life operated by a peculiar science, economics. Rather, we should turn our eyes towards the way
in which economics more and more radically transforms itself, in order
to lead the techno-scientific project of calculating the human. It is in the
same vein that we should consider how the techno-scientific approach to
man, by responding *in its own way* to the demand for performance, meets
the techno-scientific project of the natural sciences. This meeting, which
is neither a casual date nor a wedding party, needs to be understood as a
work in progress, whose manifestations are nevertheless numerous and
important: ranging from the ever more strict links between psychological and neurological sciences and behavioural economics, to the role of
these sciences in the measurement of human well-being, to the project
aimed at ensuring the undetermined extension of the duration of life.

This project, this calculation of the human I am speaking of, cannot be
understood in immediately quantitative terms, nor immediately in terms
of a quantification of quality, although it proceeds through a calculative
transformation of quality.[17]

Access to the properly calculative trait of calculation is instead constituted by a *nuance* which hides an abyss: the nuance which distinguishes
the unconditional measurement of everything with everything from
the dimension of measure.

Let us start again from an apparently distant point: from a passage in
the *Principle* where Heidegger speaks about a poet. He invites us to listen
to Hölderlin, who speaks of a calculation that has to do with the production of beauty. Commenting on the *Antigone* by Sophocles, the poet
refers to a *calculable law* and an equilibrium as elements of the tragedy.
It seems that Greek tragedy does have a measure, *its own measure.*

Here something speaks of a minus and a plus, of a relationship
between a minus and a plus, of a balance between a minus and a plus,
of a *calculable*[18] law that has to do with this equilibrium. And it speaks
about this in the language of a poet.

We acknowledge with extreme difficulty that the poetic has something
to do with measure, although poetry is, in essence, about metrics. This is
because we understand equilibrium and measure *on the basis* of measurement, and not vice versa. We feel measure and equilibrium as the *result*
(or the stabilizing point) of measurement; or we acknowledge sometimes
that a process based on unconditionally measuring everything with everything does not have any measure, nor any equilibrium.

Language and measure, then; language and measure, language and
money: do they have anything to do with the incalculable? And do

they have anything to do with calculation? As Amato suggests in his contribution to this volume, is not the fact that they are both forced to speak the language of calculation a decisive trait of our epoch?

The *Principle of Reason*, again: the epoch of the completeness of calculation is the epoch in which 'the representation of human language as an instrument of information increasingly gains the upper hand' (Heidegger 1996, p. 124). *Information* is, according to Heidegger, the basic word for the epoch of the history of humanity which works for safeguarding life, for making it secure. The representation of the totality of beings as something that can be treated in terms of information is what steers the perfection of calculation.

The epoch of calculation – the epoch in which ratio is taken to perfection as calculative reason – is the age of information. It is the age in which language must be more and more completely formatted as a means of information and communication; the epoch in which language as information must appear as an obviousness.

The relationship between information and calculation is after all quite precisely experienced in our societies, whenever the process of calculating life, through quality assurance, appears as a movement oriented towards a hyper-utterability of the human.

A very broad socio-anthropological reflection describes the managerial regime of quality assurance and auditing as a regime which makes social and organizational life (including interpersonal relations, emotions, or the relationship between a teacher and student) hyper-explicit. This making explicit is in my view what we ought to consider at the very core of what one thread of anthropological studies refers to as a *tyranny of transparency* (see Strathern 2000). The reaction against the imperative of quality control, whose most precise configuration is the coercive requirement of information on the quality of everything, often tends to take the form of an appeal to the *un*utterability of quality.

All this should be understood by looking at the movement of the assurance of language in the dimension of information. What is constantly obliterated in this dimension is silence, as something which does not coincide at all with an absence of language. But silence and money are linked by a native nexus; a nexus that has to do with nothing less than the difference between two possibilities of being human. Does human progress imply the more and more complete information and communication of our irreducibly specific differences, of our irreducibly specific human qualities? Or does another possibility of being human pass through the relationship that humans have with what is other to them, by virtue of a language which is still able to measure up to silence?

The traditional analogy between language and money, language and measure, still speaks to us. Language and money, just in the age of their extreme calculability, point to a dimension of radical inassurability.

They point to the possibility of a measured relationship with the unassurable, which is the possibility of an economic relationship with other humans and other beings.

Conclusions: calculation and limit

Let us try, by way of a conclusion, to develop some other considerations on the issue which extend this contribution, concerning the relationship between calculation and limit. Can we think of this relationship in terms of a limit that we can put on the calculation of life?

Let us step back to where we started from. In the above-mentioned book, Boltanski and Chiapello write: 'In the age of the commodification of difference, one task is obviously unavoidable on the authenticity front: restricting the extension of the commodity sphere, particularly in the direction of a commodification of the human' (Boltanski and Chiapello 2005, pp. 470–471).

I would call this obviousness into question. Not because I do not acknowledge the importance of the issue of commodification, nor because I do not understand the demand for de-limitation which speaks in the proposal for a juridical prohibition of the commodification of certain goods, with the aim of protecting their specific *dignity*. Nor do I intend to deny the fact that the calculation of the human has found in commodification an eminent field of development; a field in which, particularly in the frame of calculation of labour as a commodity, a number of crucial issues concerning social justice have emerged and continue to emerge.

What I have tried to do in this contribution is simply to interrogate the meaning of the demand of calculation in contemporary society. It is on the basis of such an interrogation (although it might appear uncomfortable or disturbing) that it might be perhaps possible to gain a sober position with respect to a number of phenomena which social science understandably considers disquieting.

It is in this perspective, and through the dialogue with phenomenological thought, that the calculation of the human has appeared as something which is not of the order of a reduction *of* the human (nor even its reduction to a commodity). Calculation, precisely in its totalizing and undeterminable form, responds to a demand which is constitutively human, as it constitutes a possibility which properly belongs to the history of humanity. But another possibility, which is not the contrary or the opposite of the latter, belongs to the humanity: the possibility of measuring up to the incalculable. This possibility is intimately concerned with the relationship which humanity has with the dimension of limit and measure.

Rather than a delimitation of calculation in the name of the incalculable, what an understanding of the essence of calculation points towards is precisely the consideration of the relationship between calculation, the incalculable, limit and measure – a relationship which still and always requires an effort of thinking. It is from this perspective that it will perhaps be possible to gain a more measured relationship with beings, goods and commodities, which is most necessary in order simply to exist.

Such an approach does not argue therefore in favour of an 'institutional critique' of calculative capitalism to be added to the *social* and *artistic* critiques. It instead points towards the very nexus between the incalculable and the institutional dimension, and particularly towards the constitutive institutional dimension of economic life. This nexus is not at all evident and appears instead as disturbing, in an era in which assurance and control are presented as the supreme ethical values. It is quite difficult in fact to understand how any institutional element rests on something radically incalculable. Yet a number of voices in the history of Western thought, including economic thought, allude to this uncomfortable issue; and a dialogue with these voices is still possible and fruitful, particularly for the sciences of economics and management, for proceeding along what is surely an unassurable path. Concerning the nature of the latter, I believe, fully agreeing with Amato (2010), that what is needed is not a *return* to a measure that we never had,[19] nor a return to any traditional way of living.

What is at stake is instead a possibility, which from the beginning has belonged to humanity, and which, even in the age of the perfection of calculability, remains as a task. Although this possibility takes the shape of an abyssal appeal and does not easily lead to comprehensive ready-made solutions, any attempt to understand what is really at stake in calculating life and money might be useful.

Notes

Part of the research activity on which this paper is based has been carried out when the author was Fellow at the *Nantes Institute for Advanced Studies*. The author thanks Suez Environment that sponsored the chair.

1. See Power (2004).
2. A critique which, according to the French scholars, could be reformulated and renewed today. See Boltanski and Chiapello (2005).
3. See the *Oxford English Dictionary*.

4. On the notion of *human resource development* which has emerged in the field of managerial studies see Brooks and Nafukho (2006).
5. See, on this point, Perulli (2000).
6. See Hardt and Negri (2000, 2004) and Negri (1999, 2003).
7. For a critique of the thesis of immeasurability, from the perspective of managerial and accounting studies, see Toms (2008).
8. The report has been produced by the *Commission on the Measurement of Economic Performance and Social Progress*, which has been created in 2008 on French government's initiative.
9. The report identifies three macro-sides: classical GDP issues, quality of life, and sustainable development and environment. See Stiglitz, Sen and Fitoussi (2009).
10. Concerning the measurement of the objective features of QoL, the report identifies two main conceptual and methodological issues, based on Sen's *capability* approach and on the fair allocation theory.
11. See on this point the dialogue between Michel Callon and John Law (2005).
12. Although the issue cannot be properly addressed in this contribution, the role of quality (and the discursive and technological universe of quality assurance, quality control and quality management) is pivotal. This is confirmed by the fact that quality measurement pervades a growing number of social domains outside the sphere of private business (including education, public services, health and cultural policies) and is the object of numerous lines of critical reflection, focusing on quality management and auditing as evidently controversial forms of hyper-managerial control; see, for example, Loughlin (1993) and Morley (2003). In my view, the role of quality in the context of contemporary calculation should not be addressed looking at quality as a sort of ideological mask under which quantitative calculation continues to reign. Nor should attention merely be directed towards the quantification of quality. We should instead understand the movement by which quality (a category which throughout Western history has been considered peculiarly close to the incalculable) is subjected to a sort of calculative transformation; by virtue of the latter it comes to be more and more completely accepted in the regime of calculation, together with quantity. At the very core of the ubiquitous demand for quality assurance there is, in other words, a movement aimed at assuring quality, so that it can speak the language of calculation.
13. The authors of the report are extremely prudent in respect of the production of a single measure of well-being, on the basis of the impossibility of summarizing in a single indicator something as *complex* as the well-being of members of society.
14. See, on this point, Amato (2010).
15. What, in the perspective of *socio-calculation* (see Vormbusch 2008), is approached as a communicative mobilization of human resources towards the constant development of the self, can be addressed by my perspective, considering how the whole of working (and social) life is mobilized towards a plus of performance.
16. On how the contemporary project of constructing a science of *human development*, which takes into account all human capacities and qualities, can be

confronted with Marx's thoughts on the development of the totality of the manifestations of human life, see Bee (forthcoming).
17. I refer here to the argument briefly developed in note 12.
18. We cannot avoid noting that here the term *calculable* seems to have a completely different meaning.
19. See Amato (2010) on how no traditional economic system has been properly founded on money as an institution.

References

Amato, M. (2010) *L'enigma della moneta e l'inizio dell'economia* (Milan: et al. edizioni Milano).
Bee, M. (forthcoming) *Senza alcun bisogno. Studio sullo sviluppo umano* (Lecce: Pensa Multimedia).
Boltanski, L. and Chiapello, E. (2005) *The New Spirit of Capitalism* (trans. G. Elliott) (London: Verso).
Brooks, K. and Nafukho, F. M. (2006) 'Human Resource Development, Social Capital, Emotional Intelligence', *Journal of European Industrial Training*, 20 (2), 117–128.
Bryan, D. and Rafferty, M. (2007) 'Financial Derivatives and the Theory of Money', *Economy and Society*, 36 (1), 134–158.
Bryan D. and Rafferty M. 'A Time and a Place for Everything: Foundations of Commodity Money' in this volume.
Callon, M. and Law, J. (2005) 'On Qualculation, Agency, and Otherness', *Environment and Planning D: Society and Space*, 23 (5), 717–733.
Cochoy, F. (2002) *Une Sociologie du Packaging ou l'Âne de Buridan Face au Marché* (Paris: Presses Universitaires de France).
Fantacci L. 'What Kind of Calculation Is Implied in the Money Rate of Interest?' in this volume.
Hardt, M. and Negri, A. (2000) *Empire* (Cambridge, MA: Harvard University Press).
Hardt, M. and Negri, A. (2004) *Multitude: War and Democracy in the Age of Empire* (New York: Penguin).
Heidegger, M. (1996) *The Principle of Reason* (trans. Reginald Lilly) (Bloomington, IL and Indianapolis, IN: Indiana University Press).
Loughlin, M. (1993) 'The Illusion of Quality', *Health Care Analysis* 1 (1), 69–73.
Morley, L. (2003) *Quality and Power in Higher Education* (Maidenhead: Open University Press).
Negri, A. (1999) *Value and Affect* (trans. M. Hardt) *boundary 2*, 26 (2), 77–88.
Negri, A. (2003) *A Time for Revolution* (London: Continuum).
Negri A. (2008) *Empire and Beyond* (trans. Ed Emery) (Cambridge: Polity).
Perulli, P. (2000) *La città delle reti. Forme di governo nel postfordismo* (Torino: Bollati Boringhieri).
Power, M. (2004) 'Counting, Control and Calculation: Reflections on Measuring and Management', *Human Relations*, 57 (6), 765–783.
Stiglitz, J. E., Sen, A. and Fitoussi, J. P. (2009) *Report by the Commission on the Measurement of Economic Performance and Social Progress*. Web site for the Report (English version): http://www.stiglitz-sen-fitoussi.fr/documents/rapport_anglais.pdf, accesssed 16 july 2010.

Strathern, M. (2000) 'The Tyranny of Transparency', *British Educational Research Journal*, 26 (3), 309–321.

Toms, S. (2008) '"Immeasurability": A Critique of Hardt and Negri', Paper for Presentation at the Conference of Practical Criticism in the Managerial Social Sciences, Leicester University Management School, 15–17 January.

Vormbusch, U. (2008) 'Talking Numbers – Governing Immaterial Labour', *Economic Sociology_the European Electronic Newsletter*, 10 (1), 8–11. Website: http://econsoc.mpifg.de/archive/econ_soc_10-1.pdf, accessed 19 july 2010.

8
Repressed Futures: Financial Derivatives' Theological Unconscious

Bill Maurer

Variously-positioned scholars make big claims for financial derivatives.[1] This essay does not refute the claims so much as point to their moral and epistemological unconscious.[2] Derivatives are a particular kind of tradable contract. Their trade value is tied to the value of other assets, historically bulk commodities but also corporate shares and currencies. The most familiar derivative contracts are futures contracts, forward contracts and option contracts. A simple options contract, for example, is a contract to sell a commodity at the market price at the moment of the contract's origination within a specified time period in the future. If the market price of the underlying commodity goes up during the term of the contract, the value of the contract decreases, since the owner would then have the essentially worthless right to sell the commodity at a price lower than market price. If the market price of the underlying commodity goes down during the term of the contract, the value of the contract increases, since the contract would specify a price higher than the market price and the owner could still make a profit despite lower current market prices. Derivatives can thus function as a hedge against risk or a form of insurance against market fluctuations. They can also be traded in secondary markets, disconnected from plans to actually purchase the commodities from which their value derives, and thus can be tools for speculation. A trader might purchase 'futures' in a particular commodity with no intention of ever using the contract to buy the commodity itself, but rather to speculate on the commodity's price fluctuations: betting, for example, that market prices will increase, thereby increasing the value of the derivative on the secondary market.

Max Weber's 1896 essay on the stock exchange lingered over the concern that derivative contracts encouraged speculation and increased market instability. But he also argued that while 'speculators who lack both judgement and capital' might, with access to derivatives trading, succumb to an 'increased temptation to gamble', derivatives nevertheless allowed a 'widening of the market', a democratization of it, that he felt was of 'positive importance for the national economy' (Weber 1978, pp. 375–376).[3] Indeed, the stock exchange was a weapon in 'the relentless and ineluctable economic struggle for national existence and economic power' (p. 377) among nations. Without overarching international agreements to abolish derivative trading, doing so in one country, or 'unilateral disarmament' (ibid.) – in the interests of quelling speculation or promoting what Weber mockingly termed 'ethical culture' (ibid.) – would be economic suicide.

The discursive connection Weber forged between derivatives trading and the sovereignty of the national economy resonates in late-twentieth-century fears about markets and money. Many view the global shift away from Keynesian models of state-based economic development and toward neoliberal models of 'free' markets as trumping the sovereignty of nation-states to set economic policy and fulfil their obligations to their citizens. Given some very high-profile scandals and losses associated with derivatives trading – one aspect of global financial liberalization – many name derivatives themselves as the culprit in eroding state sovereignty. The most prominent exponent of this idea on the world stage is probably Malaysian prime minister Mohammad Mahathir, who blamed the Asian currency crisis of 1998 on derivatives traders and currency speculators.

> Neoliberal promoters, for their part, portray derivatives as mere technique. They may be a complicated technique – such that derivatives traders have been labelled 'rocket scientists' (Jorion 1995) – but still, to neoliberals, derivatives are simply instruments. For example, the *Economist* opines that derivatives are simply another financial and managerial tool which financiers and managers need to use properly. True, some of those instruments are too powerful for inexperienced or unsupervised hands. Their innards can sometimes be complicated. But then the same could be said for a motor car, and few people would advance that as an argument for more traffic lights. (quoted in Tickell 2000, p. 89)

As Adam Tickell argues in an insightful article about derivatives and the regulatory challenge of financial liberalization, the *Economist*'s analogy is a bad one, since global derivatives trading potentially threatens not just single institutions or even countries, but rather the entire global financial network (Tickell 2000). A wild driver might take out a few pedestrians, but is unlikely to demolish the entire interstate highway system. However, this version of the story of derivatives – derivatives as technique, and technique as a closed black box, under the bonnet of the car, as it were – seems in need of analysis.

Critical writings also leave the black box of technique closed, while assuming derivatives to *index* something else. Such writings generally take as their starting point the phenomenal increase in derivatives trading worldwide since the 1980s, and the increasingly explosive effects such trading seems to have had.[4] For example, scholars argue that derivatives index (i) contingent articulations of politics and economics (Tickell 2000); (ii) the valorization of a culture of risk-taking (Green 2000); (iii) an increased rationalization and socialization of risk that produces a new monetary imaginary (Pryke and Allen 2000); (iv) a semiotic shift that abolishes the myth of anteriority, which is the presumed basis of numerical and linguistic referentiality (Rotman 1987); (v) a near-total separation of exchange from production in 'speculative tournaments' built on 'meta-fetishization' and a competitive ethos (Appadurai 1986).[5]

I borrow the term 'index' from linguistic anthropology (via the nineteenth-century American pragmatist, Charles S. Peirce), which makes a distinction between *referential* terms and *indexical* terms. Referential terms are words that refer to things. Indexical terms are words that refer to the aspect, or truth-value, or spatio-temporal co-ordinates of the things that other words refer to, such as 'that' or 'here' (Silverstein 1976, p. 25). Critical writing on derivatives often elides the distinction between referentiality and indexicality precisely because derivatives themselves call into question the referentialist categories of language. Consider Brian Rotman's (1987) discussion of derivatives at the end of his account of the semiotics of zero. The figure zero, Rotman argues, unsettles the metaphysical claim that 'things' precede the 'signs' humans create to account for them. This referentialist logic is belied, in the domain of number, by zero's non-referentiality. Zero is a sign (of 'nothing'). In that capacity, however, it is a sign about signs, indicating the absence of the other signs that belong to its sign system. Thus, zero is also a meta-sign that indexes the potentiality of enumeration, the whole sign-system of number and the subject who counts. It is the meta-sign, and not the presence of countable 'things', that enables enumeration.

Rotman carries his account of zero through the development of the algebraic variable, the vanishing point in perspectival art and imaginary money – money redeemable only for another copy of itself instead of gold or silver (see also Shell 1982). This self-referential character of imaginary money, Rotman argues, is taken to another level in contemporary currency trading that relies on derivatives. Futures in currencies concoct the *medium* of exchange – money – as a *good* to be exchanged. In doing so, they disrupt money's presumed ability simply to index the 'value' of exchangeable goods and services. There is no distinction between the prior things and the signs that represent things, a referentialist paradox that becomes even more pronounced when money's current value, its signifying capacity, is determined by its potential future states: when currency derivatives dependent on future expectations and values determine present configurations of value, risk and profit. The 'scandal'[6] of imaginary money in the nineteenth century was that it could be increased by fiat without backing by inconvertible specie such as gold or silver. It created itself out of nothing. The 'scandal' of what Rotman calls 'xenomoney', or money concocted by derivative instruments of the late twentieth and early twenty-first century, 'is the fact that it is a sign which creates itself out of the future':

> any particular future state of money when it arrives will not be something 'objective', a referent waiting out there, determined by 'real' trade forces, but will have been brought into being by the very money-market activity designed to predict its value. The strategies provided by options and futures for speculation and insurance against money loss caused by volatility of exchange and interest rates become an inextricable part of what determines those rates. (Rotman 1987, p. 96)

The myths of anteriority and referentiality – that there are things prior to the signs that represent them – are revealed in their irrevocable loss, their utter deconstruction.

Rotman's analysis, however, depends on precisely the referentialist metaphysics he debunks. In a telling passage, Rotman effects a separation of the 'real' from the 'semiotic' that rests on his bracketing of the mathematics of derivatives, the technique, in order for him to make claims about derivatives' own indexicality, their pointing toward a semiotic shift in signs and meta-signs. 'A realistic description of the workings' of phenomena of contemporary international finance, he writes, 'lies far outside the scope of this book' (Rotman 1987, p. 88). Indeed, 'the phenomena themselves...are operationally simple' (ibid.). For Rotman, who is 'interested in identifying changes in money as a *sign, only their semiotic characteristics* need by explicated' (ibid., emphasis added). Leaving aside the operational aspects, leaving out 'description' of technique itself in favor of 'semiotics', conjures a world of 'real' practices and 'signifying' practices. It permits the false separation of description from interpretation and explanation. Rotman, in leaving the 'phenomena themselves' inside a black box, represses the 'real(istic)' and at the same time grants it an inordinate amount of power to destabilize his own analysis and the sign systems that form his object.

Consider also Stephen Green's (2000) account of the culture of modern risk in contemporary finance. Green is not interested in semiotic aspects of derivatives so much as 'cultural' and 'intersubjective' aspects. To disrupt standard economic narratives, Green wants to get "beneath" the formal architecture of finance to the ideational and cultural principals [sic] which are constitutive of the modern financial order' (Green 2000, p. 77). He is interested in the ways participants in modern financial markets are socialized into valorizing certain kinds of risk-taking, and focuses on the 'highly intersubjective and reflexive' nature of financial markets that prevents them from 'being completely comprehended by risk calculations' (p. 87). Like Rotman, Green brackets the mathematical technique of risk calculation itself. As he puts it, 'I take a step back from the amazing array of mathematical energy, institutional resources, and technological weaponry currently deployed to "manage" risk and ask the question of how and why "risk" itself is constructed as the central co-ordinating social mechanism for financial actors' (p.78). Taking such a step back, however, leaves the mathematical energy and technological weaponry (calculators and computers) as somehow beyond culture, beyond the intersubjective arena that interests Green, reinstating the same referentialist fallacy that Rotman falls into: the distinction between certain 'real' practices – here, mathematical and technological – that are beyond interpretation, and 'cultural' or 'intersubjective' practices.

Finally, consider Michael Pryke and John Allen's (2000) essay on money's 'new imaginary'. Pryke and Allen reflect on Rotman's observations about money's futurity and its loss of anteriority. They argue that derivatives call forth a new kind of 'monetized time-space [that] presuppose[s] a particular rationalization of money and risk' (p. 265). Money's new imaginary involves a monetization and quantification of time-space, rendering the future 'calculable' (following Simmel 1990, p. 270). The new monetary imaginary is spatial, too, for derivative instruments make present economic returns dependent not just on the future, but on the 'future performance of distant spaces' – as, for instance,

when a pensioner's income is determined in part by 'Japanese inflation rates and general economic performance in twelve months' time'
(p. 273). Like Rotman and Green, Pryke and Allen bracket the mathematical technique of calculating that future performance of distant
spaces. They admit that 'the judgement about the pricing of the future
is supposedly based on a financial model' but insist upon '*[l]eaving to
one side the intricacies of the model*' (p. 272, emphasis added).[7] Flagging
with the word 'supposedly' the important point that the mathematical
model does not necessarily actually price the future, Pryke and Allen
later in their essay still fall into the referentialist fallacy by accepting
the 'apparent transformation of the randomness of distant events into
the near-to-hand statistical, intensive, "accelerated transport" of information' (p. 281, reference omitted). That apparent transformation into
close-to-hand statistical information occurs through mathematical
techniques that Rotman, Green, and Pryke and Allen all 'lay outside',
'take a step back from' and 'leave to one side of' their analytical focus.

My main argument in this paper is that derivatives can take on the
indexical power they do in critical and neoliberal accounts only if their
operational, mathematical technique is left in the black box, shut away,
bracketed or repressed. I am not making a mathematical claim that the
technique actually functions the way some might say it does – that it
actually determines the price of a derivative contract. I am also not
making a social claim that derivatives traders even use the mathematical technique when they price derivatives. They might not. Rather, I am
claiming that, regardless of the mathematical technique's use or efficacy, its being 'left aside' allows it to maintain a very privileged status
in any account of contemporary derivatives. I am further arguing that
its repression, exclusion, bracketing from analytical and neoliberal scrutiny does a certain kind of work that allows derivatives to take on their
putative stability as financial *entities*[8] and also to take on the peculiar
indexical power with which they have been invested, especially since the
1980s and 1990s as they have become more visible and more important
to world financial markets – the power to point toward big changes
afoot, to the aspect, state or truth-value of other phenomena. As we
know from Freud, that which we repress always comes back to haunt us.
I will argue that derivatives' indexical power in critical and neoliberal
accounts alike is a symptom of the trauma that led to the repression of
mathematical technique from discussions of derivatives.[9]

The Freudian conception of trauma holds that a founding act of
violence or an 'originary wound', while covered over in its immediate
occurrence, returns as a symptom. And it does so repeatedly, playing out

the dynamics of subject-constitution that the originary trauma permitted, reiterating them and thus stabilizing them – to the extent that traumatic repetition could be called 'stable' – in regular symptomologies. In *Moses and Monotheism*, Freud provided the following illustration:

> It may happen that someone gets away, apparently unharmed, from the spot where he has suffered a shocking accident, for instance a train collision. In the course of the following weeks, however, he develops a series of grave psychical and motor symptoms, which can be ascribed only to his shock or whatever else happened at the time of the accident. He has developed a 'traumatic neurosis'. (Freud 1939, p. 84)

What might be the founding traumatic event that causes the repression of the mathematical technique for derivatives? What follows is a partial attempt to answer this question. It involves opening up the black box of the mathematical technique, and listening to number without forcing it to refer to anything other than itself. Like Freud, I will argue that the founding trauma here institutes a theology. Specifically, I will show that the founding trauma is the separation of religion from the technical procedures of mathematics, the stochastic models that give form to derivatives trading. Derivatives' indexical power is a symptom of this trauma of separation, and the symptomology, like the images in dreams, an unconscious misrecognition. In addition, each of the sections that follow begins with a quotation from the business and popular press. These quotations, presented in chronological order and headed by the titles of the articles in which they appeared, document the rise and spectacular fall of Long Term Capital Management, a venture based on derivatives trading founded by two of the men central to the development of the mathematical technique behind it. Taken on their own, these titles and quotations chart their own theology, a casuistry of and for the divine, and provide a glimpse perhaps of the founding trauma underlying it.

The Black-Scholes Formula and efficient markets theory

Formula for Success

The chaps behind the formula [Myron Scholes, Fischer Black and Robert Merton] hit upon it on an autumn afternoon in 1969...It took them four years and several rejections to get their formula published. Today, every MBA candidate is taught the formula. Any joint projects between [Scholes and Black] in the works? 'Not while we're at Goldman and Salomon, I suppose,' laughs Black. (Kripalani 1991, p. 203)

In 1973, Myron Scholes and Fischer Black published a formula for the pricing of options in the *Journal of Political Economy* (Black and Scholes 1973). The formula was developed with the assistance of Robert Merton.[10] It fostered a tremendous expansion of the options market, because it seemed to allow a sure method for options pricing and an investment strategy based on using options to hedge against risk. Prior to the Black-Scholes formula, options pricing relied on a combination of broker experience and guesswork. The advent of the formula allowed traders to compare the price of stocks on the market with the predictions of the Black-Scholes model as they developed their investment and risk-hedging strategies, so that options trading could become a win-win situation. As the Federal Reserve Bank of St Louis put it in an article aimed at corporate managers, 'Knowing the trading strategy means that the model is not only someone's best guess; it is also possible to profit if the model is wrong. If the model price is lower than the price in the economy, we can sell the option, [and] pocket the excess over the model price...If the model price is higher than the price in the economy, we follow the hedging strategy in reverse.' In other words 'buying or selling the option and following either the trading strategy or the reverse of the trading strategy will make money'! (Dybvig and Marshall 1997).

The Black-Scholes formula is based on formulas from particle physics, and although that fact is not mentioned in the original Black and Scholes publication, it became fodder for the business press and the textbooks that teach the formula to armies of MBA students (e.g., Hull 1993). The formula is a partial differential equation for dealing with random processes. It is virtually identical to those used in physics for understanding Brownian motion, the random behaviour of small particles bumping against each other in a solution or a gas, and the subject of one of Einstein's earliest papers (Einstein 1926). Intriguingly, the model of Brownian motion created by Einstein was anticipated in a 1900 dissertation about options pricing, written by Louis Bachelier (1900). There is no evidence that Einstein or any other physicist or mathematician read Bachelier's work, although Bachelier himself seemed to think his model would apply to some problems in physics (Dimand 1993). This convergence is itself symptomatic of the trauma I am attempting to sketch out: that someone interested in the foundational building blocks of the universe and someone interested in, of all things, finance, would hit on the same mathematical formula to model their objects.

The analogy between stock prices and particles in Brownian motion requires two key assumptions. The first is an assumption about randomness, or stochastic processes. As Black and Scholes put it in their original article, assuming 'ideal conditions' in the market, 'The stock price follows a random walk in continuous time with a variance rate proportional to the square of the stock price. Thus the distribution of positive stock prices at the end of any finite interval is log-normal. The variance rate of the return on the stock is constant' (Black and Scholes 1973, p. 640). The outcome of randomness of stock prices and particle motion, in other words, is a regular distribution – plot prices or particle positions as points, take the log of the points on the curve, and you get a classic normal-distribution bell curve, given enough time and enough points in the universe.

It follows that a key variable for predicting the position of a particle or the price of a stock after a specified interval of time $t+n$ is the position of the particle or the price of the stock at time t. In other words, because the distribution of stock prices is log-normal at time $t+n$, all you need in order to predict the probability of a price rising or falling is the position or price at time t. Since an option is a bet against the future price of a stock, then, the key to determining the value of an option is the price of the stock at time t and the temporal interval to time $t+1$. As Black and Scholes wrote, 'the value of the option will depend only on the price of the stock and time and on variables that are taken to be known constants' (ibid. p. 641).

The second assumption is about the market. In order for the model to work, we need to know that the price at time t is the 'correct' price. This went unstated in Black and Scholes's original paper but was elaborated by Scholes in a later lecture. Today's stock price cannot be the result of, say, an accountant's irresponsible fib or a government's interventionist inflation of a particular industry's assets. The market must be 'efficient' in that it is allowed to operate without constraint, and trading must be free and fair, so that 'the best estimate of the value of a security is today's price' (Scholes 1998, p. 352). Bachelier, in 1900, summarized this: 'At a given instance, the market believes in neither a rise nor a fall of true prices...Clearly the price considered most likely by the market is the current true price: if the market judged otherwise, it would quote not this price, but another price higher or lower' (Bachelier 1900, p. 26).

Stochastic processes and the weight of divine argument

Dream Team: John Meriwether's Brain Trust Made Billions at Salomon. Can They Do It On Their Own?

[John Meriwether has] hired experts in mathematics, computer science, economics and stock trading [namely, Myron Scholes and Robert Merton,] in the hopes that his [new] company will become a leader in computer-assisted bond trading. (Spiro 1994, p. 50)

The Black-Scholes formula, as a probability function, is a product of what Philip Mirowski has termed the 'probabilistic counter-revolution' in neoclassical economic theory (Mirowski 1989a). Mirowski has traced the rise of probability theory in economics to a repudiation of strictly determinist models and an elaboration of statistical procedures designed to deal with real-world numbers and to 'eventually achieve numerical results' (Schumpeter 1954, p. 962). Stochastic procedures were a key component in the twentieth-century transformation of neoclassical economics.

Such procedures entered into economics as the discipline tracked changes in physics for its own model-building. In a quest to achieve scientific status, economics in the late nineteenth and early twentieth centuries borrowed heavily from deterministic energy concepts in physics (Mirowski 1989b). By the 1920s, however, physics itself turned toward probabilistic models via the new field of quantum mechanics. Economics at first was reluctant to abandon determinism. But 'by the 1930s, any culturally literate layperson could not turn around without bumping into some denunciation of determinism and praise of stochastic concepts' (Mirowski 1989a, p. 219). As Eddington wrote of physics in 1935, in a particularly rich passage:

[Classical determinism] was the gold standard in the vaults; [statistical laws were] the paper currency actually used. But everyone still adhered to the traditional view that paper currency needs to be backed by gold. As physics progressed the occasions when the gold was actually produced became rarer until they ceased altogether. Then it occurred to some of us to question whether there still was a hoard of gold in the vaults or whether its existence was a mythical tradition. The dramatic ending of the story would be that the vaults were opened and found to be empty. The actual ending is not quite so simple. It turns out that the key has been lost, and no one can say for certain whether there is any gold in the vaults or not. But I think it is clear that, with either termination, present-day physics is *off the gold standard.* (Eddington 1935, p. 81, in Mirowski 1989a, p. 219, italics in original)

Neoclassical economics was wedded to a vision of utility as potential energy and a vision of explanation as causal and deterministic. It could not escape mechanistic models without abandoning stasis assumptions and without adopting time series data. The new field of econometrics imported stochastic models from the new physics, and began the task of not merely explaining the mechanisms of the economy, but forecasting economic processes (Mirowski 1989a).

What did it mean for physics – and later, economics – to go 'off the gold standard'? It meant, up to a point, an embrace of indeterminacy and an anti-necessitarian world view. But only up to a point: neither Einstein nor the econometricians abandoned realism, embraced radical contingency, or deconstructed referentiality.[11] The introduction of temporal variables explicit in stochastic problems did not cause either field to leave causality by the wayside. Physical and economic entities were held to 'have a continuous, objective, observer-independent existence', and the introduction of temporality meant 'event-by-event causality' – x happens because a_1, then z happens because a_2, then y happens because a_3 – and a commitment to 'locality', or the idea that the variables effecting a process are not separated from the process by great distances of space or time (Cushing 1998, p. 352). In sum, then, the variables introduced through a recognition of stochastic processes were assumed (i) to be real variables in the world; (ii) to be located at a particular point in space and (iii) to be moving along a temporal trajectory. The fact that variables were assumed to be real variables in the world also meant a very particular and traumatic reading of probability theory. The normal distribution 'bell curve' had to be taken as a real reflection of the characteristics of nature, whether that nature be physical, social, biological or informatic.

Abraham de Moivre (1733), the early eighteenth-century inventor of the bell curve, devised his model to account for errors of measurement – for instance, one can measure a desk 100 times and use the model to mitigate against errors in order to obtain a reasonably accurate measurement (Langley 1971). The purpose of the normal distribution model, for de Moivre, was akin to the hypothetical desk-measuring problem. De Moivre was interested in the distribution of 'error'. He had a particular kind of error in mind, believing that in modelling errors in 'nature' he would be 'determining the frequency of irregularities from the Original

Design of the Deity' (Pearson 1924, p. 404). Furthermore, against the charge that his book – made up almost entirely of examples drawn from gambling and games of chance – would encourage 'play', de Moivre wrote that 'so far from encouraging Play', the book was 'rather a Guard against it' (de Moivre 1733, 'Dedication'). His 'doctrine of chances', de Moivre believed, would lead people away from their belief in 'Luck' and toward an appreciation of God: 'the Doctrine of Chances may likewise be a help to cure a Kind of Superstition, which has been of long standing in the World, viz. that there is in Play such a thing as Luck, good or bad' (p. iii). He continued, 'we may learn, in ma[n]y Cases, how to distinguish between Events which are the effect of Chance, from those which are produced by Design' (p. v). And in de Moivre's conviction, Design always wins any bets placed against Chance.

After de Moivre, the normal distribution curve was also found sometimes to describe patterns of natural variation. It soon became used to predict and explain natural variation. In a quick survey of introductory college statistics textbooks, I found that some were careful to stress the distinction and to warn the short-cut-seeking undergraduate against throwing out data points from an experiment simply to produce the coveted bell curve. Most, however, especially most of the more recent books, were not. At a general level the model has become a fetish, used merely to describe and reflect real-world variables, rather than as a model helpful for predicting or explaining them for the purposes of a particular argument. The fetishization of the model is particularly apparent in Black-Scholes.

Consider a variable in stochastic econometrics as an arrow shot from an archer's bow with the winds influencing its trajectory – stable entities whose motion is affected by local forces inflecting their movement through space over time. The word stochastic derives from the Greek *stokhastes*, meaning archer, but also diviner; *stochos* refers to an archer's target, but also a stable state or equilibrium. The etymology of the term stochastic recalls the connection in the history of ideas between games of chance and divination. Florence Nightengale David (1962), in her *Games, Gods and Gambling*, even argues that gambling may have been the first human invention (see Hacking 1975, p. 1).[12] Yet while all cultures seem to use randomizers like tali, dice, chicken innards and so forth to read the intentions of the gods and to gamble against the gods' plans for the future, nevertheless '*theories* of frequency, betting, randomness and probability appear only recently' (Hacking 1975, p. 2, emphasis added). Rather than speculating on this apparent lack, I follow Ian Hacking, who interrogates the 'preconditions for the emergence of probability' which, in turn, 'determined the space of possible theories about probability' (ibid. p. 9).[13]

The family of words derived from the Latin *probabilis* originally had no connection to the concept of randomness. That connection emerged in the 1600s. Previously, 'probable' meant something like 'worthy of approbation' – a 'probable doctor' was a 'medical man who could be trusted' (Hacking 1975, p. 18). It is not until the ascendance of mathematical concepts of probability that the link between probability and approval transmuted into something else.

This is not to suggest, however, that the older conception of probability is of no relevance here. Far from it. That conception figured centrally in religious debates over the status of knowledge and opinion. The probable, where opinion was concerned, derived from the position of the person offering it. For Aquinas, for instance, probability did not refer to something supported by 'evidence', but rather something approved of or accepted by 'intelligent people' (ibid. p. 22) – an 'opinion commended by authorities', one which may in fact be incorrect but is still, by this definition, probable (ibid. p. 22–23). Opinion in this sense was not knowledge, for knowledge had to do with universal truths beyond accepted opinion, and was therefore not part of the domain of medieval probability. Instead, opinion had to do with degrees of belief based on the weight of an argument. Since opinion occupied a different epistemological and moral space from that of knowledge, then, what about opinion?

Medieval opinion depended upon the citing of authority, and theologians' debates centred on which authorities to rely on and when to rely on certain authorities as opposed to others. Suffice to say, 'evidence' did not have a place in these decisions. For the Jesuits, authority derived from a process of weighing the moral consequences of following one or another authoritative opinion. For the Jansenists, authority derived from scripture and natural reason alone. The Jansenists won the theological debate, and Blaise Pascal's *Provincial Letters* represented an attack on the casuistry of the Jesuits and a defence of natural reason (ibid. p. 25). What was the nature of this 'natural reason'?

One of Hacking's chief contributions is to demonstrate that the medieval conception of opinion and probability derived not from medieval 'high sciences' like physics, but the 'low sciences' such as alchemy. In a world where the authority of theologians was no longer a valid source for opinion, but where one had to rely on scripture and one's natural reason, natural reason had to look for 'signs' of nature to gauge the probable. The notion of the sign here derived from alchemical conceptions of the universe, a universe authored, animated and marked by the Author of Nature with signs of resemblance so that Man may come to know God's mind (G. Colliern.d.). Medieval alchemists relied on the testimony of things, not people, to arrive at their conclusions about the order of the cosmos. Things testified to each other through relations of similitude – a liver-shaped leaf must bear some relationship to the liver in the body, for instance (Foucault 1973; Hacking 1975, p. 44). Hacking shows how similitude concocts 'evidence' as a new sort of object about which new knowledges may be made possible. These are knowledges of probability, not in the sense of weight of argument but in the sense of the inductive evidence of things. Arguments were still probable based on the authorities backing them, but the authorities now were the signs of nature which, more often than not, guaranteed at least the semblance of correct predictions about observable phenomena. Alchemists were a small step away from the notion of probabilistic knowledge derived from statistical frequencies based on the evidence of the world.

In Hacking's account, the dual nature of probability – weight of argument or degrees of belief on the one hand, and processes productive of stable long-term statistical frequencies on the other – was stitched together to form modern conceptions of probability in the work of Blaise Pascal in the late 1600s. Pascal's 'wager' in favour of acting as if God existed depended on the weight-of-argument epistemological side of the coin. His correspondence with Fermat, on how to divide the stakes in a game of chance that has been interrupted before its completion, depended on the aleatory, chance-dependent side of the problem. On the epistemological side, Pascal was concerned with the nature of God, who may or may not exist. On the stochastic or aleatory side, Pascal was concerned with the God of Nature, who has placed signs in the world and set the world into motion along a temporal trajectory with a Beginning and an End. Hacking's achievement is to show that, despite the ascendance of the stochastic side of probability after Pascal, the epistemological side remains, albeit often hidden, repressed.[14] Contemporary probability is thus a moral argument. The argument now involves the traumatic sundering of the stochastic from the epistemological process, and the repression of the latter.

Efficient markets, equilibrium and the fall of man

The Right Option: The Nobel Prize for Economics

Economists may sometimes seem about as useful as a chocolate teapot, but as this year's Nobel Prize for economics shows, it isn't always so. On October 14th, the \$1m prize was awarded to two Americans, Robert Merton, of Harvard University, and Myron Scholes, of Stanford University [Fischer Black having died since the development of the formula in 1973]. Their prize-winning work involves precisely the sort of mind-boggling mathematical formulae that usually cause non-economists either to snooze or scream. That is too bad, for it ranks among the most useful work that economics has produced. (*Economist* 1997, p. 75)

The stochastic move in economics did not count among its adherents some of the era's most prominent figures. John Maynard Keynes, and after him Joan Robinson, fervently argued against the statistical conception of probability and in favour of the epistemological conception. Robinson cleverly articulated the logical errors of neoclassical economics' marriage to stochastic probability theory, and also delightfully exposed its repressed theological underpinnings.

Robinson voiced exasperation with one of the fundamental tenets of efficient markets theory: the principle of equilibrium. This tenet is today perhaps the most commonsensical of all economic theories. It simply states that price tends toward the equilibrium of supply and demand. Robinson is short and devastating: equilibrium theory in economics 'uses a metaphor based on space to explain a process which takes place in time' (Robinson 1953, p. 255). Consider a pendulum swinging back and forth: over time, it will achieve equilibrium and stop moving. Robinson writes, 'If you give your bodies time, they actually do get into equilibrium. Time will help you with space' (ibid. p. 256). Economic processes such as the relationship between supply and demand, however, unfold over time, and the purported equilibrium point toward which things are 'tending' is a projected point of time in the future and not, as with a pendulum, a resting place in space. 'Take as much space as you like,' Robinson notes: '– how is that going to help you with time' (ibid.)?

Equilibrium theory fails, for Robinson, because it fails to take account of the role of the past and the future in phenomena of the present. It is the wrong tool for the job, for the job demands good arguments, not collections of 'facts'. In the *Treatise on Probability*, Keynes argued that probability was about the weight of arguments, not statistical frequencies (Keynes 1921, Maurer 2002). It appeared to him that before even attempting to assess frequencies of phenomena in the world, one needed to know, in a literal sense, what one was talking about. The argument was about logic and language. Economistic conclusions in equilibrium models, for Keynes, ignored the temporal contingency of social life and thus had less 'weight' than conclusions based on epistemological probabilistic claims. As Rotheim points out, 'words such as tendency, if used in an equilibrium framework, only have meaning if the concept of equilibrium exists, *a priori*. One cannot move in time when the language emanates from an equilibrium system, because in the latter we start with an equilibrium, define the appropriate premise structure, and then rest assured that we will return to the equilibrium unscathed' (Rotheim 1988, p. 98). He continues

> When we more into a framework of time, we start with the premises and move forward as we interact along the way causing us to change our premises and change our path. The two thought processes reflect different, incompatible language structures; between those based on atomistic systems where probabilistic statements are valid, and those which are organic, where uncertainty prevails, and where knowledge of the real, social world evolves in an interactionist configuration. (Rotheim 1988, p. 98)

Robinson, inimitably, states this same point more directly, in a passage that is worth quoting at length:

> Never talk about a system *getting into* equilibrium, for equilibrium has no meaning unless you are in it already. By think of a system *being* in equilibrium and having been there as far back as Adam and you find it useful to go:
>
> Fall of Man   → E
>
> so that every *ex ante* expectation about today ever held in the past is being fulfilled today. And the *ex ante* expectation today is that the future will be like the past. (Robinson 1953, p. 262)

Contingencies of fact and value

Crony Capitalism

Alan Greenspan patted himself on the back before the Senate Budget Committee on September 23, declaring the successful creation of 'a very efficient and very effective global economic financial system' with derivatives under careful control of banks. Greenspan might as well have been smashing a champagne bottle over the prow of the Titanic as it slid down the ramp into the harbor. Only hours later the New York Fed was orchestrating the $3.65 billion bailout of Long-Term Capital Management, the Greenwich, Connecticut-based hedge fund started by Nobel Prize-winners [Myron Scholes and Robert Merton] and star traders. LTCM's portfolio was estimated in the *New York Times* as having been worth $1.25 trillion some weeks ago – or more than China's annual economic output. (*Nation* 1998, p. 3)

I am arguing, essentially, that the separation of stochastic probability and epistemological probability was a traumatic event, and that the repressed epistemological side returns to haunt contemporary accounts of financial derivatives. When critical analysts of derivatives 'leave to one side' the black box of the mathematical model, the repressed returns in terms of a symptomology that grants derivatives indexical power, the power to point toward and refer to the truth-value of some other phenomena. Truth-value becomes a positive statement about the empirical world, not a moral statement within a language game. This is a misrecognition of the model's power as a moral argument. The model is a deontology of the way things 'ought' to be, not an ontology of the way things 'are'.

Probability theory, emerging from the 'low' sciences, came into being around a particular problem about the status of knowledge and opinion – the problem of the existence and nature of God. The fetishization of the normal distribution curve makes a certain sense in this context. If it is taken as a prediction and explanation of reality, it reveals an order to the signs of nature, the writing animating the universe. Even the 'errors', the outcome of chance events, fall into the familiar bell-shaped pattern and thereby prove divine Design ('In the Beginning was the Normal Distribution ...'). The fetishization of equilibrium in economics makes the same kind of sense. Joan Robinson's point is that equilibrium is theology, an assumption about totality together with the hubris to deny that that totality is unattainable. M. Ali Khan makes much the same argument, in his re-reading of Samuelson's reflections on economics as language. Equilibrium in economics 'does not correspond to any object that it itself has not already projected through its tropes' (Khan 1993, p. 795), yet it is taken for granted as a telos and a 'tendency' (compare MacKenzie 2001).

The awkward relationship between games of chance and monotheistic conceptions of divinity also begins to make sense. Divination techniques based on randomizers are equivalent in form to gambling, the only difference being intention: casting lots = playing craps, with the minor inflection that in craps you are betting against God, not merely trying to deduce his intentions. It is in this sense that the stochastic side of the coin is also inseparable from religion, and contemporary invocations of Lady Luck in Las Vegas and grain futures on the Chicago Mercantile Exchange are merely variations on the character of the unknowable. Stochastic models are bad at doing what they're supposed to do: they do not really help us deal with radical contingency – the flow of temporality unwritten by divine hand, the accident of luck non-personified. The fetishization of the bell curve and equilibrium supposedly renders predictable the unpredictable, but just as often fails. If it were successful, statisticians would have had no need of the concept of the 'outlier', and undergraduate statistics students would not be tempted to fudge their data.

The same issue of the *Journal of Political Economy* in which Black and Scholes's options pricing formula appeared contains an obituary and several short, commemorative essays for the economist Frank Knight. Best known for his book *Risk, Uncertainty and Profit* (1921) which clearly laid out the distinction and relationship between quantifiable and epistemological probability, Knight also authored a lesser-known work, *Liberalism and Christianity* (1945). The latter, published together with an essay by Thornton Merriam, is a defence of liberalism. It is also a defence of the epistemological conception of probability. 'Recognizing that truth is a value means recognizing that it is a social category,' he wrote. 'Truth is known, tested, and practically speaking defined, by agreement in some community of discourse' (Knight 1945, p. 49). Furthermore, 'real problems of fact are problems of the worth of evidence' – Knight considered the use of 'utilitarian application of positive science' to be 'the worst form of original sin, rationally defined' (ibid.). He concluded his essay with a strong statement against methodological individualism (p. 101). As noted in his obituary, Knight believed that 'a multiplicity of principles and conceptual frameworks are necessary if we are to know much about human society and hence of ourselves as the "social animal"; and it was accordingly necessary to surmount what he saw as a sort of original sin – the human propensity to be simpleminded' (Wick 1973, p. 514). As Knight himself put it, 'The position we have to combat seems to rest on the inference, characteristically drawn by the "best minds" of our race, that since natural objects are not like men, men must be like natural objects' (ibid). One might also state that the position we have to combat rests on the inference that the things 'men' make – like contracts and stock markets – must be like natural objects, and even that natural objects must be like the models of natural objects in positive science, models that rest on a repression of the moral contingencies of the human.

Conclusion: derivatives' unconscious and the traumatic separation of God from number

The Unbearable Lightness of Finance

Academic financial economists, unsurprisingly, still stand up for the science. Rene Stulz, who edits the profession's top research publication, the *Journal of Finance*, says, in a new book he is writing, that LTCM's only impact will be as 'a nice case study'. Most academics hint that LTCM's downfall had nothing to do with the financial models of [Myron Scholes and Robert Merton,] the two Nobel laureates (an argument that rather irks those Wall Street firms persuaded to invest in the hedge fund precisely because it was using their models). (*Economist* 1998, p. 83)

The separation of stochastic from epistemological probability, like the separation of facts from interpretations, things from signs, history from memory, is a moral problematic. It is foundational in Western world-makings that delineate sacred and profane, and animate liberalism and secularism by separating and excluding the religious even as they depend on the religious (see Asad 1993). Indeed, if we view the separation of stochastic from epistemological probability as a traumatic event in the Freudian sense, then the very metapragmatics of statistics hinges upon the reiteration of practices of purification that render number referential, and things prior to numbers (see Latour 1992, Daston 1994, Poovey 1998). Yet the deontological character of number, number as moral argument, asserts itself in its return as statistical 'power'. Cathy Caruth is instructive on this point: 'The experience of trauma, the fact of latency, would ... seem to consist, not in the forgetting of a reality that can hence never be fully known, but in an inherent latency within the experience itself. The historical power of the trauma is not just that the experience is repeated after its forgetting, but that it is only in and through its inherent forgetting that it is first experienced at all' (Caruth 1991, p. 187).

Furthermore, I am not merely suggesting that mathematical procedure, as Caruth says of history, 'is always a matter of distortion, a filtering of the original event through the fictions of traumatic repression, which makes the event available at best indirectly' (Caruth 1991, p. 185). Rather, attending to the founding and impossible separation of fact from value compels knowledge to confront its limit. What is knowable, here following Caruth's reading of Kant, is not knowledge of objects as such, things-in-themselves, but knowledge's *relation* to its objects.[15] 'To know [philosophy's] limits is to know that its knowledge of an object is always relational, a relation between the object and itself' (Ibid. p. 19). Yet even Caruth's conception of knowledge is inadequate to our object here, for, as Marilyn Strathern has argued, the very notion of *relation* was 'directly enabling of the kind of secular inquiry fuelled by the Enlightenment conviction that the world (nature) is open to scrutiny. For relations are produced through the very activity of understanding when that understanding has to be produced from within, that is, from within the compass of the human mind and without reference to divinity' (Strathern n.d., p. 14). We are left in a place where subjects, objects and relations deconstruct in the wake of the decomposition of fact and sign, anteriority and referentiality. This poses a problem not just for our objects but for any forms of knowing that would be adequate to them.

The idea of the fact 'before' it becomes enumerated and entered into the statistical formula demands the traumatic separation of words from things, deracinated particulars from moral commitments and the repression of that separation – or, better, the reterritorialization of that repression into the familiar (Western, bourgeois) separation of subjects from objects and into the commodity form, the form of the fact, the neatly purified world of words and things to which they refer (Deleuze and Guattari 1983). Hence my equivocation at the beginning of this essay over whether derivatives are subjects or objects. And hence my worry over whether they index anything at all. The mathematical black boxes of financial derivatives are a moral argument. Bringing the repressed to consciousness will not necessarily get rid of the symptom, the repeatedly-enacted desire to grant to statistical reason all the powers of argument. But it may give us other grounds to transform the weight of that argument.

Notes

This chapter is a slightly modified version of an article originally appeared in Economy and Society 31(1):15–36, 2002.

A very early (and rather remarkably different) version of this paper was presented at the 1999 annual meetings of the American Anthropological Association. I would like to thank Nicholas Blomley, Tom Boellstorff, Saba

Mahmood, Richard Perry, Elizabeth A. Povinelli, Annelise Riles and Katherine Verdery for their comments on that paper. I am especially grateful to Hiro Miyazaki for an incredibly close and critical reading, as well as for the suggestion of some key sources. I am also thankful for having the chance to discuss some of the ideas developed here with Roger Lee, Susan M. Roberts, Richard Schein and Adrian Smith. Research has been supported by the Program in Global Peace and Conflict Studies at the University of California at Irvine, and National Science Foundation grant SES – 9818258, Law and Social Sciences Program, 'Alternative Globalizations: Community and Conflict in New Cultures of Finance'. Writing was supported by the Department of Anthropology at the Research School of Pacific and Asian Studies and by the Centre for Women's Studies, both at the Australian National University. Any errors or inconsistencies are my responsibility alone.

1. Derivatives have cropped up in critical social scientific accounts of the breakdown of the Bretton Woods system of capital controls and fixed exchange rates (Cerny 1994, Helleiner 1994), the rise of 'flexible' modes of accumulation (Harvey 1989), the increasing dominance of exchange over production (Appadurai 1986), new monetary imaginaries and new forms of identification (Pryke and Allen 2000, Allen and Pryke 1999) and the emergence of mechanisms of governance modelled on insurance (see, e.g. O'Malley 2000, Rose 1996). For the purposes of this paper, I lump together futures and options, for they seem to function in the same manner in the discursive dynamics I examine here.

2. In the interests of full disclosure, I first became interested in derivatives pricing formulas in the course of research on Islamic banking and finance – a worldwide effort to create financial products that avoid interest and speculation, deemed religiously unacceptable in Islam. While the permissibility of derivatives from an Islamic standpoint is a topic of great debate (see Kamali 1996, 1997, 1998, Maurer 2001), some Islamic financiers employ derivatives pricing formulas in a manner that makes explicit their moral problematic. They use them to determine the proportion of a mutual fund's return that is derived from interest or interest-based activities. That amount can then be filtered out and given to charity, thus 'purifying' the fund. Using the formula this way belies its putative referentiality altogether.

3. Contrast this to John Maynard Keynes's famous assertion that the democratization of the stock market would be potentially disastrous: 'It is usually agreed that casinos should, in the public interest, be inaccessible and expensive. And perhaps the same is true of Stock Exchanges' (Keynes 1936, p. 159).

4. The Bank for International Settlements values the total volume of outstanding derivative contracts at the end of June, 1999, at US$98.7 trillion, or, as Donald MacKenzie notes, $16,000 for every man, woman and child on the planet (MacKenzie 2001, p. 122).

5. These accounts, interestingly, often run parallel to the social studies of finance literature or ethnographies of finance that study the behaviours and baggage of market participants (e.g. Abolafia 1996, Hertz 1996). These studies of finance do open the field's black boxes by exposing the networks of relations and institutions that make markets. Often, however, they do so by pointing to other forces or features 'outside' the financial

realm that structure financial markets, rather than attempting an endog-enous critique of the techniques involved in market trades. In this, they take a step initiated by actor network theory but do not necessarily carry it through to the knowledge-objects of finance like the mathematical for-mulas discussed in this paper. On these points, see Callon 1998 and Latour 1999. What makes MacKenzie's (2001) contribution unique is his attempt to bridge these disciplinary and methodological divides; it is fascinating, in terms of the emerging history of (inter-)disciplinarity for finance studies, that his paper appears in the journal of the Society for Social Studies of *Science*.

6. All quotations here are from Rotman 1987, p. 96.
7. Similarly, in their fascinating essay on Simmel and Deleuze, Allen and Pryke also invoke derivatives and also neglect their technique: 'it is not the instru-ments so much that are of concern to us here as the ideas about what they may facilitate and what different groups of people in locations distant from one another imagine themselves to be involved in' (1999, p. 52).
8. I use 'entity' instead of 'subject' or 'object' to avoid opening a particular can of worms just now; I come back to this at the end of the essay.
9. I see a convergence between my own approach in terms of traumatic repres-sion, and that of MacKenzie (2001) in his brilliant paper on the Black-Scholes formula and what he calls 'S-terms' in finance. Both of our approaches mean to highlight the problems of knowledge and referentiality in financial forms. By S-terms, MacKenzie refers to 'social-kind terms' that operate as performative speech acts and work to create what they name through posi-tive feedback loops. He demonstrates that it was the Black-Scholes formula itself that conjured forth a world after its own image, rather than naming a naturally-occurring world of finance 'out there' in advance of the formula-tion. MacKenzie is leaning on Barnes 1983 and Austin 1962, the latter of which also influences the linguistic anthropology I draw on here. I would like to thank Hiro Miyazaki for drawing my attention to MacKenzie's impor-tant paper, the only critical analysis of derivatives I have seen that actually attends in a sustained fashion to the problem of mathematical technique.
10. MacKenzie (2001) provides a rich social history of the formula's creation and effects.
11. One could compare the stochastic revolution in physics at the beginning of the twentieth century to Rotman's 'imaginary money' in the late nine-teenth century, when currencies went off the gold standard. Rotman's 'xeno-money' would then map onto more recent theories in physics, such as Bell's Theorem. Bell's Theorem essentially states that you can't have it both ways: you cannot maintain a commitment to locality and keep realism. The local-ity postulate only held when physicists assumed the existence of 'hidden variables'. Bell demonstrated that a statistical account of those hidden vari-ables was impossible (Cushing 1998, p. 325). Derivative pricing techniques, like Bell's Theorem, abandon locality. At the same time, however, they hold to a certain (theological) vision of statistical power, as I demonstrate below, and thus don't quite do away with necessitarianism and empiricism to the extent Bell might have endorsed.
12. On stochastic thinking in the Bible and the Talmud, see Sheynin 1998 – although I remain sceptical of his conclusions because he fails to differentiate

the use of randomizers like lots or tali from the development of models of random processes.
13. The following argument leans heavily on Hacking, and I refer the interested reader to his *The Emergence of Probability* and other writings for an account of the history of probability theory more nuanced than I can offer here.
14. Moivre and Bayse, and not just Pascal, developed probability theories around the question of the existence of God.
15. Elizabeth Mertz points out to me that it would be a mistake to fall into the false choice of adopting the relativity of vision, on the one hand, or the fixed points of a presumably 'shared' vision of a collectivity, on the other. Rather, she suggests an analytical strategy involving a 'calculus of relationship and effect' (Mertz, personal communication, 2001) in any attempt to bring trauma into the domain of the thinkable.

References

Abolafia, M. Y. (1996) *Making Markets: Opportunism and Restraint on Wall Street* (Cambridge, MA: Harvard University Press).
Allen, John and Pryke, Michael (1999) 'Money Cultures after Georg Simmel: Mobility, Movement, and Identity', *Environment and Planning D: Society and Space*, 17, 51–68.
Appadurai, Arjun (1986) 'Introduction: Commodities and the Politics of Value', in A. Appadurai (ed.) *The Social Life of Things* (Cambridge: Cambridge University Press), pp. 3–63.
Asad, Talal (1993) *Genealogies of Religion: Discipline and Reasons of Power in Christianity and Islam* (Baltimore, MD: Johns Hopkins University Press).
Austin, J. L. (1962) *How to Do Things with Words* (Oxford: Clarendon Press).
Bachelier, Louis (1900) 'Théorie de la spéculation', *Annales de l'Ecole Normale Supérieure*, 3ème série, 17, 22–86.
Barnes, B. (1983) 'Social Life as Bootstrapped Induction', *Sociology*, 17, 524–545.
Black, Fischer and Scholes, Myron (1973) 'The Pricing of Options and Corporate Liabilities', *Journal of Political Economy*, 81 (3), 637–654.
Callon, Michel (ed.) (1998) *The Laws of the Markets* (Oxford: Blackwell).
Caruth, Cathy (1991) 'Unclaimed Experience: Trauma and the Possibility of History', *Yale French Studies*, 79, 181–192.
Cerny, Philip (1994) 'The Dynamics of Financial Globalization: Technology, Market Structure, and Policy Response', *Policy Sciences*, 27, 319–342.
Collier, George (n.d.) 'Aboriginal Sin in the Garden of Eden', Unpublished Ms., *Department of Cultural and Social Anthropology*, Stanford University.
Cushing, James T. (1998) *Philosophical Concepts in Physics* (Cambridge: Cambridge University Press).
Daston, Lorraine (1994) 'Marvelous Facts and Miraculous Evidence in Early Modern Europe', in James Chandler, Arnold Davidson and Harry Harootunian (eds) *Questions of Evidence: Proof, Practice and Persuasion across the Disciplines* (Chicago: University of Chicago Press), pp. 243–274.
David, Florence Nightengale (1962) *Games, Gods and Gambling: The Origins and History of Probability and Statistical Ideas from the Earliest Times to the Newtonian Era* (New York: Hafner Publishing).

Deleuze, Gilles and Guattari, Félix (1983) *The Anti-Oedipus: Capitalism and Schizophrenia* (Minneapolis: University of Minnesota Press).

Dimand, R. W. (1993) 'The Case of Brownian Motion: A Note on Bachelier's Contribution', *British Journal for the History of Science*, 26 (89), 233–234.

Dybvig, Philip and Marshall, William (1997) 'The New Risk Management: The Good, the Bad, and the Ugly', *Federal Reserve Board of St. Louis Review*, 79 (6), 9–21.

Economist (1997) 'Finance and Economics: The Right Option: The Nobel Prize for Economics', The *Economist*, 345 (8039), 18 October 1997, p. 75.

Economist (1998) 'Finance and Economics: The Unbearable Lightness of Finance', The *Economist*, 349 (8097), 5 December 1998, p. 83.

Eddington, A. S. (1935) *The Nature of the Physical World* (New York: Macmillan).

Einstein, Albert (1926) *Investigations on the Theory of the Brownian Movement* (London: Methuen).

Foucault, Michel (1973) *The Order of Things: An Archaeology of the Human Sciences* (New York: Vintage Books).

Freud, Sigmund (1939) *Moses and Monotheism* (London: Hogarth Press).

Green, Stephen (2000) 'Negotiating with the Future: The Culture of Modern Risk in Global Financial Markets', *Environment and Planning D: Society and Space*, 18, 77–89.

Hacking, Ian (1975) *The Emergence of Probability* (Cambridge: Cambridge University Press).

Harvey, David (1989) *The Condition of Postmodernity* (Oxford: Basil Blackwell).

Helleiner, Eric (1994) *States and the Emergence of Global Finance* (Ithaca, NY: Cornell University Press).

Hertz, Ellen (1996) *The Trading Crowd: An Ethnography of the Shanghai Stock Exchange* (Cambridge: Cambridge University Press).

Hull, John (1993) *Options, Futures and Other Derivative Securities*, 2nd edn (Englewood Cliffs, NJ: Prentice Hall).

Jorion, Philippe (1995) *Big Bets Gone Bad: Derivatives and Bankruptcy in Orange County* (San Diego, CA: Academic Press).

Kamali, Mohammad Hashim (1996) 'Islamic Commercial Law: An Analysis of Futures', *American Journal of Islamic Social Sciences*, 13, 197–225.

Kamali, Mohammad Hashim (1997) 'Islamic Commercial Law: An Analysis of Options', *American Journal of Islamic Social Sciences*, 14, 17–39.

Kamali, Mohammad Hashim (1998) 'Prospects for an Islamic Derivatives Market in Malaysia', *Thunderbird International Business Review*, 41 (4, 5), 523–540.

Keynes, John Maynard (1921) *Treatise on Probability, Collected Writings of John Maynard Keynes*, vol. 8 (London: Macmillan).

Keynes, John Maynard (1936) *The General Theory of Employment, Interest and Money* (New York: Harcourt Brace).

Khan, M. Ali (1993) 'The Irony in/of Economic Theory', *Modern Language Notes*, 108 (4), 759–803.

Knight, Frank Hyneman (1921) *Risk, Uncertainty and Profit* (New York: Houghton Mifflin Company).

Knight, Frank Hyneman (1945) 'Liberalism and Christianity', in Frank Knight and Thornton W. Merriam (eds) *The Economic Order and Religion* (New York: Harper & Brothers).

Kripalani, Manjeet (1991) 'Formula for Success', *Forbes*, 148 (10), 28 October 1991, p. 202.

Langley, Russell (1971) *Practical Statistics for Non-Mathematical People* (New York: Drake Publishers).

Latour, Bruno (1992) *We Have Never Been Modern* (Cambridge, MA: Harvard University Press).

Latour, Bruno (1999) 'On Recalling ANT', in J. Law and J. Hassard (eds) *Actor Network Theory and After* (Oxford: Blackwell), pp. 15–25.

MacKenzie, Donald (2001) 'Physics and Finance: S-Terms and Modern Finance as a Topic for Science Studies', *Science, Technology and Human Values*, 26 (2), 115–144.

Maurer, Bill (2002) 'Redecorating the International Economy: Keynes, Grant, and the Queering of Bretton Woods', in A. Cruz-Malave and M. Manalansan (eds) *Queer Globalizations: Citizenship and the Afterlife of Colonialism* (New York: New York University Press), pp. 100–133.

Maurer, Bill (2001) 'Engineering an Islamic Future', *Anthropology Today*, 17 (1), 8–11.

Mirowski, Philip (1989a) 'The Probabilistic Counter-Revolution, or How Stochastic Concepts Came to Neoclassical Economic Theory', *Oxford Economic Papers*, 41, 217–235.

Mirowski, Philip (1989b) *More Heat than Light: Economics as Social Physics, Physics as Nature's Economics* (Cambridge: Cambridge University Press).

Moivre, Abraham de (1733) *The Doctrine of Chances, or, a Method of Calculating the Probabilities of Events in Play* (New York: Chelsea Publishing Company, reprint of the 1756 edition, 1967).

Nation (1998) 'Crony Capitalism', *The Nation*, 267 (12), 19 October 1998, p. 3.

O'Malley, Pat (2000) 'Uncertain Subjects: Risks, Liberalism and Contract', *Economy and Society*, 29 (4), 460–484.

Pearson, Karl (1924) 'Historical Note on the Origin of the Normal Curve of Errors', *Biometrika*, 16, 402–404.

Poovey, Mary (1998) *A History of the Modern Fact: Problems of Knowledge in the Sciences of Wealth and Society* (Chicago: University of Chicago Press).

Pryke, Michael and Allen, John (2000) 'Monetized Time-space: Derivatives – Money's "New Imaginary"?', *Economy and Society*, 29 (2), 264–284.

Robinson, Joan (1953) 'Lecture Delivered at Oxford by a Cambridge Economist', in Joan Robinson (ed.) *Collected Economic Papers*, vol. 4 (Oxford: Basil Blackwell), 1973, pp. 254–263.

Rose, Nikolas (1996) 'The Death of the Social? Re-Figuring the Territory of Government', *Economy and Society*, 25 (3), 327–356.

Rotheim, Roy J. (1988) 'Keynes and the Language of Probability and Uncertainty', *Journal of Post-Keynesian Economics*, 11 (1), 82–99.

Rotman, Brian (1987) *Signifying Nothing: The Semiotics of Zero* (Stanford: Stanford University Press).

Scholes, Myron (1998) 'Derivatives in a Dynamic Environment', *American Economic Review*, 88 (3), 350–370.

Schumpeter, Joseph A. (1954) *A History of Economic Analysis* (New York: Oxford University Press).

Shell, Marc (1982) *Money, Language and Thought: Literary and Philosophical Economies from the Medieval to the Modern Era* (Berkeley: University of California Press).

Sheynin, Oskar (1998) 'Stochastic Thinking in the Bible and the Talmud', *Annals of Science* 55 (2), 185–198.

Silverstein, Michael (1976) 'Shifters, Linguistic Categories, and Cultural Description', in Keith Basso and Henry Selby (eds) *Meaning in Anthropology* (Albuquerque: University of New Mexico Press), pp. 11–55.

Simmel, Georg (1990) *The Philosophy of Money* (London: Routledge).

Spiro, Leah Nathans (1994) 'Dream Team: John Meriwether's Brain Trust Made Billions at Salomon. Can They Do It on Their Own?', *Business Week*, 29 August 1994, pp. 1, 50.

Strathern, Marilyn (n.d.) 'Emergent Properties', Unpublished Ms., Department of Anthropology, University of Cambridge.

Tickell, Adam (2000) 'Dangerous Derivatives: Controlling and Creating Risks in International Money', *Geoforum*, 31, 87–99.

Weber, Max (1978) 'The Stock Exchange', in W. G. Runciman (ed.) *Max Weber: Selections in Translation* (Cambridge: Cambridge University Press), pp. 374–377.

Wick, Warner (1973) 'Frank Knight, Philosopher at Large', *Journal of Political Economy*, 81 (3), 513–515.

9
Representing and Modelling: The Case of Portfolio Management

Herbert Kalthoff and Uwe Vormbusch

Introduction

So far, financial sociology has observed only certain areas of financial markets empirically and made them accessible. In particular, these areas have the following characteristics: orientation towards traders; speed due to technically developed long-distance communications, providing simultaneous availability of information; and the formation of financial market practices based on mathematical models. This paper attempts to widen the sociological perspective on financial markets, and to describe other financial market practices.

The practice we will analyze empirically is *portfolio management*, involving the investments in funds of private or institutional investors. Depending on the customer, funds can be either *mutual* or *restricted*. Restricted funds are set out for one or more investors according to their specific requirements.

Portfolio management is a specific segment of the financial market, and has several particularities. It differs from the sectors of the financial market which have been at the centre of financial sociologists' attention until now, in a number of ways:

(a) A first difference is the temporal structure of decision-making and information procurement. As is generally known, for example, currency traders make deals within seconds based on the volatility of the market. Decisions made within seconds are rare in the area of portfolio management. Here, time is needed to prepare decisions, maintain information and develop products, in order for a personal portfolio to be constructed. Time pressure develops in another way: decisions do not need to be made quickly or in rapid sequence, but many firms and markets must be observed simultaneously and their movements reviewed regarding their significance for the portfolio. Thus, in the area of fund management, temporality is not intense due to a rapid sequence of events, but intense due to parallel processes which must occur simultaneously and which are presented on a spreadsheet.

(b) While currency traders focus on the third or fourth position after the decimal point (Zaloom 2003), portfolio managers see a price change as an occasion to ask Goffman's question: 'What is it that's going on here?' The answer leads to a decision about an investment. Thus, a portfolio manager is concerned with the development of the value of firms (through analysis of their fundamental data) and the anticipation of the price development of stocks (by considering market events, rumours, macrodevelopment, and so on).

(c) Fund management is an area that is client- and product-oriented. The acquisition of clients, the development of products and marketing are as important as for consumer markets. The analysis of portfolio management offers an intriguing contrast with the currency trade, thereby confronting financial sociologists with theoretical challenges. The first part of this paper will describe the theoretical perspectives of portfolio management, and the second part will present the empirical findings of our research.

Portfolio theories

In 1990 Harry Markowitz, Merton Miller and William Sharpe received the Nobel Prize in economics. This called public attention to the so-called modern portfolio theory (Mertens 2004) – the basis of which Markowitz and Roy had developed in the 1950s. The novel aspect of Markowitz's approach was the theoretical inclusion of the 'risk' dimension and the appropriation of a formula which made this risk quantifiable within the selection process of assets (Spremann 2006, pp. 52–55). Markowitz's work on portfolio theory greatly influenced the development of modern financial mathematics and its application in practical fields (Wang and Xia 2002). These theories from the 1950s and 1960s still form the basis of a common language for financial markets.

Markowitz's portfolio theory

The *Portfolio Selection Model* of Markowitz is based on the empirical observation that financial actors invest in a variety of values (Markowitz 1952). Such a diversification only makes sense if criteria other than the projected yield are considered when planning an investment strategy. If the focus were only on the projected yield, the logical consequence would be an investment in a single asset – the one with the highest yield probability.

However, this was confirmed by Markowitz' empirical observations. Thus, he assumed that the investment behavior of an investor was not based on a monovariable, goal-oriented function and he analysed the configuration of portfolios using two indicators: the yield (μ) and the risk (σ). The assumption was that individual actors find their personal equilibrium between the maximally expected yield and the minimally taken risk. This leads to their individual investment decision (Wang and Xia 2002).

The central concept of Markowitz' model is the 'efficient portfolio', meaning that according to the desired expected yield, one chooses the portfolio with the least risk. An investor with some readiness to accept risk will thus pick the portfolio with the highest expected yield. The term *μ-σ-efficiency* denotes this behaviour. The total of μ-σ-efficient portfolios forms the so-called 'efficient frontier'. The model does not attempt to describe the individual preferences of every single investor, because this is difficult to determine given the diversity of individual emphasis on yield and risk. Nonetheless, the investors' selections are – in this model – limited to portfolios that are on the efficient frontier (Wang and Xia 2002, p. 3, Steiner and Bruns 2002, p. 9).

Wang and Xia (2002, p. 22) observe that despite the continuing development of portfolio theory, certain problems have so far not been solved satisfactorily. Among these are transaction costs, the observation of numerous periods, incomplete information and the measurement of the influence of other factors, such as financial restrictions, changing interest rates and the relevant capital structure. Therefore, the development and optimization of theoretical models remains a clear task for economists, or for economic theory in general.

However, there have been and still are problems which impede a smooth application of portfolio management *à la* Markowitz. For example, to apply the model, investors would have to analyse every possible combination of accounts in order to find the most efficient portfolio.

To construct a portfolio from a variable number (n) of bonds, the following steps would be necessary:

- Estimation of the expected yield of every bond;
- Estimation of the variances of the bonds as well as the co-variances between the bonds;
- Decision to choose the most efficient of all possible portfolios.

In order to implement these steps, a large amount of data and estimated values are necessary. However, this data is often historical, incomplete and biased. Thus, portfolio management is systematically confronted with a lack of knowledge.

Capital Asset Pricing Model (CAPM)

The CAPM, developed by Sharpe (1963), is based on the insights of portfolio theory. The CAPM supplies an exact prognosis regarding the risk and expected yield of an investment. The main problem for the CAPM (which has a wider perspective than portfolio theory) is the expected yield of a portfolio within capital market equilibrium if – in addition to investments with risks – there is a possibility of investing without risk. The answer is found graphically in the so-called 'capital market line' (Fabozzi et al. 2006, pp. 34–37). By contrast, the 'security market line' shows the price of a security in the portfolio within the capital market equilibrium, and the risk that must be assumed for such a security (Fabozzi et al. 2006, pp. 211–212).

The CAPM is the simplest and earliest form of a *general equilibrium model* which derives from portfolio theory, and it provides a model for the construction of an ideal portfolio. The CAPM is based on a number of assumptions, including the divisibility of investments, complete competition and the homogeneous expectations of investors (Elton et al. 2003, pp. 292–293).

The validity of the model has not been confirmed or repudiated despite countless empirical studies. Nonetheless, the CAPM is the best-known explicative model for the connection between yield expectations and the risk of securities. Firstly, the model describes the *trade-off* between yield and risk; secondly, it provides performance measurement of investment fund results (Steiner and Bruns 2002, pp. 29–30).

The problems that arise when using the CAPM are similar to those that arose in connection with the theory put forward by Markowitz: The future values of yields and risks cannot be projected exactly, so must be estimated according to historical values. But the Black/Scholes model is far better to work with because it is based on two parameters that are easy to estimate and calculate: risk-free interest rates, and volatility (MacKenzie 2003). Here no calculation or estimation of the average rate of return is necessary. And it is exactly the calculation of these average rates that poses a major problem for mathematical modelling. As Fama and French (2004) have shown, the model has never been explicitly confirmed or discredited.

Notwithstanding these conceptual difficulties, Markowitz's model and CAPM both play a decisive role in everyday portfolio management decisions. In conformity with the hypothesis of efficient markets, all information is available and mirrors the respective prices of different assets. This assumption leads to the conclusion that false appraisals are non-existent. Thus, it is impossible through purposeful selection of assets to gain higher returns than the market allows. This causes some investors to follow a so-called 'passive portfolio management strategy' by trying to emulate the assumedly efficient market in one's own portfolio (Zimmermann 2006, Jones 1988). According to this strategy, the market is a very efficient portfolio: no portfolio can offer a higher yield with the same expected risk, and no portfolio with the same expected yield can offer fewer risks.

Active portfolio management repudiates the 'efficient market hypothesis': 'In active management, it is assumed that markets are not fully efficient and that a fund manager can outperform standard indices by using specific information, knowledge, and experience' (Fabozzi et al. 2006, p. 104). Accordingly, the selection of assets underestimated by the market, combined with adept buying and selling, can provide a return that is higher than the average market yield.

The use of numbers and calculation in portfolio management

So far, we have offered a basic sketch of existing economic theory regarding portfolio management. Now we present and discuss the findings of our own empirical research. We have carried out 16 qualitative interviews with fund managers, asset managers and an executive director of distribution, as well as ethnographic fieldwork.[1] Portfolio managers usually have a cubicle in an open-plan office arranged according to the asset classes they administer. Within the bank investment teams are grouped according to asset classes, typically, the investment team pensions, the investment team European bonds, and so on.

The general working climate is comparable to that on trading floors, and the informal communication between the portfolio managers plays an important role in shaping opinions about formulas, investments and market development.

We consider the investment practices of the financial market actors as 'epistemic practices'. These practices are embedded within a knowledge structure which uses historically variable and field-specific representative formats and media. Just like a particular representative format – a graph, table or timeline – the investment portfolio combines the thinking and acting patterns of the financial market actors in a paradigmatic way. In a way it is the central tool of financial market capitalism, which portfolio managers use to see what is happening on the financial market, and also to decide and act in response. The portfolio is an instrument of market construction through observation, as it simultaneously makes possible particular patterns of action: comparisons, analyses, or selection processes. The construction and use of portfolios shows that it is not only self-referential reproduction of payment processes that constitutes markets, but also structured forms of reciprocal observation and self-observation.

The modern financial market could not exist without the work carried out on investment portfolios, and the analytical concepts and instruments used for this work. From the perspective of capital market theory, as well as from the perspective of everyday investments, the portfolio delineates the central problem: maximizing yield, whilst minimizing risk and volatility for all the investments made.[2] Below we present two essential aspects of using numbers in the field of portfolio management: the epistemic status of numerical knowledge, and the variety of investment styles for constructing portfolios.

On the constructivity of numbers

Since investment decisions are based on systematic implementation of numbers, evaluating the quality of the data is a paramount task. Within this context, it is especially important for portfolio managers to observe the interface between one's own data and 'off-site' data, meaning the evaluation of incoming data compiled by analysts, information services such as Bloomberg, or subscription databases such as CSFB HOLT or FactSheet. It is especially problematic that portfolio managers do not have any control over the production and aggregation of this data, nor do they have reliable *technical* instruments for evaluating it. Instead, the evaluation of the data is based on the social capital of its producers, and on the trust portfolio managers' distinct styles of working with the data.

Data is the foundation for all formal modelling processes. The answers given regarding the quality of the data input, in the context of its use in quantitative investment models, are remarkably consistent. Several portfolio managers characterize the data input as 'merely subjective'. According to a portfolio manager who represents the approach of fundamental analysis, the 'data input for the models used are mere subjective estimates. ... Every assumption made with the DCF-model is a prognosis, an estimate'. From his point of view, however, the quality of the data input has continually decreased both *empirically* and *historically*:

> We do not get the numbers from companies. Basically, it is becoming increasingly difficult to gather reasonable information from the companies about their future. We are only given a rough sketch – there is no chance to get numbers for the five coming years. (Interview Fund Manager)

The constructivity of data is a problem that does not only pertain to incoming data. A general problem is the reproduction and/or amplification of incorrect original data during the processing. One portfolio manager explains:

> This led to the fact that the macrodata used for the model was incorrect. Everything was wrong. Garbage in, garbage out – that is our central problem. (Interview Folio Manager)

A solution to this problem could be to apply the resulting evaluation models 'in a more pragmatic way, that is, not as rigorously'. According to this approach, and somewhat paradoxically, higher accuracy for the model's results is achievable through a less precise implementation of the formal calculation model. However, this opinion – which is widespread among the portfolio managers interviewed – obviously does not solve the basic problem, but is rather a strategy of 'satisficing rationality' (March and Simon 1958, p. 141), which responds to rationality deficits in the decision-making process by lowering the expectations of rationality.

In other cases, there is an implicit separation between internal data and off-site data. This separation comes from voiced distrust regarding databases that 'are based on the subjective expectations of external analysts' (portfolio manager). That is to say that the often schematic reaction to off-site data depending on the implemented models allows for neither reflection on the context in which the data was developed nor rejection of data-conforming decisions in favour of 'softer information' on the basis of other significant factors (such as a rising oil price). Nonetheless, there are practical time limits and information restrictions which impede more viable alternatives for processing decontextualized data.

In addition to the quality of the data input and the formal models themselves, however, financial market actors are critical of investment decisions exclusively based on numerical data. In their view, those decisions are 'underdetermined' because other market dimensions have to be taken into account. Thus, investment decisions are based not only on numerical data but also on additional information, distinct investment styles and the social capital of other market actors. There are no prescriptive rules for how to get from numbers to decisions; individual methods of analysing the market prevail:

> We have a lot of freedom regarding the way we work. Everyone has their own system of spreadsheets, everyone considers different numbers important.
>
> Almost all of the fund managers interviewed have had negative experiences concerning the resilience of data compiled by companies for their compulsory publicity activites. Problems can arise in abundance: from the resilience of management prognoses to the allegation of manipulated data. (Kalthoff 2005)

Nonetheless, the fund managers must continue to observe the companies in question – on the one hand 'because things can change rapidly in that area' and on the other hand because 'we cannot uncover the fraud ourselves'. The incapacity to control the development of the data which forms the basis for investment decisions can lead to a fatalistic view. For example, a fund manager explains: 'I just use the numbers that are communicated by the companies'.

Another fund manager had a similar view on manipulated data. He was 'not very worried' about the problem:

> The numbers published by companies are entered into the spreadsheets as they are, even though I know that there is the possibility to manipulate them. I pretend that the numbers are true. (Interview Fund Manager)

That means that the fund manager temporarily brackets the correctness of numbers and thereby pragmatically eliminating the need to recalculate and double-check them. Another strategy to deal with these 'far-fetched facts' (Rottenburg 2009) consists of checking economic representations (e.g., numerical data) for consistency. This is done by

comparing data in their temporal order. However, the companies themselves often change their data to influence the comparability of their
representation. For example, one portfolio manager double-checked all
the published company data to 'uncover the possible manipulations'.
Yet he has discontinued this method because the introduction of international measures (International Financial Reporting Standards) has
given companies 'too many manipulation possibilities':

> If you take a simple model such as the DCF-Modell and concern your-
> self with it, then you will see how you can represent any opinion you
> might have using this model. (Interview Fund Manager)

For this portfolio manager, the discounted cash flow model does not
represent an 'external' reality resulting from the model, but rather something which was invisible before, namely certain opinions and attitudes
of interested actors. By determining certain contingent parameters for
the model, decisions can by manipulated. Thus, on the one hand, economic calculation does not represent economic life in a neutral and
objective way, and on the other hand it indicates alternative choices in
a specific way. The proviso of manipulation is not only valid to the use
of numbers, but also to other formats of representation. A fund manager comments thus on the practices of his colleagues:

> In their presentations, the analysts only show the charts that confirm their
> opinion. It would be easy to find charts which repudiate their opinion.
> These charts and images are simply ignored. (Interview Fund Manager)

We interpret this as evidence of the portfolio manager's predominantly
post-objectivist, rather than objective, understanding of calculative
practices despite the simultaneous *constitution* of the financial market
through a 'landslide of numbers' (Hacking 1983) or formal representations and models (Vormbusch 2008). Because of this, the numbers
are handled *pragmatically*: they are not treated as 'real' in the sense
that 'true' numbers are; they are not taken for granted as representatives of an external reality. Instead, their legitimacy arises from their
use by a multitude of other relevant financial-market actors. The value
of the measurables does not depend on their concordance with the
external reference. Rather, their value is a function of their communi-
cability: their validity is achieved interactively. Even though several of
the interviewees admitted to a certain 'unease' regarding the validity
of the data, we concluded that the data was considered valid because

(and only in this specific sense) it had no individual author but was accepted and simply deemed necessary within the system of financial market communication. Given a lack of other possibilities, confidence in the data does not arise from assessment of external validity. By contrast, it is achieved by closing the system of financial market communication to external references.

The plurality of investment styles

The central goal of portfolio management is the prognosis of price movement. The actors organize this task in a variety of ways. While some banks attempt to standardize their internal procedures, others not only tolerate a heterogeneity of calculatory styles, but even support it. This heterogeneity becomes visible because the actors use an important instrument of observation (the spreadsheet) in very individual ways, and because they treat information sources differently. Some fund managers rely on the prognoses of companies; others ignore them and concentrate on the estimates of the analysts they communicate with daily. Others employ external databases and services (e.g., Reuters and Bloomberg). The exchange of information between colleagues takes place differently as well. In small investment banks there are no formal meetings, whereas in bigger banks there are morning conferences, investment sessions and similar meetings, at regular intervals.

According to our observations, portfolio construction and investment practices are determined largely by bank-specific *investment styles*. From a sociological perspective, the term 'investment style' denotes a set of individual attitudes, social practices and strategies for generating knowledge. The styles vary regarding the significance of qualitative and quantitative evaluation models, the preferences for technical or fundamental analyses and the relevance of formal models.

The statements of the portfolio managers show a correspondingly high variance with respect to practices of portfolio construction. For its fund specializing in global and European bonds, one large bank begins by 'running the numbers listed in "MSCI World" and "Emerging Markets" through a quantitative filter'. The filter criteria are a high-dividend yield, meaning the relative coverage of the dividend by the net earnings of the firm, as well as the market capitalization and the liquidity of the bond. However, the last two criteria are not imperative. In principle, it is possible to invest if liquidity and market share are actually too low, but the dividend yield is high enough. Thus, the so-called 'complete universe' (in the words of one fund manager) is at a manageable level of complexity: 'For this limited universe, we calculate *value* and *growth*'. The next step is a quantitative evaluation:

> We appraise the quality of the management, the surrounding market as well as the market position. I include values that are fundamentally good in the portfolio. All values are measured the same way in portfolio construction. (Interview Fund Manager)

It is remarkable that portfolio managers repeatedly emphasize their autonomy with regard to formalized models and computer calculations. These 'do not restrain me: I have the freedom to deviate from them'.

By contrast, the portfolio managers of an investment enterprise define their work as 'purely stock-picking'. They do not try to emulate an index or to reproduce weighting of market segments and branches of trade; instead, they look for the 'best individual securities'. The screening process for market capitalization and liquidity precedes a fundamental and 'qualitative' evaluation of factors such as management quality. The construction of a 'working universe' (portfolio manager) of – in this case – approximately 400 companies takes place on the basis of quantitative selection criteria due to the sheer number of competing investment opportunities. Within this working universe, qualitative estimates are prioritized rather than quantitative values. These estimates attempt to encompass factors such as management quality, market position and the surrounding market, as well as growth prospects. The portfolio managers consider these estimates to be 'purely judgemental', that is, subjective evaluations that are made based on their respective experience; they are not based on a systematic method.

Operating figures do not necessarily determine whether an investment is made in a company or not. However, in the case of a large insurance company discounted cashflow models are applied and free cash flow, ROC (Risk on Capital) and price/book-ratio are calculated, though the resulting operating figures do not entirely determine the final outcome of the discussion of economic choices.

In general portfolio managers keep their distance from formal models, especially regarding the possible limitation of their decision-making autonomy through the models. Firstly, they argue that models are significant for investment practices because (i) they offer only one of several parameters for decision-making, and (ii) they protect the portfolio managers from blatant errors. Thus, the models help structure decision-making situations by suggesting alternative scenarios – but the decision itself does not derive from the algorithm of the model. Secondly, the implementation of models can offer individual risk minimization similar to the implicit processes of 'isomorphy' (Meyer and Rowan 1977). If models are employed correctly, the manager can claim to have done technically sound work even without adequate results. This legitimizing function displays its full power if the model is also understandable to laypersons, such as members of the board:

> In my opinion, this model was successful because it is so simple: Any member of the board could understand it. (Portfolio manager)

To some extent, there are notable differences in expectations regarding formal models – even within a single company. Here, a fund manager distances himself from the mere implementation of formal models:

> Naturally, it [the investment company] can do it all. They have models, the whole apparatus, as I call it. [...] They look at what the models say. If the majority of the models say OK, we start discussing: Is this a false signal? Can we understand the model's results?

This quotation depicts a reflexive understanding of formal representation. From this perspective, the actors encounter a problem of attribution: What do the model's assertions represent? Are they artefacts, mere effects of internal mathematical constructions, or do they refer in a proper way to external economic relations? Knowledgeable human actors can only stabilize the knowledge the models impart through interpretation. Hence, for the practice of portfolio management the model's statements are not just triggers for decisions, but rather, the starting point for an almost economic-hermeneutic understanding which aims at social recognition in fund management.

However, this treatment of formal models is also controversial within the field of portfolio management. Several managers of German and Swiss banks stated, for example:

> We say: Forget your portfolio theories; we need to construct products that clients buy. [...] You know, we are on the battlefield. And they [in the headquarters] are technicians. They produce rockets. But if we cannot shoot with their rockets, they are useless.
>
> Sheet in, sheet out. How should we feel about that? For us, models are only a form of support. We take note of the results and discuss. [...] The investment company uses all these formal things, but we stand for the fundamental side.

I consider models useless: All the qualitative factors we just named, such as management quality etc. are not quantifiable. They lead to a picture in my mind that can not be represented in numbers.

(i) An emphasis on the significance of fundamental data for investment decisions, (ii) limits to economic models as dysfunctional instruments and (iii) unquantifiable factors of great importance for imaginative decision-making – these three issues are at odds with the accepted image of deductive portfolio management. Cumbersome models on paper are not the focus of attention.

Conclusion

This paper has been particularly concerned with heterogeneity, that is, active ways of *'doing difference'* in the economic field of portfolio management. The heterogeneity of procedures leads to a variety of expectations, calculations and results. The participants expect this to happen: they anticipate that other actors will achieve other results with other models, and that these models are in competition. The infrastructure of the calculation culture is like a toolbox with a plethora of uses. Framed by institutional procedures, the actors follow an implicit mathematical anti-realism. If correct calculation is not possible, the maintenance of compiled data provides a simulation of the market, the funds, and so on. The representation of an external referent is insignificant. Instead, generation of knowledge about relations and connections between data, models, implementation and theory is pivotal.

Portfolio management involves a number of issues which are important for the sociology of calculation and financial markets, two of which are of particular significance. Firstly, the transfer and formatting of economic practice through economic theory – the 'performance' theory put forward by Callon (1998) – is called into question by this empirical study. The basic concept of the *actor network theory*, which claims that the world of practice is shaped by the world of economic theory, is called into question. In the case of portfolio management there is no universalcodification of calculation to detail and prescribe the calculation of a value in a standardized way. The limits of formalizability are the limits of the representational practices which Daston and Galison (2007) have identified as 'mechanical objectivity'. In other words, working on a portfolio combines systematically two forms of objectivization: the methodological objectivity of models and calculation, and the social objectivity of estimation and prognostication of values.

Secondly, we are no longer concerned with calculation in the strict sense of the word. Instead, we are concerned with the simulation of events and their development. Therefore, it is unimportant whether the actors employ homogeneous codified models, or proceed idiosyncratically: either way, they simulate the characteristics and growth prospects of their portfolios within specific market surroundings, and thereby visualize possible developments that they can react to consequentially. Therefore, in this context, simulation means the visualization of invisible aspects of prospective economic tendencies, and the generation thereby of knowledge for portfolio optimization. In this sense, simulations are natural experiments in the economic laboratory of portfolio management.

Notes

The paper is based on a research project on 'Economic Calculation' funded by the German Research Association (Deutsche Forschungsgemeinschaft; KA 1235/2–2).

1. Ekaterina Svetlova, whom we would like to thank for her work, conducted some of the interviews.
2. The third dimension of the 'magic triangle' of capital market theory is the liquidity of portfolios. However, when applying the theory one assumes a perfect capital market (with no information or transaction costs), so the question of liquidity (i.e., the temporal flexibility of investments) which is significant in practice is ignored when constructing theories (Garz et al. 2004).

References

Callon, M. (1998) 'Introduction: The Embeddedness of Economic Markets in Economics', in Callon, M. (ed.) *The Laws of the Market* (Oxford and Malden, MA: Blackwell), pp. 1–57.
Daston, L. and Galison, P. (2007) *Objectivity* (New York: Zone Books).
Elton, E., Gruber, M., Brown, S. and Goetzmann, W. (2003) *Modern Portfolio Theory and Investment Analysis* (New York: Wiley).
Fabozzi, F.J., Focardi, S.M. and Kolm, P. (2006) *Financial Modeling of the Equity Market. From CAPM to Cointegration* (Hoboken, NJ: Wiley).
Fama, E. F. and French, K. R. (2004) 'The Capital Asset Pricing Model: Theory and Evidence', *Journal of Economic Perspectives*, 18 (3), 25–46.
Hacking, I. (1983) *Representing and Intervening. Introductory Topics in the Philosophy of Natural Science* (Cambridge: Cambridge University Press).
Jones, R. C. (1988) 'The Active Versus Passive Debate: Perspectives of an Active Quant', in F. J. Fabozzi (ed.) *Active Equity Portfolio Management* (New York: McGraw-Hill Publishing), pp. 37–55.
Kalthoff, H. (2005) 'Practices of Calculation. Economic Representation and Risk Management', *Theory, Culture and Society*, 22 (2), 69–97.

188   *Herbert Kalthoff and Uwe Vormbusch*

MacKenzie, D. (2003) 'An Equation and Its Worlds. Bricolage, Exemplars, Disunity and Performativity in Financial Economics', *Social Studies of Sciences*, 33, 831–868.

March, J. G. and Simon, H. A. (1958) *Organizations* (New York: Wiley).

Markowitz, H. (1952) 'Portfolio Selection', *Journal of Finance*, 7 (1), 77–91.

Mertens, D. (2004) *Portfolio-Optimierung nach Markowitz* (Frankfurt am Main: Bankenakademie Verlag).

Meyer, J. W. and B. Rowan (1977) 'Institutionalized Organizations: Formal Structure as Myth and Ceremony', *American Journal of Sociology*, 83 (2), 340–363.

Rottenburg, R. (2009) *Far-Fetched Facts. A Parable of Development Aid* (Cambridge, MA: MIT Press).

Sharpe, W. F. (1963) 'A Simplified Model for Portfolio Analysis', *Management Science*, 9, 277–293.

Spremann, K. (2006) *Portfoliomanagement* (Munich: Oldenbourg).

Steiner, M. and Bruns, C. (2002) *Wertpapiermanagement* (Stuttgart: Schaeffer-Poeschel).

Vormbusch, U. (2008) 'Talking Numbers – Governing Immaterial Labour', *Economic Sociology Newsletter*, 10 (1), 8–11.

Wang, S. and Xia, Y. (2002) *Portfolio Selection and Asset Pricing* (Berlin: Springer).

Zaloom, C. (2003) 'Ambiguous Numbers', *American Ethnologist*, 30 (2), 258–272.

Zimmermann, H. (2006) 'Martingales and Portfolio Decisions: A User's Guide', *Financial Markets and Portfolio Management*, 20 (1) 75–101.

10
Brief Encounters: Calculation and the Interaction Order of Anonymous Electronic Markets*

Alex Preda

Introduction

Calculation has emerged in the recent debates about (financial) markets to re-focus analytical attention on the processes through which trading strategies are worked out in trading rooms (e.g. Beunza and Stark 2005, p. 92). It has been tied to the concept of agency, designating the incorporation of scripts for practical actions in (formal) economic representations and technologies (e.g. Callon 2004, p. 123, Callon 2007, pp. 337–338). Calculative agency highlights the role of classification in making economic entities suitable for formalization (Callon and Muniesa 2005, p. 1231, Muniesa and Callon 2007). Markets appear thus to be 'calculative collective devices', emphasizing the common effort put by groups of market actors into reaching various degrees of consensus on value. At the same time, calculative practices highlight the institutionalization of specific rationalization procedures within organizational structures (e.g. Miller 2008, p. 53), procedures which can change organizational dynamics and the relationships between organizations and political institutions.

At least three notions of calculation are implicit in these arguments, the first being that of cognitive operations, including classification and computation. Such operations have a sequential character, are repeatable, and their outcome can be estimated and anticipated. The second notion, which includes but is not limited to the above, is that of selecting, projecting and evaluating the outcomes of market transactions. Calculations are seen as strategies involving expectations about other actors' beliefs, the evaluation of alternative courses of action, as well as criteria for choosing and implementing courses of action. Trading strategies rely on classifications, the processing of numerical data, as well as criteria and procedures for the optimization of means with respect to transaction goals (Biggart and Castanias 2001, p. 473). Finally, calculation designates the social processes through which entities are selected and transformed in such a way that they become the object of market transactions submitted to efficiency criteria. These processes create institutions – sets of rules incorporated in artefacts and organizational structures – which provide the resources for, as well as the constraints to, (financial) transactions (Miller 2001, p. 380).

From the perspective of financial transactions as live and lived interactions, then, calculations appear as strategies (or action plans) implemented in the interaction order of trading. Is the latter then something external to such plans – a setting in which plans are realized – or is it intrinsic to transactions? More generally, what is the relationship between calculation and trading interactions?

An appropriate context for examining these questions is that of anonymous, online financial markets. In some situations at least, the interaction order seems to be reduced here to a bare minimum. Lay online traders,[1] for instance, anonymously trade financial securities on electronic platforms on their own account, earning all or a considerable part of their income from online trading activities. They are not part of any organization, and are not employed in any capacity by any financial institution. Organizational habitats are part of the traders' system but not of their 'lifeworld', understood as the traders' primary reality (Habermas 1987, Schutz and Luckmann 1974, p. 35). Moreover, anonymous electronic transactions are click-and-trade, not talk-and-trade. In a certain sense, online anonymous trading seems to come close to the normative model of isolated, calculating individuals making choices based on their strategies. By studying the apparently minimal interaction order of lay online trading, we can investigate whether or not calculation consists of implementing strategies.

In the following, I examine the above questions based on ethnographic observation (including audio and video recordings) and interviews with lay online traders. I argue that calculation remains an interaction-based achievement and can be best conceptualized as a relational and situational activity. I show how lay online traders calculate trades based on at least two interaction achievements: projection of the self, and actualization of other presences in the given situation. In anonymous, online financial markets calculation does not appear to be the application of a plan or formula, or a strategy whose outcomes are checked against projected results. Building on Erving Goffman's concept of encounter, I suggest that in anonymous online markets calculation emerges from

gaming encounters that are geared toward the display of the participants' socially relevant features. It requires bodily work different from
that of face-to-face encounters. Its main prerequisites are the stabilization of the screen and the definition of specific situations. The screen
appears to be an observational instrument, as well as a portal through
which anonymous traders 'cross over' into each other's situations. Since
the display of social attributes is achieved through price variations,
among other means, this contributes to explaining the price volatility
observed in electronic markets.

Calculation, plans and the interaction order

Calculation as planned action implies that actors implement rule-based
sequences of activity which can be evaluated against criteria of efficiency. Such sequences can include establishing the objective, considering alternative courses of action, computing the likely outcomes
and enacting the outcome 'that optimizes risk and return according to
pre-determined decision criteria' (Fenton O'Creevy, Nicholson, Soane
and Willman 2005, p. 79). This division between devising a trading
plan and implementing it seems to reflect an organizational division
of labour between fund managers, for instance, who draft plans, and
traders implementing such plans under specific constraints. Planned
actions may require the use of various technologies of evaluation and
execution (e.g. charts and software programs), the application of formulas, informational inputs and data processing activities (e.g. analyses and
price data), as well as webs of relationships, exchanges and collaborative
processes (as provided, for instance, by the division of labour found on
trading floors). Organizational contexts can provide the resources for
planned actions, but they also set constraints upon them: for instance,
organization-based networks of relationships can function as the pipes
(Podolny 2001) through which information flows, while also setting
boundaries to the circulation of information.

While institutional constraints and resources (Abolafia 1996), adhe-
sion to analytical tools or styles (Smith 1999), judgement biases (Fenton
O'Creevy, Nicholson, Soane and Willman 2005, pp. 83–86), as well as
intuitive elements (Zaloom 2006, p. 136) can affect the actual courses
of trading, the planned element is nevertheless crucial. This element
concerns not only the sequentiality of trading activities (from planning
to implementation and evaluation), but also the fact that, at any given
time in the process of trading, rules and criteria can be separated from
the lived activities which embody them. Traders' *post hoc* accounts and

rationalizations could be seen as empirical evidence for this separability, assuming that such accounts would be identical with what traders actually do. The analytically-minded observer could then detach and analyse calculative elements from actual actions, and evaluate the latter against the former. Moreover, calculative elements would have to be prior to the real, live trading: while this latter may introduce modifications and adaptations, the plan would need to be recognizable as such (Suchman 1987, p. 36) and implemented by the trader.

From the perspective of the interaction order, then, trading would be situated calculation. An observer should be able to identify and describe at least three distinct phases of calculation: plan preparation, plan implementation/adaptation and evaluation. Whether such a distinction can analytically and empirically hold would require a closer examination of the interaction order of trading.

Calculation as a situational and relational activity

Financial trading is a relational activity, grounded in an orientation toward other market actors, and relying on observational technologies: computer screens, display boards and the like. These technologies shape the boundaries of the actors' zone of operation (Schutz and Luckmann 1974, pp. 36, 44). The resources of the situation, however, are not simple vehicles for a strategic activity or a plan whose definitional features remain independent of these resources (see Goffman 1983, p. 9). It is not the same whether traders receive price data on their screens, through shouting accompanied by hand signs, via a formal letter at home, or on a paper slip left under the doormat.

In online anonymous markets, the screen constitutes the trader's 'kernel of reality' (Schutz and Luckmann 1974, p. 42, Knorr Cetina and Bruegger 2002, p. 913), as a board on which anonymously posted displays (including one's own) can be observed. Observation of price data implies awareness, or selected availability, of what is being seen (Heath et al. 2002, p. 321). It is an acknowledgment and validation of the presence of other traders which, for a moment, becomes relevant. Other traders, however, are anonymous strangers, whose position is characterized both by remoteness and closeness (Simmel 1971 [1908], p. 145). They are remote not only in the spatial sense of the word, but also because of a lack of any information about their identity, interests or intentions, as well as of the absence of any personal relationships, of the kind institutional traders can develop (Knorr Cetina and Bruegger 2002, p. 941). They are close in the sense that traders must work with the assumption of basic similarities (of knowledge and interests) between them and their unseen counterparts. But they are close also because traders, in order to transact, must face unseen strangers as real. The data flickering on screens are taken as 'appresentations' (Husserl 1995, p. 112) – representation and perception fused together – of the traders displaying them. Thus, anonymous strangers have to be co-present in the trader's situation.

The acknowledgment and validation of anonymous strangers, however, cannot be based on an immediate and direct orientation to their presence. Firstly, strangers are remote and do not have a face. Secondly, they display in a fleeting manner. Thirdly, they compete for the trader's attention. The very limited range of resources displayed on the screen (price and volume data)[2] requires a trader to draw upon additional means in the process of acknowledging and validating other presences.

Such means cannot be seen as a set of universal, fixed rules, of the kind implied by the equivalence between calculation and strategy. Fixed rules would not do justice to permanently changing displays. Such rules would have to come from somewhere; neither the screen nor the (organizational) context provides them as a resource.[3] They would have to stabilize the presence of other traders as significant, even if for a moment. A plan or a formula (as part of a plan) can hardly provide this, since it cannot include *ex ante* criteria for evaluating significance. In order to do this, a plan would have to foresee not only the order in which data will flicker on to the screen, but also its value. If we understand calculation as the application of a formula (which generates data), then that formula would have to contain the criteria according to which the significance of the generated data could be evaluated. For instance, if we see calculation as the application of a formula for options prices, then this formula would have to establish the significance of theoretical prices in the same manner for every trader. A plan would have to provide omniscient anticipations of other traders' actions, anticipations which would be then embedded and adapted within the interaction order. If a plan or calculation cannot be taken as distinct from the interaction order in which it is enacted, then it would have to be intrinsic to the trader's orientation.

This orientation, however, is not *a priori* with respect to action, but established within the interaction order.[4] If such rules or plans existed at all, they would have to emerge in this order – which contradicts the presumption of generality and universality. Within this context, calculation can hardly be seen to be following a given set of instructions, which is not among the resources at hand. Even assuming its location in the actors' consciousness, it could not support action without a set of instructions for correlating rules with the resources of the situation. From here on, however, infinite regression sets in, since correlation would require in its turn a set of specifying rules, an so on.

Calculation and trading encounters

While plans and strategies are intrinsic to games (which, indeed, have often been equated with calculations), during the playing of a game a variety of relevant interactions occur, which cannot be defined in terms of the game's rules (Goffman 1972, p. 33). This variety can be seen as a gaming encounter: the play of a game of chess, for instance, is a special abstraction from the gaming encounter between specific players. As usually presented in chess manuals, the playing abstracts, selects and re-works concrete interaction into schematic visual representations of moves. It is this re-working which allows the reference to plans and strategies. Glances, bodily movements, worded exchanges or tantrums are left out, enabling the codification of chess encounters as plays of the game of chess, with the latter being analysable in terms of moves, counter-moves and strategies.

A gaming encounter can be characterized by a problematic outcome and by sanctioned displays of socially relevant attributes (Goffman 1972, p. 61), such as dexterity, endurance, self-control, resilience to humiliation and the like. Games, then, can be seen as arrangements or conventions for 'integrating into gaming encounters... socially significant externally based matters' (Goffman 1972, p. 64), centred on specific sets of routines. Gaming encounters in chess, for instance, include sets of routines executed during competitive displays of social attributes. In such displays, participants can switch into various 'keys' (Goffman 1974, p. 49) in which they perform their routines. In a game of basketball, for instance, a player can switch from a dribble to a mock (pretend) pass in order to confuse his opponent; such re-keyings can be part and parcel of gaming encounters.

The competitive display of social attributes resonates with Clifford Geertz's notion of 'deep play' (1973, p. 433), in which cockfight routines provide the framing for engaging in status competitions by way of betting. In other words, gaming encounters bring forth value-relevant issues in relation to specific conventions and routine-like procedures (such as those of football or chess). In a chess encounter, for instance, such value-relevant issues can be 'unflippability', endurance, or quick response. Apparently unrelated gaming types, then, can provide occasions for similar value-relevant issues (think of rugby, car racing and chess, for instance, with respect to a quality such as endurance).

Face-to-face gaming encounters can be characterized by symbolic distance from the environment in which they take place (Goffman 1972, p. 65) – card games are a case in point here. In card games, participants sitting around the table distance themselves from their audience, who may have the right to look, but must remain silent and are not allowed to intervene, give advice, and so on. The audience is thus spatially near the players, and symbolically distanced from them. In other kinds of encounter, not only is the opponent/ partner not known, but their relevance as opponent/partner may not be known (blind speed-dating, for example). In the context of online trading, the relevance of somebody being a partner is not known previous to them displaying on the screen. This prevents the gaming encounter from establishing a symbolic distance from the environment. The trader has to use environmental resources – the screen, for example – in order to establish this relevance. Symbolic closeness replaces distance. This can be illustrated with floor-based trading versus online trading. In the former, the status and identity of competitors is known before they make the first hand sign (Zaloom 2006, pp. 98–103). The pit is symbolically distanced from the clerical desks and phone booths situated only a couple of steps away. In online trading, presence must be inferred from the screen displays, without them providing enough resources to clearly establish it. Hence, the encounter must be kept close to its environment. Online trading can therefore be re-keyed in ways in which floor-based trading cannot: it can be re-keyed as a café encounter (as observed by this author, among others), or as a household encounter.

The resources used by a trader in acknowledging and validating the significant presence of anonymous others can only come from the situation of which the trader is part. A major resource is the trader's own presence. A basic form of addressing the presence of the other is when the actor 'replies to himself as truly as the other person replies to him' (Mead 1964 [1934], p. 203). In carrying on a 'conversation of gestures' (Mead 1964 [1934], p. 205) with herself, as well as in talking to herself, the actor can use her own presence as a resource for establishing a meaningful orientation to the presence of (remote) others. Self-talk does not emerge as indulgence or taboo-breaking (Goffman 1978, p. 788), but as a way of embedding the assumed presence of other actors into the trader's situation and context of action. Similarly, the presence of familiar persons (or familiar strangers) in the situation can be taken both as an occasion and as a resource for bringing remote, anonymous, strange traders into the situation. By addressing others present in the situation, or simply by taking the presence of others as an occasion for addressing herself, the trader can momentarily stabilize images on screen, and validate them as significant.

Against this background, online trading encounters are anchored in the orientation toward other potentially relevant presences, and toward oneself (as a major situational resource). This action extends into the future: its aim is to process given elements in order to obtain a result which can be significantly related to other results, obtained through previous operations. Displayed data must be processed in such a way that the results of these activities can be connected to each other. Processing displayed data, in its turn, depends on actively adding, deleting, or combining existing data in new configurations and evaluating their relevance. It also depends on selecting and actualizing some displays as relevant in the given situation, while others are overlooked. This actualization process implies bringing the displayed data into the trader's situation, relating it to her own actions as relevant. It is a process of actualizing the actions of absent, anonymous traders as relevant for one's own future actions. Finally, these actualized presences have to be endowed with minimal stability, in order for one's own actions to unfold. Even if only for a brief moment, they must be maintained as significant. In order to achieve this, traders use the most elementary resources at hand: their own bodies and voices.

The traders' displays to others cannot exclude from the start socially relevant attributes; numerical screen displays have existential qualities (Vollmer 2007, p. 593) and intervene therefore in establishing social relationships. Endowing other, unknown presences with significance as the basis for actions is related to the display of such attributes through numerical data. Traders must show that they are 'there'; they must show that they are attractive to others. Endurance, even obstinacy, coolness, or attractiveness have their place among these attributes.

In online financial markets, calculation emerges as the execution, adaptation, ongoing combination and modification of specific routines (e.g. buying a put, selling a call on an index) according to the requirements of the encounter. Encounters can be seen as social relationships of short duration, characterized by competitive displays of socially relevant attributes, and having uncertain outcomes. In online trading, where participants engage with anonymous strangers through the computer screen, social attributes cannot be displayed directly to anonymous others. They can, however, be displayed in sequences of actions, like posting numbers on screen, or reacting (or not) to the numbers posted by strangers. Trading encounters therefore have at least two dimensions: the actualization of other presences in the trader's situation, and the trader's self-displays to others on the trading screen. Trading encounters are symbolically close to the environment in which they unfold. They involve bodily engagement with strangers, an engagement mediated by the screen.[5] Since the execution of trading routines requires ongoing adaptation to the characteristics of specific encounters (including competitive displays of attributes), it follows that transaction sequences cannot be predicted. These sequences will vary not only from market participant to market participant; they will also have an intrinsic variability, due to the necessity of adapting them on an ongoing basis.

Methods

An appropriate way of identifying the empirical underpinnings of the above propositions is to observe closely how calculations unfold in the live process of trading. The aim is not to find representative frequencies of types of strategies. (What is taken as a strategy often reveals itself as a *post hoc* rationalization.) Best suited for such an examination is naturally occurring data (e.g. Schegloff 1996, p. 167) – that is, observational data obtained from online anonymous traders in their natural habitat. Instead of asking lay traders, for instance, if and how they calculate while trading, visual and audio recordings of the trading process itself, together with protocols of participant observations,[6] can be used in order to identify and analyse calculative processes. This can be complemented with interview data providing more background information about the traders' past experiences, the constraints under which they operate, and so on.

Gaming encounters do not necessarily include verbalizations and explanations of actions performed by traders. Nevertheless, the presence of the ethnographer can trigger thinking aloud, or providing accounts – that is, evaluative inquiries (Scott and Lyman 1968, p. 46) of what is going on, while it is going on. In such cases the ethnographer's presence can act less as a disturbing or distorting factor and more like an opportunity – and resource – used by traders to formulate what they are doing. This means that traders will seize on the presence of the ethnographer as a pretext for describing what is going on and for making dialogues with unseen trading partners audible, dialogues which otherwise may take place in private. Since such formulations are uttered in the process of trading – where so much is at stake – they should emphatically not be seen as performing for the benefit of the ethnographer, but as concretizations of encounter moments (i.e., as making them audible). Any performance for the benefit of the ethnographer would mean interrupting an ongoing on-screen gaming encounter and engaging in a face-to-face one. Such shifts would be disruptive, would be observable, and would require repair. It is the interaction itself (i.e., the presence or absence of such repairs) which indicates whether the presence of the ethnographer is an occasion for audibility or a disruption of onscreen encounters.

An appropriate additional way for checking up on such moments is to examine interaction sequences where the ethnographer is absent. By recording trading days without the presence of the ethnographer, we can see whether verbalizations occur as intrinsic to the trading process or not. I have made recordings of full trading days (a total of ten) without my presence, and checked them against recordings of trading days when I was present. The comparison shows that traders verbalized interactions even when they were completely alone. The presence (or intervention) of family members did not appear as a disruption, but as an occasion for commentary and evaluations, and for making audible sequences of inner dialogue with unseen transaction partners. Comparing the presence/interference of family members with the presence of the ethnographer, disruptions or modifications of the trading process were not recognizable in either case.

The following analysis is primarily based on data obtained through observation of lay US traders in the period October 2005–March 2007, consisting of video and audio recordings of trading, together with protocols of participant observation. The traders used US-based electronic platforms; nevertheless, as they travelled, observations and interviews with the same traders were made both in the US and in Europe. The data discussed here consists of the following: extensive recordings of trading days (over 82 hours of recordings); video recording of trading with observation protocols (over 3 hours); observation protocols without recording (over 9 hours); observation protocols with audio recording (over 7 hours); and interviews (over 40 hours).

The use of this combination is motivated by the necessity to (i) check interaction consistencies; (ii) complement audio data with visual ones, thus gaining access to behavioural detail (Peräkylä 2006, p. 95); and complement audio and video data with interviews, thus gaining insight into the traders' operating context, background and self-perception. In addition to participant observation, recordings and interviews, this author has attended training and presentation sessions organized by the electronic brokerage firm used by the traders. The sessions were aimed at introducing lay traders to the trading software and brokerage services of the firm; they were organized in co-operation with and on the premises of a global stock exchange.

The screen as an observational and an encounter device

In the cases discussed here, lay traders logged in on a NASDAQ level II screen, which looks like a grid of differently coloured cells, revealing the bids and offers for every anonymous market participant posting quotes. Observation and trading do not necessarily overlap: for instance, if traders transact derivatives, they will also monitor the underlying asset. In addition to information about bids and asks, traders need to monitor their asset balance and liquidity, which is automatically updated. Due to the physical limitations of the screen, multiple windows can display various kinds of information: price charts, news and expert recommendations from specialized services, as well as a chat room. This last capability was not used by the traders observed by the author.

Not all activities of traders consist of calculation: searching for news, perusing expert recommendations, narrating past relevant events or interpretation of charts are some of the activities which take place during a trading day. But the most important moments are those of engagement with other traders. They are important not only because there is considerably more excitement, and sometimes even tension, in such encounters, but also because the trader's financial situation changes as a direct consequence of them.

The screen appears thus as a laminated object (Goffman 1974, pp. 82, 156–157), framing together various layers of activity, some of which are oriented toward anonymous strangers, and some toward searching for information which should enable this orientation. Some of these layers enable contemplation, some enable experimentation and some enable engagement. Some zones of the screen contain durable data (e.g., the codenames of securities), while others contain highly variable data (e.g., prices and volumes). Traders can set up different combinations of securities to be observed, can increase the number of combinations and can seek out encounters with various combinations of trades. Thus, at any given time, each trading screen is unique, in the sense that it incorporates unique combinations of anonymous presences and unique responses to them.

Calculation as bodily work and material co-ordination

Orientation toward and interaction with the screen is crucial for engaging in encounters. The traders' attitude is far from a passive, contemplative one. Observing the screen is more than 'looking at'; it implies physical closeness and active bodily engagement:

> Trader: [16"] [points finger to screen cell with underlying asset on which he trades puts] still there quite a bit *though* I *mea*n [moves cursor up].hh but I have stuff next month so.hh [13"] [brings cursor back down] [moves cursor up, opens portfolio window] not a *pre*tty month for me.hh I'll say *that* much [4"] *th*at might not be as *ba*d as it looks, I mean [points with finger to index cell] if that *fi*nishes even above *seventy*seven [2"] it will wipe out all *the*se [points with finger down to row of puts he has put up for sale] you *know* I mean I won't have to buy'em *ba*ck↑ [opens again portfolio window] but that's the *pro*blem with getting the squeeze, you know what I *me*an

In the above sequence, the trader must decide whether to buy back a bunch of puts he has sold earlier. He must decide upon (or calculate) the implications of his actions, with respect to present as well as to future situations. Calculation appears neither as a set of purely mental operations, nor as the application of a plan. It is not recognizable as the implementation of a (standard) move, nor taken as such by the trader. In order to establish what they are going to do next, traders have to define their situation at a given moment. Defining the situation, however, is not simply a matter of words: good, bad, acceptable, or whatever. Nor is it a matter of comparing data with a template, or evaluating them according to a set of criteria. It is a matter of identifying relevant spots on the screen and correlating across spots, so that actions can be adapted to an ever-changing display with multiple, co-ordinated sites, where relevant encounters might happen. Hitches, response cries (Goffman 1978) and hand movements are used to mark places and moments of relevance for future actions, and to support calculations. The entire body, although strapped to the chair, is geared toward such operations: leaning forward, pointing at the screen with the finger, clicking the mouse, sighing are among the bodily actions marking relevant moments in calculative activities.

This marking is important in an ever-changing environment, and allows the trader to stabilize, if only for a moment, the spots on the screen which need to be correlated and accounted for. The very activity of accounting for a screen flickering – intrinsic to encounters – cannot dispense with bodily work. In lines 5–6 above, the trader does exactly this – he projects the relevance of a spot on the screen for his future situation by engaging his body in interaction with the screen (through co-ordination of hand and eye movements with vocalizations) and by describing his own movements *in relation to* the screen spots. In this perspective, encounters are prepared and sustained by material and discursive co-ordination with the device, based on stabilizing observations, defining situations and projecting future consequences of present situations.

Calculation in anonymous encounters

Within the experimental field incorporated in the trading screen, participants display their trades, waiting for an anonymous stranger to appear and engage with them. Before this happens, traders cannot know whether their posted trades are relevant to others or not. Knowing this, however, is essential for deciding on future trades: which products, at what prices and for what expiry dates (in the case of derivatives) should traders post? The answer depends on the success of the trades already posted, as well as on the traders' reactions to anonymous others. Engaging with others is essential for evaluating the relevance of numbers seen on the screen, as well as for the question of what to do next. Engagements imply making others present in the situation, in spite of their remoteness and anonymity.

One tool for bringing strangers in is talk: by talking to absent strangers, traders create the conditions for calculating their trades not as abstract and impersonal computations, nor as the application of a pre-established plan, but as responses to relevant presences. The encounter, however brief, stabilizes the numbers flickering on the screen and enables their manipulation and rationalization as responses within an interaction frame. Transactions come out of such brief, anonymous encounters, which can be framed by soliloquies. Like somebody waiting in the street for a blind date which could be late or fail to appear, and who eyes unknown passersby saying privately 'is this the one?', 'this one looks like s/he might be', and so on, traders project relationships by means of internal conversations (Mead 1934), and act according to such projections.

Making strangers present in the situation can mean addressing them, talking to them, as indicative of their acceptance or refusal to engage. Such talk, which cannot of course be heard through the screen, often includes response cries, marking relevant moments in the encounter (Goffman 1978, p. 814; see also Hutchins 1995, p. 313):

> Trader: [15″] hah. [10″] [music playing] *Ra*king in the cash!↑ haha↑ I'm *ta*king *ca*sh *for* risk. Hrrh hah. Dim digidim digidim dim dim [slaps hand] [32″] *Oh*kay.↓ *Oh*kay.↓ We're going to learn how it works *ou*t. Haha haha hh. [45″] [music playing, tapping, computer sounds] *Oh*kay.↑ I'm not *ha*ving that kind of day, *bu*d. hihi Give me a *ca*ll. [pushes chair]

The trader is here completely alone. He has just sold a batch of derivatives when an anonymous presence on the screen attracts his attention: he refuses to engage in the encounter (i.e., to take the trade posted by the stranger) by addressing this directly, as the 'bud' who should maybe call later. It is not recognizable here that the refusal is part of an overall strategy of rejecting particular kinds of trades, or that it follows any criteria for evaluating the implications or the attractiveness of the posted trade. The rejection comes because, after having sold, the trader does not have 'that kind of day'. This is linked to what had happened immediately before, not to any general decision-making frame. It should be noted here that the outcome of the previous transaction is still open, but it is the previous successful encounter which makes the trader decline a new one. Display of disinterest as a socially relevant attribute, similar to somebody not returning a glance in the street, or ignoring the remark of a stranger, is intrinsic to this sequence of trading activity.

In the following sequence, towards the end of the trading day, a trader engages in a conversation while talking to his wife in front of the active trading screen:

> Trader: We're playing a little mad over trades. [1″] It's like, whatever, *du*de. I might, I might nibble a little more, but [2″] I mean [.5″] obviously he sold *the*se at a much cheaper *pri*ce↓, but, you know, hahaha I might just *say*, well, give me *tho*se *ba*ck↓, I'll sell you a few [1″] I didn't really want you to sell it to me at eightyfive, I count, I think seventyfive is more appropriate, further *ou*t, but you've *go*t to pay me more↑ than you would for the eightyfives, because, you *kno*w, it's ten dollars cheaper that you can sell it to me for. *So* you've got to give me more money for it. *Tha*t's my attitude↑. hihihi you with me? [7″] This sure is a *cra*zy market time↑. I guess to*da*y's everybody's, everybody decided today's not a good *da*y to buy. Hehe.

Immediately before this sequence, the wife has entered the room saying that the dogs are barking outside, which might mean that a code enforcement officer (a county inspector) is in the neighbourhood. The trader uses the question to change the topic to his situation, and, having elicited interest, utters the above sequence. He had bought options on a company stock at a specific strike price and wants to sell options on the same stock at a different strike price. What is the appropriate price to ask for each strike price? Instead of using a general formula for calculating options prices, the trader relates to the anonymous 'dude' he has traded with earlier and thus tries to make sense of his own real intentions as a basis for identifying the right asking price for each strike price. At least in this instance, calculation does not appear to be the mechanical application of a formula (which traders might even ignore), but to be grounded in establishing a social relationship with a counterpart.

The first step is to create the encounter by bringing in the anonymous 'dude', in a conversation embedded in the conversation with the trader's partner. Then, the 'right' asking prices for two different strike prices (seventy-five and eighty-five) are made dependent on a change of mind ('I didn't really want') and on fairness imperatives ('you've got to give me more money for it'). Finally, this calculation is rationalized by the trader's describing his attitude to outside, uncontrollable constraints ('crazy market time') and with the unwillingness of passers-by to give him a glance ('nobody's willing to buy').

All this happens while the algorithm for calculating options prices, embedded in the trading software, is at hand; at the click of a screen button, prices can be obtained for any strike price and any underlying asset. Yet, there is a fundamental tension between using a trading screen provided as a device for engaging in anonymous, brief encounters, on the one hand, and using a formula on the other hand. Since traders' activity is geared towards successful encounters, price calculation must unfold within this frame, bracketing out algorithms (see also Lave 1988, p. 122). The right price therefore becomes dependent on fairness issues, on the traders' changing their mind, on them not really meaning it – in short, on well-known interaction and relational issues which can surface when encountering strangers.

The price emerges in a direct negotiation with the unseen trading partner, in a way similar to that in which participants in a gaming encounter of cards, sitting around the table, can ask each other to put more money on the table before they reveal their hands. This is not the price generated by a formula which is only a couple of clicks away, but by personal interaction. Trading means engaging with 'guys', 'dudes' and 'buds', not following onscreen instructions. As engagement with 'guys', trading relies on displaying socially relevant features. 'Coolness' may be one of them, in the same way in which a game of poker may be at least as much about social rankings as it is about money.

Seeking out encounters

In order to safeguard margin, traders need to calculate how the price dynamics of the underlying asset is affecting the options they have sold. They will sometimes need to buy some options back, in order to stay within margin. If they have sold puts with an expiration date in the following month, buying them back now will affect the situation in a month from now. The task is to calculate the price of the underlying asset at which the puts will be wiped out – that is, they will have to take a loss next month. The trades (put sales) are displayed in cells on the screen. The cells need to be correlated among themselves, but this correlation cannot be done without establishing first the link between a cell, or position, and what is in that position – a reflexive work (Schegloff 2006, p. 154) which cannot follow any pre-established plan. In a situation of fundamental instability, when cells flicker all the time without any apparent rhythm, this becomes very important.

Any margin-maintenance intervention (in order to avoid forced liquidation of positions) will entail a corresponding adjustment of other related positions; this adjustment will affect the margin of other positions, which will require correction; this correction, in its turn, will trigger a re-adjustment of the portfolio, which may affect other margins, to cause further readjustments, and so on. The trader's situation is one of flow (Knorr Cetina and Preda 2007, p. 137), where the next sequence of action modifies projections of future situations, leading to other actions and other modifications, continuously. All these re-adjustments will take place within an ever-changing setting: the screen flickers permanently. Calculating trades means correlating present situations to projections of future ones, and modifying these correlations with every step of action. Thus, the trader's task is that of tuning positions to a continuously changing display board (knowing well that these adjustments will introduce additional changes into this state), while trying to avoid random, uncontrolled shifts (such as would be caused by a forced liquidation). Under these circumstances, calculating according to a preset plan is futile: no such plan can forecast how the next changes on the screen, triggered by the interventions of anonymous strangers, will affect the trader's positions and, with them, his margin. In such situations, open engagement with others is required. Like a person waiting for an encounter in the street, who decides to become active in approaching strangers, traders may need to actively display their presence to anonymous others:

Trader: [after having checked portfolio page again] ↓That's easy, *I'm* still in *ma*rgin [3″] I'm *ti*red of this *shit.* [1′40″] [cursor moves across price cells for puts on the underlying asset, lingers on them: $0.70, $0.79, then moves over to $1.54 and transforms it into $1.55, then moves over to $0.5 and changes the order limit from 1 to 4, then moves on 'T', clicks, selling at $0.5. Then opens portfolio page, checks. A yellow strip is there.].ah shit, back in the *ma*rgin suit.hh ↑ha hahaha ha [continues moving the cursor across price cells. Changes a price, clicks 'T'. Then opens the portfolio page.] [35″] *fuh*ckhhh!

Ethnographer: the yellow.

Trader: *ye*ah. All right, well, then I *gue*ss we gonna get some, get some bad *ass*↑ on this.// Ya know, it's called *git*tin the *baa*dass↑.

Ethnographer: //.hh [19″]

Trader: [10″] ↑dadadadadaaadahdahaa tootoo tatatatatataataa↓ [48″] Allright, *so* oh I'm getting down *the*re. *Bu*t we might just have to roll all *the*se all *down*↓ [11″] Can't wait fore*ve*r, noone waits fore*ve*r [3″] [moves the cursor, changes the limit order to 20 for $1.67, there is a buy cell on the right of the limit cell] twen*tee* freaking sell twenty [then moves the cursor down to the sell order for the same price and positions the cursor on the limit cell, waits there. Does not click, but moves the cursor up, lingers with it in the $1.65 cell, then moves it to the right and opens the portfolio page. The yellow strip is still there.] Son of a ↓*bit*chhh! *Oh*key,. hhhhh [16″]:hhohhohhohoho.hh tatata tatata tatatattaataataa tatatatatatataaa [slaps hand on knee repeatedly] all*righ*t, we are not gonna wait too *long* [moves cursor upwards next to a buy cell, changes limit to 50 for a $77 put, then prepares to moves to the price cell]

Ethnographer: You're buying now?//

Trader: //I have to it's strrr *tth* [4″] all right *we*ll [5″] actually, seventy or seventynine pu*ts* [moves cursor, scrolls page down, inserts new put at $79. Clicks 'Buy', sets limit at 10, sets price at $2.59, moves cursor to 'T', moves cursor back to price, changes it to $2.60, moves cursor back to 'T', clicks, checks portfolio page, moves upwards to 'sell' at \$1.00, clicks 'T', moves upwards to 'sell' at \$0.56, clicks 'T', checks portfolio, moves cursor down to 'sell' at \$1.70, clicks 'T', moves cursor upwards to sell at \$0.56, clicks 'T' again, checks portfolio. Operations continue for 3'39"]

In the above situation, the trader decides to make his presence visible to others, to display himself without waiting for anonymous others to appear first. Such a display means posting trades to be seen by others: every trade displayed can affect other positions, and the trader's task is to balance various positions so as to make the yellow strip disappear while not (entirely) disrupting his future trades.

Making the yellow band disappear is not something which can be simply done by clicking a series of buttons on the screen, according to a set of pre-existing rules. It involves glosses which make bodily actions (such as placing the cursor on a specific cell) accountable. It is structured by hesitations, rhythmic vocalizations and response cries (like 'son of a bitch'). It involves the trader repeatedly announcing his presence to others ('we are going to get bad ass'; 'we are not gonna wait too long') as a means of defining the situation and of making potential, remote and anonymous partners present in his situation. Announcements of the own presence and acceptance of other presences as relevant ('all right well') are intrinsic to accomplishing the task at hand. The display to others is repeatedly announced by vocalizations, situational definitions and self-summonses (lines 14–16, 22–23).

Calculation is oriented here toward two interrelated tasks: making the yellow band disappear, and finding relevant encounters quickly. The latter contributes to the former, but should not be exaggerated: once enough quick encounters have been found, this should stop. Hence the step-by-step and recursive character of the calculative process: making a transaction, checking on the yellow strip, making another couple of trades, checking again. There is no overarching goal to this, only immediate, step- and sequence-relevant goals, analogous to what Edwin Hutchins calls 'evolutionary search' (Hutchins 1995, p. 349). If necessary, the trader transacts with himself – that is, buys back the puts he has posted earlier for sale – thus becoming his immediately available other. Choices – buying at a strike price of seventy or seventy-nine, for \$2.59 or \$2.60 – seem to be determined by available presences, as well as by the necessity of quick displays to potential anonymous partners.

The process-like, unplanned (and unplannable) character of this flow of reciprocal adjustments makes trading into something which is developed ad hoc, depending on and drawing upon the resources of the situation. The trader cannot directly and immediately recognize screen changes as expressions of an underlying plan (Suchman 1987, p. 33; Hutchby 2001, p. 138), to which he should adhere or react. The trader has an array of put options on the underlying asset (an industrial index) which he had previously sold and which he is forced to buy back now. The prices of puts, as well as the strike prices of the underlying asset, vary. For instance, the trader can decide to buy puts priced at, for example, $0.50 or $0.65, on strike prices of the underlying asset of $77, $75, or $79. He has plastered various combinations on the trading screen and needs to decide among them. Every trade, however, changes the situation, which needs to be continuously assessed and then modified again. Put simply, the task is to make the yellow strip – which indicates combinations of transactions gone awry – disappear from the portfolio window.

Adjustments are relational: they are conducted through brief, anonymous encounters, which require displaying oneself to others and reacting to the displays of others. Their unfolding does not follow pre-set steps; adjustments will have to be defined and justified in this very process. Definition implies here not only an answer to the question 'what is going on?' but also anticipatory elements of the responses to the trader's action (Smith 1999, p. 135). A situational definition may require forms of talk drawing on the mundane presence of other actors, the trader's own presence, or the potentially relevant presence of anonymous traders.

From this step-by-step process emerge interaction forms which, while firmly anchored in the situation, are not reduced to the physical presence of the trader, but combine it with absent presences – that is, with anonymous others who are brought into the situation. At the same time, traders can cross over to the other side of the screen, so to speak, when their presence has to be displayed more forcefully:

Trader: [16"] Okay↑, I guess that's enough selling for *one* day [5"]. *hh* hahaha ha [16"] I guess I'm gonna *go ba*ck and *try* again [13"] [drinks] so what's my *ave*rage [points finger to screen] it's seven-*ty*nine↑, not very *goo*d, [finger moves up and to the left on 'buy'] fifty*two*, not very good [continues buying at different prices and limits] [30"] I said I'm in mar*gin* it's not *s*elling lately [22"].hh [6"] ah donno pretty *ugl*y, pretty ↓*down ugly* [checks portfolio again. Yellow strip has reappeared.] *yeah*, here we go↑ *here* we go↑ [31"] [scrolls down the page, inserts buying puts at $79, sets limit to 3,

cursor on 'T', goes back, changes price to $2.01] *oh*key↑, let's see
if it's *fou*nd a floor *now* [14″] [checks portfolio, yellow band still
there] ↓*ug*ly, mister, *bitch* ugly, ↓all I can *say.*

The announcement about withdrawing from encounters ('enough
selling') is immediately followed by a second, contradictory one ('try
again'), conditional upon locating averages, which in turn leads to a definition of the situation ('pretty down ugly') and then to an announcement of engaging in further encounters ('here we go'). This latter fails,
and the trader addresses remote others as a means of justifying the failure ('ugly, all I can say').

Finding the average means here the average price at which the trader
has bought back the puts he had previously sold. Though a simple
arithmetical operation, it has to be done in real time – that is, while
adjusting to the changing situation through continuously buying and
selling. Here, the identification of the average price on screen (through
pointing at the respective price slots) requires concomitant judgement:
further actions depend on whether the average is seen as good or bad.
This identification is achieved by bringing others into the situation: not
only is the ethnographer's display of availability taken advantage of,
but anonymous others are brought into the situation to make the failed
action accountable. The trader, who has announced several times his
intention to stop, continues trading (and fails to make the yellow strip
disappear) because the situation is still 'bitch ugly'. Such insults and
imprecations, while leaving the impression that the market is treated
in an anthropomorphic fashion and endowed with a gender, serve in
the first place situation-specific accountability purposes, and help orient the trader's actions. The talk during trading interactions (intrinsic to the tasks of defining what is going on, calculating and judging)
includes mundane, vernacular expressions ('bitch', 'baby', 'bad ass') as
consequential situational markers.

Conclusion

The interaction order of anonymous online markets has at least the following features: (i) bodily work oriented towards the screen as a means
of stabilizing and correlating data displays; (ii) bringing anonymous
strangers into the trader's situation; (iii) self-displays to others. While
previous ethnographic work has identified face-to-face (Abolafia 1996,
Zaloom 2006) and face-to-screen (Knorr Cetina and Bruegger 2002) as
forms of the interaction order in floor-based and trading room-based

transactions, respectively, a third form can be suggested here: that of presence-in-absence, characterized by brief, anonymous encounters within the trader's situation.

The screen presents itself as an observational and experimental instrument, but also as a tool for crossing over: an interface through which strangers can be 'pulled' into the situation of the traders, who display themselves to the strangers. The fundamental instability of this instrument, subject to external constraints and continuous interventions, and uncontrollable by a single trader, makes stabilization a crucial task. Stabilization involves a variety of situational resources, including the trader's own body, as well as vocal interventions in the trading process.

In anonymous online trading, calculations are not identical with preset plans. Neither are they identical with the application of a formula, the results of which determine trading decisions. While the institutional adoption of economic models (including formulas) has been recently debated in the context of performativity (see, for instance, MacKenzie, Muniesa and Siu 2007), the actual uses of models and formulas do not follow automatically from their institutionalization.

Calculations are situational actions, geared toward brief anonymous encounters. Such encounters are realized by making absent strangers present in the traders' situations, as well as by the latter 'crossing over' to display themselves to unknown others. While online traders employ routines such as doing a straddle or trading index options, these routines do not represent strategic applications based on anticipations of the opponents' moves or on the evaluation of the latter according to criteria of efficacy. An analogy can make this point clear: basketball players can employ routines such as passes or dribbles, but ultimately have to engage in encounters with other players on the field, encounters which will determine not only the character of a dribble and its outcome, but also the subsequent sequences of action. Performing a specific routine (a dribble or a straddle) appears to be less a decision enacted in specific situations, and more like the outcome of encounters in which participants engage with each other in socially relevant ways. On the trading screen, where strangers come close to each other, socially relevant attributes relate to, for example, acceptance, rejection or resilience.

Games of acceptance and rejection appear to be significant in online trading, but they are not unknown in institutional trading either. To give but one recent example: the huge losses incurred by the French bank Société Génerale appear to have been caused by a trader's drive to become accepted in the circle of the 'big guys' who earn big bonuses.

Yet, returning to Geertz's notion of 'deep play', the kinds of play taking place in online anonymous markets appear to be different from those of institutional trading: the latter seem to be about status competitions within relatively small groups, the members of which know each other. Here, indeed, the analogy with Geertz's cockfight arena could be pushed further, pointing to the need to examine in detail the interaction order of status competitions, together with the associated rituals (and consequences), within financial organizations.

Non-institutional online trading seems to be more about repeatedly occurring short bursts of social competitiveness among strangers. If, in Geertz's (1973, p. 449) interpretation, the cockfight was to be seen as a Balinese reading of the Balinese experience, online markets can be regarded as the story which a highly individualized, fragmented, competitive society tells itself.

Another relevant aspect is how price variations emerge in the interaction order of online trading. Such variations have been tied, among other factors, to ambiguous classifications made by analysts (Zuckerman 2004) or, in the case of lay traders, to shared judgement errors due to a lack of sophistication (e.g. Shleifer 2000, p. 12). This latter would imply unavoidably bad calculations on the part of non-institutional traders. The examination of the interaction order of trading, however, reveals that price variations are an intrinsic feature of trading encounters. Their anonymity and individual character include, if not outright require individualized price displays, a feature supported by the capabilities of the trading software. Since rejection and acceptance play a significant role, traders are encouraged to vary their prices as a means of encountering other traders. The sources of price volatility, then, should be sought less in imperfect calculations than in the essential characteristics of the interaction order. This points to competitive rituals as a possible source of price volatility within institutional trading. It is perhaps ironic that online financial markets, with an unprecedented degree of technological penetration and the explicit aim of attracting more and more laypeople into financial activities, emerges as a platform for brief encounters, therefore exposing calculation as social competition.

Notes

An extended version of this paper has been published in *Accounting, Organization and Society*, 34 (5) (2009), 675–693.

1. Lay traders are usually referred to in the popular media as 'day traders'. This term is perceived as pejorative; moreover, day trading designates a set

of specific techniques not always used by lay traders. Therefore, I will refer throughout this paper to 'lay', in the sense of non-professional – albeit full-time or near-full-time – traders.

2. Traders can infer categorical identities from this data (e.g., whether displays are made by individual or by institutional traders); they can also ask the brokerage house to reveal *post hoc* the identity of their counterparts for specific trades. This identification is a longer bureaucratic process which can unfold only after the trading moment, when it will have lost its relevance. The observed traders did not use it, preferring, for all practical purposes, anonymity.

3. Science and technology studies point to the ways in which plans, such as engineering blueprints, schemes, drawings, can act as props for action. These are not simply representations or sets of instructions for actors, but rather technologies of social interaction (for a recent example, see Vertesi 2008).

4. Similarly, in auctions prices emerge through the participants' interactions (Heath and Luff 2007, p. 81).

5. Conversely, in boxing, which apparently is exclusively body-centric, talk plays a significant role (Wacquant 2004, p. 66).

6. While participant observation cannot be regarded as naturally occurring data in the strict sense of the term, it can capture situation-relevant elements, such as gestures, which cannot be retained by an audio recording. Video recordings certainly allow the analysis of such elements, but they usually offer a restricted angle which is not identical with the vision field of the observer. In many cases, a combination of video recording and participant observation has the potential for better data yields.

References

Abolafia, M. (1996) *Making Markets: Opportunism and Restraint on Wall Street* (Cambridge, MA: Harvard University Press).

Beunza, D. and Stark, D. (2005) 'How to Recognize Opportunities. Heterarchical Search in a Trading Room', in K. Knorr Cetina and A. Preda (eds) *The Sociology of Financial Markets* (Oxford: Oxford University Press), pp. 84–101.

Biggart, N. W. and Catanias, R. P. (2001) 'Collateralized Social Relations. The Social in Economic Calculations', *American Journal of Economics and Sociology*, 60 (2), 471–500.

Callon, M. (2004) 'Europe Wrestling with Technology', *Economy and Society*, 33 (1), 121–134.

Callon, M. (2007) 'What Does It Mean to Say that Economics Is Performative?', in F. Muniesa MacKenzie and L. Siu (eds) *Do Economists Make Markets? On the Performativity of Economics* (Princeton, NJ and Oxford: Princeton University Press), 311–357.

Callon, M. and Muniesa, F. (2005) 'Economic Markets as Calculative Collective Devices', *Organization Studies*, 26 (8), 1229–1250.

Fenton O'Creevy, M., Nicholson, N., Soane, E. and Willman, P. (2005) *Traders, Risks, Decisions, and Management in Financial Markets* (Oxford: Oxford University Press).

Geertz, C. (1973) *The Interpretation of Cultures* (New York: Basic Books).

Goffman, E. (1972) *Encounters. Two Studies in the Sociology of Interaction* (Harmondsworth: Penguin).

Goffman, E. (1974) *Frame Analysis* (New York: Harper).

Goffman, E. (1978) 'Response Cries', *Language*, 54 (4), 787–815.

Goffman, E. (1983) 'The Interaction Order', *American Sociological Review*, 48 (1), 1–17.

Habermas, J. (1987) *The Theory of Communicative Action. Vol. 2, Lifeworld and System: A Critique of Functionalist Reason* (Cambridge: Polity).

Heath, C. and Luff, P. (2007) 'Ordering Competition. The Interactional Accomplishment of the Sale of Art and Antiques at Auction', *British Journal of Sociology*, 58 (1), 63–85.

Heath, C., Svensson, M. S., Hindmarsh, J., Luff, P. and vom Lehn, D. (2002) 'Configuring Awareness', *Computer-supported Cooperative Work*, 11, 317–347.

Husserl, E. (1995) *Cartesianische Meditationen* (Hamburg: Felix Meiner).

Hutchby, I. (2001) *Conversation and Technology. From the Telephone to the Internet* (Cambridge: Polity).

Hutchins, E. (1995) *Cognition in the Wild* (Cambridge, MA: MIT Press).

Knorr Cetina, K. and Bruegger, U. (2002) 'Global Microstructures: The Virtual Societies of Financial Markets', *American Journal of Sociology*, 107 (4), 905–950.

Knorr Cetina, K. and Preda, A. (2007) 'The Temporalization of Financial Markets. From Network to Flow', *Theory, Culture and Society*, 24 (7–8), 123–145.

Lave, J. (1988) *Cognition in Practice. Mind, Mathematics and Culture in Everyday Life* (Cambridge: Cambridge University Press).

MacKenzie, D., Muniesa, F. and Siu, L. (eds) (2007) *Do Economists Make Markets? On the Performativity of Economics* (Princeton, NJ and Oxford: Princeton University Press).

Mead, G. H. (1934) *Mind, Self and Society* (Chicago: University of Chicago Press).

Mead, G. H. (1964 [1934]) *On Social Psychology* (Chicago: University of Chicago Press).

Miller, P. (2001) 'Governing by Numbers. Why Calculative Practices Matter', *Social Research*, 68 (2), 379–396.

Miller, P. (2008) 'Calculating Economic Life', *Journal of Cultural Economy* 1 (1), 51–64.

Muniesa, F. and Callon, M. (2007) 'Economic Experiments and the Construction of Markets', in D. MacKenzie, F. Muniesa and L. Siu (eds) *Do Economists Make Markets? On the Performativity of Economics* (Princeton, NJ and Oxford: Princeton University Press), pp. 163–189.

Peräkylä, Anssi (2006) 'Observation, Video, and Ethnography. Case Studies in AIDS Counseling and Greetings', in Paul Drew, Geoffrey Raymond, and Darin Weinberg (eds), *Talk and Interaction in Social Research Methods* (London: Sage), pp. 81–96.

Podolny, J. (2001) 'Networks as the Pipes and Prisms of the Market', *American Journal of Sociology*, 107 (1), 33–60.

Schegloff, E. (1996) 'Confirming Allusions. Towards an Empirical Account of Action', *American Journal of Sociology*, 102 (1), 161–216.

Schegloff, E. (2006) 'On Possibilities', *Discourse Studies*, (8/1), 141–157.

Schutz, A. and Luckmann, T. (1974) *The Structures of the Life-World* (London: Heinemann).

Scott, M. B. and Lyman, S. (1968) 'Accounts', *American Sociological Review*, 33 (1), 46–62.

Shleifer, A. (2000) *Inefficient Markets. An Introduction to Behavioral Finance* (Oxford: Oxford University Press).

Simmel, G. (1971 [1908]) 'The Stranger', in Donald N. Levine (ed.) *On Individuality and Social Forms* (Chicago: University of Chicago Press), pp. 143–149.

Smith, C. W. (1999) *Success and Survival on Wall Street. Understanding the Mind of the Market* (Lanham, MD: Rowman & Littlefield).

Suchmau, L. (1987) *Plans and Situated Actions* (Cambridge: Cambridge University Press).

Vertesi, J. (2008) 'Mind the Gap. The London Underground Map and Users' Representations of Urban Space', *Social Studies of Science*, 38 (1), 7–33.

Vollmer, H. (2007) 'How to Do More with Numbers. Elementary Stakes, Framing, Keying, and the Three-Dimensional Character of Numerical Signs', *Accounting, Organizations and Society*, 32, 577–600.

Wacquant, L. (2004) *Body and Soul. Notebooks of an Apprentice Boxer* (Oxford: Oxford University Press).

Zaloom, C. (2006) *Out of the Pits. Traders and Technology from Chicago to London* (Chicago: University of Chicago Press).

Zuckerman, E. (2004) 'Structural Incoherence and Stock Market Activity', *American Sociological Review*, 69, 405–432.

Index